Breaking Ground

Lynda V. Mapes

Breaking Ground

The Lower Elwha Klallam Tribe and the Unearthing of Tse-whit-zen Village

FOREWORD BY *Frances Charles*

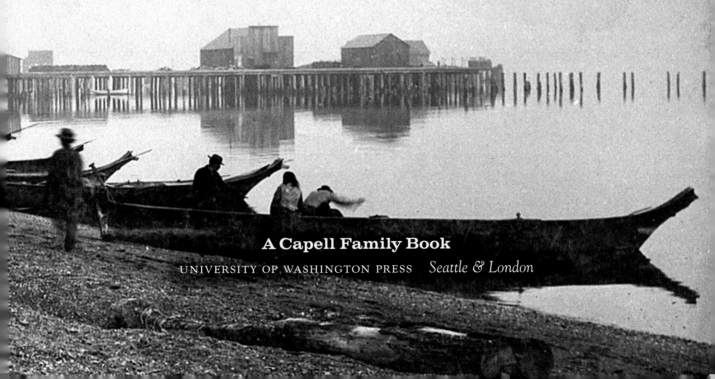

A Capell Family Book

UNIVERSITY OF WASHINGTON PRESS   *Seattle & London*

THE CAPELL FAMILY ENDOWED BOOK FUND supports the publication of books that deepen the understanding of social justice through historical, cultural, and environmental studies.

UNIVERSITY OF WASHINGTON PRESS
www.washington.edu/uwpress

The paper used in this publication is acid-free and 90 percent recycled from at least 50 percent post-consumer waste. It meets the minimum requirements of American National Standard for Information Sciences—Permanence of Paper for Printed Library Materials, ANSI Z39.48–1984.

LIBRARY OF CONGRESS
CATALOGING-IN-PUBLICATION DATA

Mapes, Lynda, 1959–

Breaking ground : the Lower Elwha Klallam tribe and the unearthing of Tse-whit-zen Village / Lynda V. Mapes ; foreword by Frances Charles. — 1st ed.
    p. cm.
Includes bibliographical references and index.
ISBN 978-0-295-98878-8 (pbk. : alk. paper)
1. Tse-whit-zen Village Site (Wash.) 2. Clallam Indians—Washington (State)—Port Angeles—Antiquities. 3. Clallam Indians—Antiquities—Collection and preservation—Moral and ethical aspects—Washington (State)—Port Angeles. 4. Excavations (Archaeology)—Washington (State)—Port Angeles. 5. Lower Elwha Tribal Community of the Lower Elwha Reservation, Washington—Interviews. 6. Clallam Indians—Washington (State)—Port Angeles—Pictorial works. 7. Port Angeles (Wash.)—Antiquities. 8. Port Angeles (Wash.)—Ethnic relations. I. Title.
E99.C82M36 2009   979.7'99—dc22   2008050111

FRONTISPIECE Hollywood Beach, Port Angeles, Washington, ca. 1900. Indian canoes and encampments on the beach are haunting reminders of the Indian people who are being displaced from their homeland on the waterfront as the city of Port Angeles begins to rise around them. Bert Kellogg Collection, North Olympic Library System, INDN ACTV 002.

PAGE VI The Elwha River in 1887. Bert Kellogg Collection, North Olympic Library System, ELWA RIVR 005.

To the memory of my mother,
Georgette S. Mapes,
who gave me my first books

In the early days of my grandfather, there was an ancient law. It was to keep the knowledge and memories of our ancestors alive. If a person did not do this they would become poor, destitute, have no past or identity. They would be a nobody. They would be unable to have a guardian spirit board. They would have no foundation in their lives. They would have to borrow someone else's culture. This was a truly sad state of affairs for a people to endure, for they would have no resiliency.

—*Gerald subiyay Bruce Miller*, Skokomish/Yakama

He brought me to the Elwha River every morning to bathe. . . . And it was to make you strong, not only in your body, but in your mind and spirit. And I believe that's what helped me to survive everything that was to come.

—*Johnson Charles Jr.*, Lower Elwha Klallam

Contents

Tribal members and local residents walk the drydock site one last time in a December 2004 healing ceremony after the project was shut down. Courtesy Steve Ringman, *Seattle Times*.

THE TRUE HISTORY UNDER EVERY FOOTFALL, ALONG EVERY SHORELINE, IS OFTEN silenced by collective amnesia. But here, on a twenty-two-acre waterfront property in Port Angeles, Washington, the ground spoke: of the Indian village here, and of a river that once sustained an entire ecosystem and way of life. Of uncounted Indian burials, ancestors of the Klallam people. Of the sawmill built right over their village and cemetery, transforming the look, but not the truth, of this ground.

When a Washington State agency broke ground here in August 2003 for a bridge repair project, the burials and village site were inadvertently unearthed. That discovery, and all it would lead to, actually broke ground for a different sort of bridge altogether— a shared sense of history, with the potential to heal wounds festering not only here but across America since first contact. This book is the story of that struggle.

Foreword

LESSONS FROM TSE-WHIT-ZEN

Frances Charles, *Lower Elwha Klallam Tribal Chairwoman*

SINCE OUR VILLAGE OF TSE-WHIT-ZEN WAS UNCOVERED ON THE PORT ANGELES waterfront, a lot of people have asked, "How could that have happened, how could they have not known about us?" A lot of the misunderstanding is no misunderstanding. This is something we know that non-Natives need to know. It is the frustration about the denial in the community, denial about the presence of the Klallam people. We know that they knew about us, as well as all other Native peoples along the shores. Even in the earlier stages, whether it was the 1800s or the 1900s, which is not that long ago, whites wouldn't believe Natives existed. They were treated worse than dogs at the time. But, we too are human. We have feelings. And we have pride today, in today's society; pride in who we are and where we come from, and pride in being able to carry that message from the elders' generation to our generation and to the youth who are not even born yet. To be able to teach them and train them and have them learn and be proud of who they are and where they come from. To not look at the ground and look low. But to be proud, because it is their culture and heritage. It is the pride, and the heritage, and the dignity of our elders and ancestors that has carried us for generations.

Everyone is reborn and re-created in one way or another. And there has been a re-creation of the lives that we learned from this process. The grounds themselves have spoken for us and defended us. The ancestors stood up for us, and they still are. Even some of our own people today tell us that we didn't do these things, that we didn't have this culture. They say this because of what happened to our elders, how they were beaten and punished so they would never say those words and had to bury the culture so deep in their souls and try to forget about it. But the ground itself and the village were able to bring it out.

This book is about the true history. We opened our homes, our hearts, our tribal archives, and family photo albums to tell it, because we want it known. I think it is in many ways the history that was never gone and has always been there. But it has been hidden in many ways. What we want is for people to look not in a tunnel but at their surroundings. At what is around them. There is not one path. There are many paths. Take the opportunity to ask why, and stop and understand what the true history is about. Look forward to a future that isn't only for us; it's for everyone. The teaching, the learning, and the education is about what was there and what was once plentiful for everyone. This book is an opportunity to continue that education, so that the youth and young adults will know who we are. To be proud for the sharing of the culture and the heritage. It is also an opportunity to have that unity, to be as one. What we see is the division of the colors and the races. But we all share Mother Earth itself. It's the teachings that we have to continue with, for the younger ones to the old, to be able to share the knowledge. Not to be afraid to ask the questions or to try to hide the knowledge.

It is detrimental to everyone, not just to us, to not know that history. It impacts everyone. If people had known, if it had been part of our school curriculum over the generations and had been taught instead of ignored, we wouldn't have had this problem. Even some of the tribal council people born and raised here didn't know. It is something that has been pushed away.

The battle is still going on over who can tell the true history. Somehow it's believed that we are not at the same human level, to be able to tell history. What we have is "just stories." Or "oral history." And somehow that is not real. There is a lot of frustration, a lot of hurt in that. But what I say is, Read our words in this book. And put yourself in our shoes. Be open-minded. See how our ancestors' remains were used as backfill in pipeline trenches. Think about that reality, of how you would like your loved ones treated with respect in what they thought was their final destination and final resting place. Think about my expression as I stood with our tribal youth and those pipeline trenches and the bones of our ancestors were uncovered, and I tried to be strong and their backbone at that time. As I tried to explain how people could have treated another human being like this. And think about their anger and confusion and frustration that there were no laws and no rules, for years and years. And that people don't even always follow their own rules today.

But I have hope because I go back to the old man who came down to the site when we were working and said there was something he needed to clear from his heart and soul. He came down and said there was something he had been carrying for many years. It was hurtful to listen to, but he had to acknowledge that he knew, when they were building the mills down there, that they were just throwing the bones of our ancestors around. And then when this new construction project began, it started opening that up. It's that awareness in the community, that understanding, that we want. It was heavy in his heart, and he had to let it go. That is why the denial of this history, the refusal to look at it, has to stop. And then let things go, or you make yourself sick. That's why we say that what happened in the past happened in the past. Don't carry it with you.

We don't want the generations behind us to go through what we did. We want to be able to stand and say we did the best we could, and to carry on and educate the community and whoever its leaders might be. To look at the partnerships and the collaborations that everyone needs to work things out. Because we are not going to go anywhere. We have said time and time again, we will always be here and we have no intention of moving. This is our land, our waters, and our home base. Our teachings and our culture are here. Our history and our heritage. We want to be able to protect what we were taught; it doesn't matter what generation it is.

For too long, people have been cheated. They never learned any of this in school. The history books were tainted. They were tainted so that people would believe the tribes did not exist, that Native people had no existence here. The knowledge that this village was here shouldn't have to come from us. It should come from the outside communities. Even the current history books have nothing in them about the Native peoples; it is all denial. Look at the pictures in this book, which our elders provided, of their homesteads that were destroyed, homes that were bulldozed. And people are still telling that fib, not making it clear that Indians existed here. Even today, they take our material, but they don't use it. Or they don't listen. Why do they even ask?

Listen to the elders speak in this book. Listen to our youth. Look into the faces in the pictures. Look at the belongings of our elders, the pieces of the village that still remain at the site. And remember that we are not in this little box. When you listen to the stories from our elders, hear that we had villages and camps all along the shores. All up into the Elwha River Valley, there were no borders and boundaries like people want to believe today. We were enclosed in this little land base of the reservation, but it was not a choice that we made willingly; it was a choice that was made for us. We had thousands and thousands of acres that were known to be Klallam territory. It is frustrating to look at what once was ours and to be on such a little base. And look at us today: we have to buy back our land with money meant to meet the economic needs of the community, and not only of our community but of everyone.

Read this book and think about resilience and holding on to what is most important. That is what we have done. And now it is what we all must do. We can all learn from Tse-whit-zen and the damage that has been done to a culture and an environment in just two hundred years. The sea life in the harbor is not safe to eat; it's contaminated to toxic levels because of the pollution. The Elwha River is still not free because of the dams. Our salmon have gone, and we have wiped out the herbs and the roots and the berries with logging and development. We forget about what our true needs are.

It's that defragmentation that we need now. We need to look at the whole picture again, ask the questions, and not be afraid. Open your mind and heart. Look at the whole picture. Listen to what our elders tell us: You have to know your past in order to build your future.

Preface

STORIES CAN BE STUBBORN THINGS. SOME WANT TO BE TOLD MORE THAN OTH-ers. Some have their own life and power. This one was like that. My job as the writer was to show up, in the fullest sense, and stay there until the telling was done. My work was, at root, an act of careful conveyance. It was the carrying of people's thoughts, emotions, and yearning over contested ground, trying not to spill a drop of meaning.

This book is a work of nonfiction, and it is a diary as much as anything. In ten chapters, organized in three sections, what unfolds are the emotional journeys of many people, captured in the moment and set in the context of larger historical forces. Ultimately, this is a story about conflicting values and, as such, it spends much time in the interior of people's hearts and minds and in their emerging understanding of the events that enmesh them.

A few features of the book require explanation. First is my heavy reliance on interviews in telling this story. The reader is invited into my extended conversations with members of the Lower Elwha Klallam Tribe, officials at the Washington State Department of Transportation (WSDOT), and Port Angeles community leaders as the state began, then walked away from, a major construction project inadvertently sited atop an ancient Klallam village and burial ground.

These talks took place in homes on the reservation and at the site as tribal members dug their ancestors from the ground, clearing the way for construction. There were long talks with agency officials in their offices, their homes, and amid my work rooting through government documents. My own interaction with the landscape that holds the history of the site is here, too. The land, I discovered, speaks quite well for itself. All of these conversations shape the flow of the book, with the history fitted around them for context.

Photos make up the second factor in the distinctive shape and feel of this book. I am not a photographer, but I have long been convinced of the power of photography to tell stories. This book needed a rich visual telling, and with a lot of work and much help and generosity, offered here is a powerful photographic document recounting the history of this corner of the Pacific Northwest and its people, from the present day back to artifacts from aboriginal times. Many of these photos have never been published in any book, and I invite readers to linger over them. They allow us all to literally look into the face of history.

Permission to use most of these photos was gifted by the *Seattle Times* and the Lower Elwha Klallam Tribe, which provided access to their troves of photos shot during the archaeological dig and the unraveling of the project. Both archaeological firms involved in the project also offered their photos, as did the Department of Transportation and the editor of the *Muckleshoot Monthly*, the tribal newspaper for the Muckleshoot Indian Tribe. I dug some photos out of local historical archives in Port Angeles. Most special of all were the personal family albums that tribal elders at the reservation allowed me to borrow and the pictures I was permitted to take (briefly) out of the frames on their living room walls to make digital scans. Absent from all of the photos are human remains at the burial ground. That omission is total, at the request of the tribe, which did not want the bones of their family members offered for public view.

Another decision I made with the tribe was to include Native words for certain concepts, places, people, and things. The purpose of using the tribe's language was to illuminate the worldview embodied in the Klallam language, kept alive through the work of the tribe and its elders. It is significant that some Klallam words have no translation and that some English words do not exist in Klallam. There is, for instance, no Klallam word for "exhume" or "disinter." In the tribe's culture, that just didn't happen. There is a glossary at the back of the book for ready reference. Some place-names are also provided in Klallam and translated. To call a place "Pysht" is one thing. To know it means "Place Where the Wind Blows All the Time" is quite another.

Finally, for those who would like it, what follows is a brief roadmap of the book. The structure is nothing fancy; I chose a straightforward chronological telling. The exception is the first chapter, which starts right in the middle of work on the state's dry dock. My purpose in letting the reader walk around the construction site with a tribal member employed as a night security guard is to convey from the start a Native sense of place and spirituality. For this tribal member, and many others, the place was not just a construction site. It was sacred ground, alive with the spirits of his ancestors, with whom he was in active communication. It was also his homeland. It's worth getting this straight from the beginning, as this value system underlies everything that happens in the book.

Lower Elwha Klallam elders Bea Charles and Adeline Smith are crucial narrators in this story. They were eighty-six and eighty-seven years old when I reported this story for the newspaper and followed up with more interviews for the book. They had lost none of their faculties, and their memories and power of expression were sharp and rich. They were also generous and brave in telling their stories and answered every question, even the uncomfortable ones. Both women had lived away from the reservation for many years, first at the Chemawa boarding school for Indian students in Oregon and later in Seattle, where they went to find work as maids. When they returned to Port Angeles much later in life, they found a community that lived in separate worlds, Indian and non-Indian. To their amazement, many in Port Angeles seemed not to know the tribe even existed. "We was supposed to have died," is how Smith sometimes put it.

Much of this story is told through their oral history, including their knowledge, passed on to them by their elders, that a burial ground lay beneath the site the state selected for its dry dock. Charles and Smith close the first chapter by saying that no one should have been surprised to find the remains of an Indian village and burial ground at Tse-whit-zen. The site at the head of the harbor, crooked in the sheltering arm of the Ediz Hook, had always been a center of wealth for the entire region. Indians weren't stupid, they said. They knew where to live. And that place was Tse-whit-zen, some of the finest real estate in the aboriginal world.

The second chapter steps back to the beginning of the story and lets it unspool from there. The landscape that is the battleground of this story is the logical place to begin. Chapter 2 explores the natural history of the site, from the creation of the sand spit that cradles the harbor to the ecology of the Elwha River and watershed. I tell this history through elders on the reservation, who recount their parents' memories of the Elwha before it was dammed. They also offer teachings from their elders about the tribe's spiritual connection to the river and its salmon. The archaeological record of the site also helps tell this piece of the story, through the tools the Elwha people used to harvest the abundance of their homeland. Skeletons of the animals they harvested document the rich food web that provided the early Klallam people with the original diversified portfolio: something to eat in every season.

In the third chapter, I detail the arrival in 1790 of the first known European explorers, with the Manuel Quimper expedition. I use ship's logs and other primary sources and scholars' interpretations of them to re-create the explorers' travels up and down the Strait of Juan de Fuca and their first encounters with the Klallam people. In this chapter, I relate the coming of the diseases that would kill an estimated 80 percent of the coastal Indians in the first century of contact. The historical record helps tell this story, but so, too, does the archaeology at Tse-whit-zen. One of the most intriguing questions about the site is whether it provides a record of that fearful time and perhaps even depicts a cultural response to an epidemic. If so—and it is still a matter of debate and interpretation among experts—that would make the site all the more important for what it can teach us about this turning point in Northwest history.

In chapter 3, I recount the making of the Treaty of Point No Point, between the U.S. government and the Klallams and other tribes, and how tribal members were dispossessed of their waterfront home. Relying on the oral history of elders on the reservation, I tell a story not of victims but of a people who refused to be banished, as the treaty required, to a reservation one hundred miles from their homeland. Instead most Klallams stayed, adapted, and found ways to survive.

In chapter 4, I begin telling of the transformation of the Klallam people's homeland into prime industrial land. Tse-whit-zen would once again be a center of wealth for the region, this time for the newcomers who would make and count their wealth in money and jobs. The chapter opens with the damming of the Elwha River by Thomas Aldwell, who tells much of this part of the story best in his autobiography, so aptly titled *Conquering the Last Frontier*. I use oral history offered by elders at Lower Elwha as well as newspaper clippings of the day to document the mind-set among the newcomers, prevalent in that time, that the Indian people were a puzzling presence. A nostalgic presence, at best, to be flicked out of the path of progress if necessary. In this chapter, I also document the state's complicity in the damming of the Elwha

River with no provision for fish passage, despite clear laws, even then, requiring it. I quote from documents in the state archives to show that state officials not only knew they were breaking the law, they also knew it would lead to the demise of the mighty Elwha tyee, or chinook salmon, one of the greatest salmon runs the region has ever known. The record shows we cannot comfort ourselves by believing otherwise; the choice was a deliberate one. I rely on tribal members' stories of growing up by the river and their enduring attachment to it to let their sense of loss speak for itself.

Chapter 5 continues the story of the industrialization of the waterfront, with the building of the Big Mill, the largest sawmill of its day, right atop the Tse-whit-zen village site. In this chapter, I also discuss an often overlooked stage of the transformation of the Klallam homeland: the filling of tide flats that had sustained the tribe for thousands of years with shellfish and was one of its most valuable food sources. Here I rely on the expertise of anthropologists who have written eloquently on the importance of shellfish in the diet and culture of the Klallam people. Filling the tidelands and starving the beaches for sediment trapped behind the dams on the Elwha completed the destruction of the Klallam people's food supply. Like the salmon, the Klallam people were confined to a smaller and smaller homeland and a restricted food web. The chapter includes the construction of a second sawmill directly to the west of the Big Mill, to soak up the juice generated by the dams on the Elwha. I use newspaper clippings and internal newsletters from the Crown Zellerbach Corporation to capture the sense of casual necessity as builders literally tossed the bones of Indian people out of the way of construction. Period newspaper clippings recount residents being burned out of so-called squatters shacks on the Ediz Hook, right as the first fall rains began. Charles and Smith tell, too, of how the Klallam people, pushed away from the waterfront, settled on homesteads in the floodplain of the Elwha and farther out on the peninsula, at Pysht, until they were run out of there, too, this time by a logging company. The two women eventually moved to Seattle to work rather than stay in Port Angeles, where, as Smith said, "If you didn't look Indian, you never admitted it."

Some 150 years of disease, dispossession, industrial development, and forced assimilation took their toll. Within the tribe, a cultural gap opened, as tribal members left to find work and elders decided not to pass their culture on. They didn't want more children to suffer as they had. So deliberately dug, it's a cultural gap that this town, this state, and this tribe soon fell into together. In chapter 6, the WSDOT enters the picture. Here, department policy leaders explain the urgent need to fix the Hood Canal

Bridge and their search for a suitable site for building gigantic concrete components for the repair. City officials enter the story as well, recounting their efforts to bring the dry dock project, and the construction jobs associated with it, to Port Angeles. It is here that I explain the state's and the city's assumptions about the site, as well as the mistakes made in the initial archaeological survey that turned up no showstoppers at the site. But it's also in this chapter that tribal leaders talk about their own mistakes. They didn't dig into tribal archives to investigate the history of the site or talk to their elders about the proposed project. Instead, when the state forwarded its flawed survey finding no concerns about the site, the tribe counseled caution but agreed with the report and gave the project the go-ahead.

Tribal Chairwoman Frances Charles speaks of the state consultant's shallow survey, in which not a single tribal member was even telephoned. And she speaks as well of the elders' reluctance, as the project got under way, to come forward when they had never been listened to in the past. The failure to know what is to come next is a shared one.

The ground first speaks in chapter 7, when construction workers, within days of beginning work, unearthed a shell midden. Next, human bone fragments were dug up, and ten days after the job began, Douglas MacDonald, secretary of the WSDOT, shut the project down. It is here in this chapter that the story diverges from the past. This inadvertent discovery didn't happen in 1930 or 1950. This was the year 2003, at a publicly funded construction project two hours away from Seattle. Instead of just going ahead with construction, as had happened at this site many times before, the department offered an unusual gesture of reconciliation. At the tribe's invitation and at taxpayer expense, the department participated in a burning ceremony, the first held at Lower Elwha in many years. The ceremony marked the first stage of negotiations between the state and the tribe over if and how the project could continue.

I rely on transportation officials' personal recollection, correspondence, and even midnight diary entries to take the reader inside hearts and minds at the highest levels of the department, where nobody thought saving the project was going to be easy. In chapter 8, I pull back the curtain on six months of negotiations between the state and the tribe on restarting construction. The struggle on both sides to reach common ground, with the bitter taste of history still in their mouths, is expressed through recollections of tribal and agency policy makers at the negotiating table. Finally, the tribe gave its assent and construction resumed. Workers uprooted the first intact Indian burial within a week.

Chapter 9 details how the agency's project began to unravel. Tribal members hired to work alongside archaeologists at the site speak of their initial excitement as they encountered the bones and belongings of their ancestors. But as the number of burials disturbed by construction mounted, feelings shifted. Tribal members told the agency they could not bear the disruption and separation of their ancestors as they dug some skeletons from the ground, because they were in the path of construction, and left others behind, because they were not. Take every bone out, the tribe insisted, or the spirits of our ancestors will search forever for the loved ones left behind.

Already behind schedule and over budget, agency policy makers resisted. Meanwhile, word of what was going on at the project started to spread. The Centennial Accord, the annual meeting of tribes around Washington to talk policy with the governor and cabinet members, turned into a referendum on the dry dock project. By the end of the day, Tribal Chairwoman Charles told Secretary MacDonald that she would be sending him a letter asking him to stop the project. MacDonald, after later consulting with the congressional delegation and the governor, took a deep breath and walked away from more than $90 million in public funds that had been sunk into this ground. Enough was simply enough.

Chapter 10 puts the reader inside the union halls and town meetings in Port Angeles, where the tribe and the department are excoriated for shutting the job down. To town leaders, the project became a kind of toxic cloud over the future development of the waterfront. As the dispute ground on, the tribe, stymied in its request to rebury its ancestors, sued. After two tries at negotiation, the tribe finally settled with the state and gained a parcel of land at the site for reburial. But the celebration of the agreement rang hollow. Stopping this project had merely illuminated the need for another: building a bridge of reconciliation. Whether that work will be successful is yet to be seen.

The epilogue sets forth the lessons taken from Tse-whit-zen by people across the country, where the department's decision was widely regarded as long overdue and precedent setting. But this is not a book with a neat, happy ending. What remains in the end is a sense of the work ahead, building a shared vision of our history and our future. Perhaps from it can come a new meaning for progress.

Acknowledgments

THIS BOOK COULD NOT HAVE BEEN WRITTEN WITHOUT THE HELP AND ENCOURagement of the Lower Elwha Klallam people and tribal members around Puget Sound who opened their homes and hearts to me.

Elders Bea Charles and Adeline Smith allowed me to spend many hours at their homes, recording the stories of their lives growing up in the Pacific Northwest during the time of forced assimilation. I am grateful for their courage and generosity. I am also grateful for their permission to use family photographs to illustrate the book. I could not have written this book without their insight, stories, knowledge, and encouragement.

Elder Johnson Charles Jr. welcomed me into his home, his heart, and his memories, sharing his upbringing along the Elwha and the stories and teachings of that river. He also permitted me to use a precious photograph of his father in this book.

Tribal Chairwoman Frances Charles allowed me to work at the reservation as well as at the Tse-whit-zen site. This book would not have been possible without her generosity of heart and spirit and her support for this project. Her commitment to the telling of this story was total; she could not have been more helpful. She and her husband, Jerry, also opened their home to me while I was at the reservation, turning what could have been long slogs away from home into fond memories.

I am also deeply honored to have been allowed to spend time in the presence of the tribe's ancestors as well as to witness private moments and ceremonies both at Lower Elwha and at the smokehouse in Esquimalt, just outside Victoria in British Columbia. This privilege was crucial to helping me understand some of the cultural aspects of life at Lower Elwha and the inseparable spiritual dimension of the dry dock dilemma. But let me be clear: All of the stories and the cultural and traditional knowledge shared by tribal members in this book are their intellectual property, and they are their sole authorities and owners.

Spiritual leader Mary Anne Thomas and her husband, Andy, chief of the Esquimalt Nation in British Columbia, invited me to attend winter ceremonial dances at the Big House in Esquimalt and helped me understand the ties of blood and culture that, since time immemorial, have bound them across the water to the Lower Elwha people.

Tribal members Lonnie Charles, Mark Charles, Arlene Wheeler, Derek Charles, Teresa Sanders, Wendy Sampson, Mike Watson, Carmen Watson-Charles, and Michael Q. Langland shared their deeply personal stories of working at the Tse-whit-zen site and talked about how it changed their lives.

Tribal council member Dennis Sullivan bravely opened his heart about negotiations with state and federal officials as the tribe wrestled with the decision as to whether to allow construction of the dry dock to continue. He was tribal chairman then, and his candid descriptions of his regrets over the handling of the project made for a much stronger, truer story.

Douglas B. MacDonald, former secretary of the Washington State Department of Transportation, was generous with his time and insights and went above and beyond to connect me with other people at the department who had important knowledge and feelings to share. Our peculiar encounter, as he called it, taught me once and for all that one story well told and heard always leads to another.

I owe a particular debt to Colleen Jollie, Randy Hain, and Steve Reinmuth at the Department of Transportation for the time and heart they offered. Jo Aldrich, executive assistant for the department, got me to the documents, people, and appointments I needed, with warmth, humor, and efficiency. Lloyd Brown, director of communications for the department, handled my many requests with a spirit of generosity. Linda Mullen, former director of communications for the department, was kind enough to read a draft of the manuscript after she left the agency. She contributed important insights into this complex story and its players.

John Loftus, editor of the tribal newspaper *Muckleshoot Monthly*, gave me photos he had taken at the Tse-whit-zen site to illustrate this book.

Glenn Hartmann of Western Shores Heritage Services spent many hours explaining his firm's controversial role in this story, when he didn't have to talk to me at all.

Archaeologists Dennis Lewarch and Lynn Larson helped in countless ways, and Allyson Brooks, director of the state Department of Archaeology and Historic Preservation, steered me to the documents I needed and answered my questions with refreshing candor.

Scholar and author Robert Boyd of Portland, Oregon, shared his expertise and notes on the infectious diseases that ravaged the peoples of the Northwest Coast. He also took time from his own work to review the chapter on smallpox as well as to help *Seattle Times* artist Mark Nowlin create the map illustrating the spread of that disease in the Northwest.

Brian Winter of the National Park Service spent a day explaining the remarkable Lower Elwha ecosystem and the dam removal project to me.

Olympic Park Institute field research project manager Darek Staab invited me to join Lower Elwha teens and tribal elders for their summer 2006 exploration of the Lower Elwha, enriching my sense of the tribe's connection to the river.

Jamie Valadez of the Lower Elwha Klallam tribe emptied her library for me and gave me access to her voluminous notes and files on the Elwha River, greatly enhancing my understanding of the river from the tribe's perspective. She also helped me make crucial connections to elders at Lower Elwha and helped me locate information in the tribal archives I would not have found on my own. Her support for this project was crucial.

Kathy Monds, executive director at the Clallam County Historical Society, and Dona Cloud, the society's research librarian, were patient and helpful beyond measure as I dug through their trove of old newspapers, photographs, and other material on Port Angeles.

I also thank *Seattle Times* publisher Frank Blethen, who supported seven months of work at the paper on the Tse-whit-zen story, printed first as breaking news in the *Seattle Times* during the fall and winter of 2004 and then as a four-part series in the spring of 2005. Without support at the top for sensitive, time-consuming, in-depth work, stories like this simply do not get published in the mainstream press.

Seattle Times photo editor Fred Nelson brought his sharp eye and aesthetic sense to the photo edit for the book. *Times* managing editor Suki Dardarian, managing editor Jim Simon, metro editor Mark Higgins, and assistant metro editor Ian Ith also provided unwavering support. *Times* photographer Steve Ringman could not have brought more talent or heart to this story. Special thanks to Evelyn Edens of the *Times* for her tireless persistence and attention to detail in securing permission for use of the photographs from the *Times*, and for her marketing finesse. No author could hope for better support.

The newspaper also generously granted me access without charge to much of the superb photography and illustrations that appeared originally in the newspaper, adding enormously to this book's emotional and explanatory power.

Photographer Terry Donnelly of Vashon Island gave up hours of his time and lent his first-class equipment and expertise to help me organize hundreds of digital images and scan tribal members' treasured family photographs.

Photographer Ed Hosselkus of Port Angeles turned around my request for dozens of digital scans in a blink to help me make a deadline. The research staff at the Port Angeles branch of the North Olympic Library System endured my many questions and helped me navigate their rich trove of images in the Bert Kellogg Collection.

My deep thanks go to friends at Skokomish, who were among the first to instruct and encourage me in my work as a journalist with Indian people. Michael Pavel embraced me as a friend, mentored me, and welcomed me into his remarkable family. Gordon Nielsen first brought me the Tse-whit-zen story and then encouraged me to write this book. The late subiyay Bruce Miller taught, inspired, and challenged me.

My editor at the University of Washington Press, Jacqueline Ettinger, and former executive editor Michael Duckworth proposed doing this book in the first place. They offered clear-minded assessment and sincere encouragement throughout the process.

I am also grateful to the Press for its willingness to support top-notch photo illustration for this book. It meant more work and expense, but everyone involved wanted to do this book right. No author could ask for more.

I also offer deep thanks to Peter and Linda Capell of Seattle for their generous decision to create an endowment at the University of Washington Press for publication of books in the field of human rights and social justice, beginning with this one.

Finally, I thank my friends and family for supporting me in this project. I could not have done this without the love, encouragement, and help of each and every one of them.

I

Tse-whit-zen (čixʷícən)

1

Buried Past Comes Alive

THEY LIE FACING EAST, IN A WINDOWLESS ROOM, IN THE HALF-LIGHT OF FLICK-ering fluorescent bulbs. The buzz of the lights sounds like breathing. Candles burn on a makeshift altar, two-by-fours arranged in a cross painted white. An upholstered bench seat from a van shares the entryway with a defunct control center for this concrete-block bunker, a relic from the Second World War. The console has dials and switches and buttons, like something for the man behind the curtain in *The Wizard of Oz*. The Honeywell Supervisory Data Center, with controls for a water storage tank, master oil storage, decontamination fan, and emergency all-clear siren, looks ready for any calamity but this one. Next to it is a control center of quite another sort: a bolt of white blanket fabric in which to wrap human remains. A jar that once held oysters now half filled with red ochre powder, to paint around the eyes and wrists for spiritual protection.

Just a few steps inside the door, the smell of cedar is sharp, penetrating. And then there they are, behind a blue plastic tarp hung from the ceiling for privacy: more than 335 handmade boxes, each filled with the bones of the ancestors of the Lower Elwha

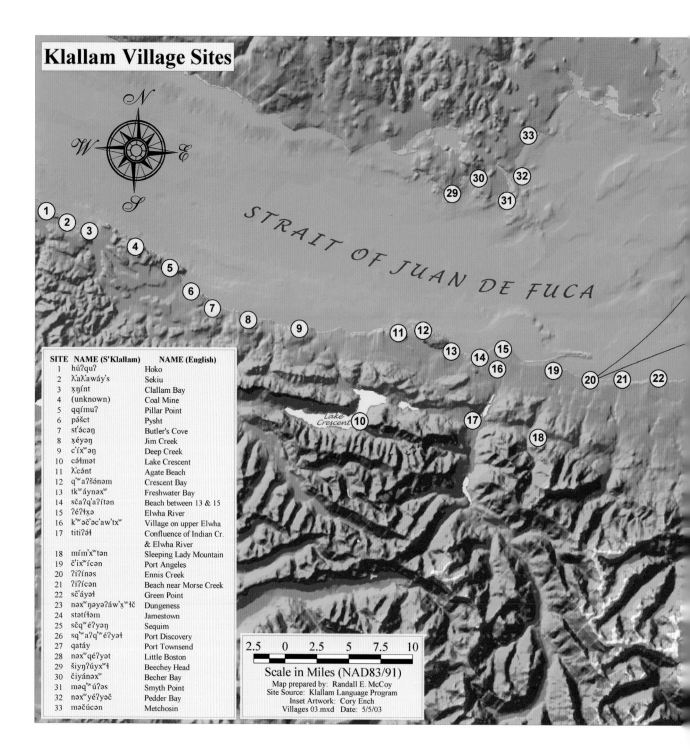

Klallam Village Sites

SITE	NAME (S'Klallam)	NAME (English)
1	húʔquʔ	Hoko
2	ƛ̓aƛ̓awáy's	Sekiu
3	x̣ŋínt	Clallam Bay
4	(unknown)	Coal Mine
5	qqímuʔ	Pillar Point
6	pə́šct	Pysht
7	st̓ə́cəŋ	Butler's Cove
8	x̣éyəŋ	Jim Creek
9	c̓íx̣ʷəŋ	Deep Creek
10	cə́łmət	Lake Crescent
11	ƛ̓cə́nt	Agate Beach
12	qʷaʔšónəm	Crescent Bay
13	tkʷáynəx̣ʷ	Freshwater Bay
14	sčaʔq̓aʔítən	Beach between 13 & 15
15	ʔéʔłxə	Elwha River
16	kʷəč̓əc̓aw'txʷ	Village on upper Elwha
17	titiʔə́ł	Confluence of Indian Cr. & Elwha River
18	mím'x̣ʷtən	Sleeping Lady Mountain
19	č̓ix̣ʷícən	Port Angeles
20	ʔiʔínəs	Ennis Creek
21	ʔiʔícən	Beach near Morse Creek
22	sč̓áyəł	Green Point
23	nəx̣ʷŋəyəʔáw'x̣ʷłč	Dungeness
24	stətíłəm	Jamestown
25	sčq̓ʷéʔyəŋ	Sequim
26	sqʷaʔqʷéʔyəł	Port Discovery
27	qatáy	Port Townsend
28	nəx̣ʷqéʔyət	Little Boston
29	šiyŋʔúyx̣ʷł	Beechey Head
30	čiyánəx̣ʷ	Becher Bay
31	məqʷúʔəs	Smyth Point
32	nəx̣ʷyéʔyəč	Pedder Bay
33	məčúcən	Metchosin

Scale in Miles (NAD83/91)

2.5 0 2.5 5 7.5 10

Map prepared by: Randall E. McCoy
Site Source: Klallam Language Program
Inset Artwork: Cory Ench
Villages 03.mxd Date: 5/5/03

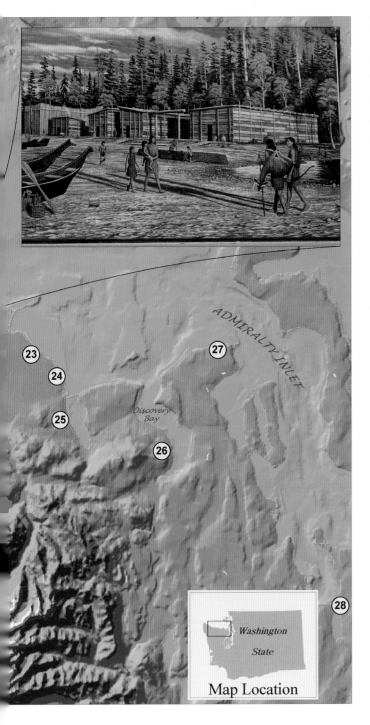

Klallam Tribe. "One person," says a small handwritten tag on a box, hand-carved like all the others and fitted with yellow cedar pegs that fasten its red cedar planks. The boxes are sanded smooth as skin and have simple rope handles threaded through each end. Crosses are carved in every lid, a reflection of the Indian Shaker Church faith adopted by many here at the Lower Elwha Klallam reservation, just outside downtown Port Angeles.

"Three people," reads the tag on another box. "One person, age, sex unknown." "One person's foot." "Two infants." Large, smooth, rounded gray rocks, the headstones found with the graves that held these bones, are heaped in plastic tubs along one wall. Jackets, shirts, pants, and other clothing, donated by tribal members, spill from plastic garbage bags piled in a corner, to be burned on split cedar tables along with complete dinners of salmon, oysters, and clams. Offerings for these ancestors, to be carried on the smoke of the burning table to the spirit world. The boxes are all sizes: small as a cradle and tinier, like a hatbox. Big as the seat of a bench, even as large as a closet door. Inside that box, the headless skeleton of a medicine man, laid out on his back, glitters with mica.

Darrell Charles Jr., one of the carvers at the Lower Elwha Klallam Tribe, is pulling all-nighters with Clark Mundy, a non-Indian friend, to make these boxes. They craft one after another, strong enough to carry two hundred pounds if necessary, including earth

The Klallam people's aboriginal territory included thirty-three known villages on both sides of the Strait of Juan de Fuca, along the Elwha River, and into the Olympic Mountains. Courtesy Lower Elwha Klallam Tribe.

taken with the bones. "It was kind of hard to do. It felt draining, but it got easier because there is such a need," Charles says. "What was the alternative? Bagging and crating? I just couldn't see that. Now we are making about thirty a week at a time, and they ask us to do special sizes, for multiple individuals, burials that run into each other, or with a large number of artifacts." He arrives to deliver the boxes in a rez car packed with friends, talking on his cell phone, his jeans caked with cedar sawdust. He knows his is no ordinary job. "I've got to start with a good attitude or not at all. We're rehousing the ancestors, that's what it is," Charles says. Tribal member Linda Wiechman joins him, walking over from the waterfront site where she is working with more than one hundred tribal members alongside construction workers and archaeologists to help dig her ancestors' bones and belongings out of the path of heavy equipment.

The Washington State Department of Transportation (WSDOT) chose this area to build a dry dock, inadvertently placing it atop the tribe's largest waterfront village, Tse-whit-zen, today called Port Angeles. The village name in Klallam is čxʷícən, translated as "area inside the spit." The village would turn out to be one of the most important archaeological finds in the Northwest and the burial ground for an uncounted number of Indian souls. By November 2004, as Charles and Mundy are pulling their all-nighters, the workers had unearthed the remains of an estimated 369 ancestors, including as many as 223 burials discovered in the course of building the project. Some had been disturbed by earlier development but many appeared to have been intact. This was nothing anyone had intended or even imagined back when the work began in August 2003. Wiechman makes offerings of eagle down, sage, olive shells, and daily prayers to ask her ancestors for permission to be on this ground, doing this work, digging their graves. When she talks with her ancestors, she gets disturbing answers back. She feels haunted. "The spirits are not happy. They said it's not over by a long shot, because you are removing them from Mother Earth," Wiechman says. "We are removing them from the womb."

My first visit to the village site came after tribal member Carmen Watson-Charles, then just twenty-three, decided to phone me at the urging of a friend from another tribe. A cell phone call from a tribal member at an Indian burial ground, with the sounds of heavy equipment operating in the background, is the sort of thing that gets a newspaper reporter's attention. Already extensively written up in the *Port Angeles Daily News*, the story of the discovery of the burial ground and Klallam village, parts of it in use for at least 2,700 years, had not yet reached a wider audience. "They are uncovering whole skeletons intact. They are finding infants that were used as backfill," Watson-Charles says on that first phone call, her voice shaky with emotion. She tells me about separating the skeletons of a couple who had been buried together, their faces turned to each other and arms locked in an embrace. She describes breaking their bones apart, one at a time, to fit them in a box. "I'll have to live with that the rest of my life," she says.

After I hang up I sit quietly for a moment. This is how it goes in newsrooms everywhere. One moment you're working on a story about mad cow disease and the rebound of the Washington beef industry. Researching meat prices and the Atkins diet craze. Dialing around for a rancher who still drives cattle on horseback, looking for pictures to go with the story. Then the phone rings with news of an Indian burial ground that somehow is also a state construction project and an archaeological dig all at once. That's not making any sense to me. How can it be all three? What is the state doing uprooting intact Indian burials by the hundreds? If that's really true, how could it still be going on? If the village is that important, why is it being destroyed? How in this day and age did a public construction project—paid for mostly with federal money—wind up in the middle of an ancient Indian village? I don't even know exactly where the site is yet. But I'm pretty sure that whatever this story is about, it's going to be filling the front page and several blanks of the Sunday newspaper four days from now.

The next morning breaks clear and cold. I cross the salt water of Puget Sound by ferry to begin the two-hour drive to Port Angeles—P.A. as it's known locally. Along the way, I cross the Hood Canal Bridge, the longest floating bridge over salt water anywhere in the world. A mile-and-a-half-long two-lane strand, the bridge spans the cold, slate blue of Puget Sound and is a critical connection between the state's urbanized western side and the more rural Olympic Peninsula. The Olympic Mountains, mantled with the first snows of fall, rear up over the water to the west. I drive past construction workers operating heavy equipment and working at repairs. The bridge, opened in 1961, is undergoing improvements to the west half, but the east half is slated for total replacement. It's already past its useful life: One of its cables had snapped, and the drawbridge span was no longer reliable. The $471 million replacement project was one of the state's most urgent priorities. The transportation department chose the Port Angeles site for building new concrete pontoons, which float the road surface of the bridge, and concrete anchors that tether the whole thing to the bottom of Puget Sound.

The first step in the project was to build a dry dock at the site, so the completed

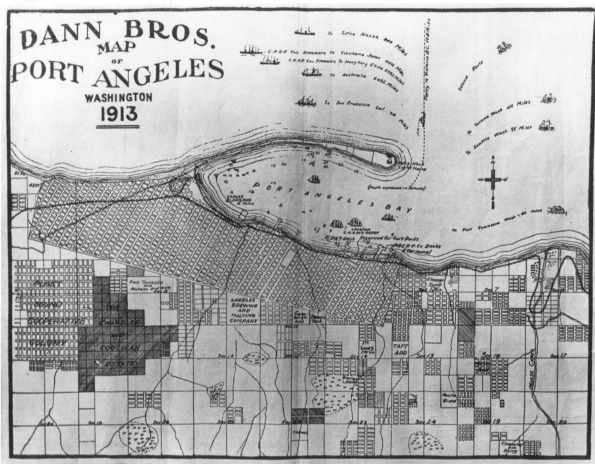

The Greatest Future Shipping Port of the Pacific Coast

PORT ANGELES, WASHINGTON
The Coming Coast City
The Natural Terminus of all TRANSCONTINENTAL ROADS North of California

Port Angeles, 1913. Boosters envisioned a prosperous city in the heart of what had been the homeland of the Klallam people for generations uncounted. The land claim of Alexander Sampson is in the same location as the Tse-whit-zen village site. Later, a large sawmill and then the state's construction project were placed on the site. Courtesy Klallam County Historical Society.

pontoons and anchors could be floated out to open water and towed to the bridge where they would replace the old pontoons. Once I reach the other side of the bridge, thick fir forests crowding the road showed the deep bites of clear-cuts. Logging trucks blast past me, making my small car shudder. Logging has shaped the land and people on the peninsula for more than one hundred years. I pass the totem poles that mark the entrance to a casino, one of the few obvious reminders of the Indian people who still call this region home, more than 150 years after ceding most of their lands to white settlement in the Treaty of Point No Point. As I finally hit the downgrade to the waterfront in P.A., the town's main street quickly gives way to the log yards and mill buildings on the west end of the waterfront.

Most people here would tell you that Port Angeles is not an Indian town. Go to Taholah, on the Washington coast; or to Nespelem, amid the dryland ponderosa forests in northeastern Washington; or to Neah Bay, at the state's farthest northwestern tip. Those are Indian towns, with their free-ranging rez dogs, fishing boats in the front yards, and Indian people everywhere. Not Port Angeles, a town built atop the remains of Indian villages along its waterfront and physically transformed by a century of fill, riprap, logging, sawmills, and pulp plants. Port Angeles is big rigs and fat tires and hickory shirts. It's broad shoulders and pickups, logging trucks thundering down the two-lane. It's a waterfront where you can't see the water for the industrial buildings roaring with the sound of the work everyone wants. It's windsocks of smoke and steam; it's rusty metal pipes and smokestacks and growling machinery. Chain link and broken asphalt. Tires stacked as tall as the roof of a station wagon, with tread that would swallow a finger to the knuckle. Not many Volvos here. It's mountains of logs, ready to ship; it's men carrying hot dogs wrapped in foil, bought at the gas station take-out counter and eaten walking back to the job site. It looks, in fact, like the perfect place to build an industrial-scale dry dock. Once part of a thriving timber and mill town, today this waterfront, with its acreage of empty lots, idle machinery, and a marina crowded with listing boats going nowhere, yearns for jobs and paychecks. What's under this parking lot? That mill building? What do those pipes thrust through, those pilings, those utility lines, tie-downs, and foundations? Who wants to know? No one knows; everyone knows.

Nothing in this town had ever been stopped because of anything Indian. Even as the body count rose with each shovelful of dirt turned, the decision by state, federal, and tribal leaders to shut down the project, lay off every worker, and walk away from about $90 million in state and federal tax dollars already spent at the site hit Port Angeles like a bomb. But it's the invisibility of the Lower Elwha Klallam Tribe, here for more than 10,000 years, that is the real surprise. The ancient beach where they lived and buried their dead is long forgotten under layers of fill dirt, stacked with battlements of logs. The people who drive these pickups, log trucks, and front-end loaders with clanking jaws taking another bite of logs are mostly men and mostly white. They don't know šášk'ʷu (Adeline Smith) and ƛíƛ̓ixc̓ə (Bea Charles), Lower Elwha Klallam elders who could tell anyone who asks just what is under this industrialized waterfront. But nobody asks.

Newcomers in Port Angeles and its Native people have learned to largely do without each other. Just miles apart, they live in parallel worlds. Not a single tribal member has ever served on the city council, the port commission, the school board, the county commission or in the legislature. Why bother? Outside the public school system, where the tribe and public school educators have gone to great lengths to make Indian students feel at home, the civic life of Port Angeles is not a place of concern to the tribe, any more than the tribe is of concern to the city of Port Angeles. Unless the tribe gets in the way of something the city wants to do. And that has never been tolerated for long. The division in this town is well symbolized by the damming of ʔéʔɬxʷə stúʔwiʔ (the Elwha River). Just west of town, the river cascades from the heart of the Olympic Mountains all the way to the salt water of the Strait of Juan de Fuca. The lifeblood of this tribe for millennia, the Elwha was once home to the biggest salmon in Puget Sound. The mighty June Hog chinook, some reaching a weight of one hundred pounds, were sacrificed to build hydropower dams with no fish ladders, which powered mills constructed atop the tribe's waterfront villages. Industrialization would continue to displace, drown, and bury this tribe's homeland on the Elwha and Port Angeles waterfront for the next century. By the time the WSDOT showed up to scout a location for its construction project, the waterfront site offered by city business and political leaders wasn't known as an Indian anything. It was thought about, valued, and sold to the state as prime industrial land.

The Native sense of this place was unknown, disregarded, easy to ignore, but still very much alive: the salt tide still sluices through the cobble here on the sand spit of the Ediz Hook, easing and bubbling up the beach. Smooth and rounded by the sea, the beach stones are the right size to chip into a knife that fits just so in the hand. Used for butchering the salmon that surged by here, these cobble spalls still can be found by the hundreds in the ground at Tse-whit-zen. No mute, inert repository of human action, the ground is dimensional in its memory. The diary of all that has

Tse-whit-zen (čixʷícən), aerial view, 2004. When the Washington State Department of Transportation chose this spot for its project, it did not know a major Klallam village and uncounted number of graves lay just below the fill dirt covering the site. Courtesy Washington State Department of Transportation.

happened here is recorded in the land the Creator brought forth to provide a home for the tree people and animal people who in turn were created and entrusted with the care and feeding of the last, most fragile ones: us. The plant and animal people who helped sustain Tse-whit-zen all knew this village, and they remember it well. To many Indian people, this ground also speaks through the guardian spirit helpers that are still very much a part of their lives. And it speaks of the ancestral spirits that inhabit the ground today, as dynamically as when they walked the Earth here as humans 2,700 years ago.

The Indians' songs and stories, gifted in dreams, vision quests, and oral tradition, tell of canoes entering the bay sheltered by the spit from the great waters of the Strait of Juan de Fuca. They tell of residents of the village, returning with salmon, halibut, and woven baskets full of clams. Of travelers, stopping off at Tse-whit-zen to trade before crossing over to the other side of the Strait. Invited guests from throughout the region came for ceremonies in the big house, right on the water. There would be days of feasting, oratory, singing, and dancing, perhaps to celebrate the gifting of a name or the coming-out of a guardian spirit dancer and to demonstrate the wealth of the high-class families in this village. The web of memory in the ground goes broader and deeper, entwining the descendants of tribal members who lived at Tse-whit-zen. It includes the təwánəxʷ (Skokomish) people along Hood Canal and tribes all over the Olympic Peninsula and across the salt water into Canada. Peoples all around the Salish Sea, as Puget Sound is also called, have family members buried here. Their ancestors gathered food here. They traded for the smoked, sweet, fat clams dug from the tide flats at this village. And they savored the roasted haunches of deer and the herring roe combed from emerald green eelgrass with the tiny teeth of rakes fashioned from bone. Tse-whit-zen was a crossroads of aboriginal travel and culture, nurtured by ties to

Tribal members and archaeologists were astonished to find museum-quality artifacts at the village site nearly every day. This comb (tšéʔqʷən) was carved from bone on both sides and was found nearly intact by tribal construction monitors. Courtesy Washington State Department of Transportation.

the four directions. The people of the southern sound and the outer coast, the northern tribes from Canada and Alaska, and peoples from east of the Cascade mountains all knew this place.

Songs, passed by inheritance from generation to generation, are still sung today throughout Puget Sound country by relatives of the people of this village. And more songs are still coming home to Lower Elwha, gifted back by tribes who inherited them through ties of blood and marriage. Indian names, traced through family trees stretching back hundreds of years, find their roots in the sqʷəyíyəšháwtxʷ (dancehouse) that stood at this village, where marriages and syəẃən (winter dances) were held close to the sound of the tide. The night would be filled with the sound of songs, kʷčmín (rattles) made of deer hooves on dancers' poles, and the beating of drums. And it would be punctuated with sparks, thrown by great fires built on the earthen floor, lifting orange and bright into the night sky through smoke holes in the cedar plank roof. The sound of the tide rinsing through the beach cobble is the only living thing

Lower Elwha tribal member Mark Charles, known as Hammer on the reservation, painstakingly searches for human remains, 2004. Tribal members worked alongside archaeologists to remove their ancestors' bones from the ground, out of the path of construction. Courtesy Lower Elwha Klallam Tribe.

left from those days at Tse-whit-zen. It's a sound that must be sought out, at the water's edge, where it meets riprap and fill, and listened for over the din of industrial equipment. Or you can still hear it on a small strip of natural beach that still survives on the Ediz Hook, between a pulp mill and a Coast Guard station. For beginning in 1790, in different ways and for different reasons, xʷanítəm (non-Indians), like the Native people before them, made this place a center of wealth for their people. And as they did so, they steadily, completely transformed this place. By the time the Department of Transportation showed up in 2002, looking for a place to build pontoons and anchors to fix the Hood Canal Bridge, this place, like so many others in the Northwest, was no longer known by its Indian name. The animal people, the plant people, even the descendants of this village were long gone. The sčiyúʔis (ancestors) and their village were still here. A buried but never obliterated truth held in this ground, they would speak for themselves in time, for the land can't be silent forever.* In August 2003, when the department broke ground at the site, the buried past came alive.

Lower Elwha tribal member Derek Charles considers himself one of the lucky ones: The ancestors would show themselves to him. Formerly a $7.35-an-hour donation attendant at the Goodwill Industries in Port Angeles, he was one of more than one hundred tribal members hired by the WSDOT to work at the dry dock site on the Port Angeles waterfront after the village was unearthed. Charles, thirty-two, had dropped out of auto mechanic school and taken college courses in business administration. The $12-an-hour job at the dry dock was the best one he had ever had.

Diagnosed with cancer at age three, Charles felt lucky to be alive. Surgery after surgery filled his childhood. "They started on my left leg. Then my bladder. Then my

* Dr. Michael Pavel, Skokomish, gifted the author with this understanding of Tse-whit-zen during a conversation in Port Angeles, Washington, July 2005.

In this December 2004 meeting with state transportation officials, members of the Port Angeles Chamber of Commerce are not happy to learn that the dry dock project that brought high-paying jobs to town is being shut down to protect Indian graves. Never before had anything been stopped here because of anything Indian. Steve Ringman, courtesy *Seattle Times*.

brain. It was eight, nine years of treatments and staying at the hospital. From growing up, I knew I was left here for a reason." Charles worked as a security guard at the dry dock site for more than a year. His post was a construction trailer, set aside for the exclusive use of tribal members while the project was under way. The Love Shack, they called it. With a dish of təməɬ (red ochre) for spiritual protection, and a candle burning in honor of his ancestors, Charles spent all night keeping watch over this ground. Slowly, line by line, he filled page after page of a notebook with the tag number of every car that came and left and logged every person who visited. And while their elders taught them they weren't supposed to be on this ground after sundown, when the spirits of their ancestors crowded in thick, Charles, a night watchman for the construction site, had no choice. "The first night, I wouldn't leave the shack," Charles said. "It was pretty freaky; it was scary out there, even with a flashlight. Finally I said, 'OK. I'll go out there where they were digging.' I'd go wandering around." With red ochre touched on his face, he ventured out into the night. "My curiosity got the better of me, to go out there and see what's going on. That's when I got my experience of the spirits, walking around. It was like they were grabbing my arms and legs and walking around with me. I didn't know what was going on. I just put my hands up and said, 'I am here to make sure you guys are safe, make sure no one stomps on you, or walks all over you.'"

An annual meeting of state officials and tribal leaders from across Washington becomes a referendum on the construction project as controversy about it spreads, December 2004. Tribal Chairwoman Frances Charles (*center*) tells former Washington Governor Gary Locke (*left*) and former secretary of transportation Douglas B. MacDonald that the disturbance of her people's graves is unbearable. Steve Ringman, courtesy *Seattle Times*.

On a wet, blowing night, he walked to the west end of the site, where, in a space the size of a two-car garage, tribal members were working to remove more than 103 skeletons crowded in the ground. Tribal members believe it is a smallpox grave. "Something twisted me around from my normal route; I just did a U-turn," Charles said. "I walked past a big pile of dirt, and something happened. All of a sudden I just needed to cry. Then I walked back to the shack and just cried for a good hour. After I started crying, I knew it was my ancestors. I heard a couple of them. They said, 'Derek, we are getting tired of this.' It's like they were talking to me as I was walking back to the shack." He called his brother and a few close friends for help. "They came down, and I was shaking and shaking. I said, 'I don't know what was going on. The ancestors spoke to me and said they are getting tired of what's going on down here, they were upset and disturbed and tired and sad at all the bickering and fighting, that it has got to stop.'"

Back home, still shaking, he went next door, to Johnson Charles Jr., a tribal elder. Concerned, Johnson called some tribal leaders of the Indian Shaker Church at Lower Elwha to come over and spiritually cleanse Charles. "They said my spirit was still down there, and they had to bring it back to where I was," Derek Charles said. He sat down in a chair and shut his eyes as the Shakers went to work on him. They knew what was needed: powerful song, sung together, with no one leaving or breaking concentration until the ceremony was over. Prayer and hands swept over Charles's head and body, to brush him off. And bells, rung at the threshold of pain, to bring his spirit back from the site and return it to his body. It took hard work, together, to send that song and prayer and the sound of the bells to the spirits, disturbed from their rest and holding Charles in a dangerous grip. For the spirit world of the tribe's ancestors is embodied not in some distant place, reached after death. It is right here, right now, in the ground with their remains, at the site. And those spirits, when disturbed or violated, are deeply powerful, even dangerous. But none of that first experience with his ancestors scared him so much as it changed him, Charles said. Swift Waters—his Indian name—understood that from then on, while he was the only one assigned to work the night shift at the site, he wouldn't be working alone. "After that, I felt like they were always around me when I was doing my patrol. I'd feel them on me, hugging me, here around my chest. I'd say, 'All right, ride's over.' It was like a comfort, like a security blanket, that they would keep me safe, that there was someone with me. I'd go out, and this particular time, I was walking along and I saw something standing. It was a full figure, but it was like a shadow, black. A little taller than I was. I think it was a man. Just standing there. I don't really know why they communicated with me," Charles said of his ancestors. "But I know it was real. They know who I am; obviously they had probably known me for quite a while. I don't know why they picked me, but they did. It made me feel better that they knew who I was and why I was there." He felt sorry about what was happening at the site, even though he wanted the work to continue for the good of his tribe and the people of this town.

Charles knew that separating some of the spirits from the others still in the ground was a problem. "They have been around each other for so many years, it would be like your best friend moving away. I'm sure they are not happy that their family's or friend's remains were taken out of there. Their relatives are gone. They are up at the bunker. You never know, maybe that was one of the ones that was walking around here, following me home. I don't sleep in the dark; that's when they start talking with me. I knew they were angry. I would tell them we are doing all we can. And they would understand. After I figured out what was going on, it didn't scare me anymore."

As the construction project continued, the tribe struggled to get others to understand how real their native connection to this land, and these spirits, is. To realize that illnesses and accidents were happening because the spirits were being disturbed in their resting place. The death rate on Route 101 climbed higher and higher. Tribal members believed they knew why.

Burial tents dot the site, as archaeologists and tribal members work to move the bones of the Klallam people's ancestors out of the path of construction, November 2004. Hundreds of burials were taken from their resting place during the course of the dry dock project. The rocks with red tape are headstones. Steve Ringman, courtesy *Seattle Times*.

By the time I met Tribal Chairwoman Frances Charles at the gate to the site in November 2004, work had been going on since March. I'd never met her before, but as I arrived, she tore into our first moments together like the former firefighter she is. Charles is a common name at Lower Elwha, with family members related by marriage and blood for generations uncounted. The tribe's most powerful elected official, from one of the largest, most influential families on the reservation, Frances Charles pulled no punches. "This is a sacred cemetery," she said as she began taking me around the site. "We have our village being destroyed as we talk. It's sad to witness and watch workers excavating our ancestral remains. We have been asked to give and give, and I don't think anyone has given more than the tribe has already in allowing the project to continue. We were told it's all disturbed, so we are not going to find anything here because of the mills that were built here. We've found burials with pipes and posts right through them." Even more painful than the historic desecrations from the first industrialization of the site in 1912, when the largest sawmill in the country was built

here, were the modern utility trenches. Tribal members found coaxial cable and PVC pipe snaked right through bone fragments in the backfill covering the trenches. Charles's father, Jerry Charles Sr., like most of the elders in the Lower Elwha Klallam tribe, knew Port Angeles had been settled atop the tribe's largest village and its burial ground. Jerry Charles was the tribe's gravedigger. He always wondered where the ancient burial ground at Tse-whit-zen was. He even worked in a mill built right atop the village and burial ground and never knew it.

But some elders here say they knew where the cemetery was. And they knew the state's transportation project was not the first time bones had been disturbed in this ground. They remembered when their people's bones had been thrown aside to build the mills on the waterfront. "I knew it wasn't the first bone," said elder Beatrice Charles, when the state first unearthed human remains at the site in August 2003. "And I knew it would not be the last." But really, they also say, why should anyone have been surprised to find Tse-whit-zen? As hundreds of burials were unearthed,

Tribal spiritual leader Mary Anne Thomas (*right*) carries a candle as she escorts human remains from the site to a temporary storage trailer, November 2004. All the remains of the ancestors (sčiyúʔis) were wrapped in white blankets and placed in cedar boxes along with any gifts and belongings found with them. Steve Ringman, courtesy *Seattle Times*.

along with longhouses, structures, cooking areas, and more than 10,000 artifacts, why should anyone have been shocked? This had always been some of the most valuable land in Port Angeles. "Indian people aren't stupid," Beatrice Charles said. "We knew where to live." And that place was Tse-whit-zen: some of the finest real estate in the aboriginal world, with its protected deepwater bay, the salt water of the Strait of Juan de Fuca, tide flats alive with shellfish, a tidal lagoon, and a marsh. All of it nourished by the Elwha River.

2

Abundance

WHEN IT IS TIME TO PRAY, JOHNSON CHARLES JR. GOES TO THE RIVER. FRESH, green, cold, the Lower Elwha receives his daily offering. And, sometimes, even seems to respond. "My wife, Georgia, and I go down to the beach and we say prayers. Almost every day we do that," Charles said. "We go down by the river, farther down there, closer to the river. One time we were down at the mouth of the river, and she was just standing there by the river, and she had her hands up, and she was praying. I said a prayer and started singing in a real low tone." Seated on the couch in his living room, Charles's face took on a faraway look; he heard and saw the river in his mind. Felt it, as if he were right there, and he told his story slowly, hypnotically as the glide of the river. "The waves were just coming in and splashing on the beach where we were standing. When I started singing that song, the river just calmed right down. The waves stopped splashing and got real calm. I kept singing that song; I sang it through three times. And as soon as I stopped that song, the waves started splashing again, and the river started swirling. That is the way it is in our life—you pray and you sing, and it calms you down, it calms everything down

Lower Elwha Klallam elder Johnson Charles Jr. and his flute were a gentling presence at the construction site, where workers found the soothing tones of his music a welcome balm, November 2004. In the background, a pile of matrix dug from the site awaits sorting by archaeologists, who would later pick through it for bits of bone, shell, and artifacts. Steve Ringman, courtesy *Seattle Times*.

like that. That was the Elwha River down there, too."

Johnson, as everyone calls him on the reservation, has a voice and a manner as soothing as the river's. When it got rough down at the dry dock site, when tribal members were in tears, confused, hurting as they dug their ancestors' bones from the ground, Johnson helped console them. He always carried his wooden flute down to the site, to be ready for times like that. Born by the Elwha River, Johnson, a tribal elder, went as far as eleventh grade at the high school in Port Angeles, then left the reservation to make a living. He worked in Alaska, Canada, and all over the Olympic Peninsula at hard jobs. Planting trees, logging, mostly. "The only hard part was climbing up and down the mountains; I never really did get hurt." Finally, he came back home to the reservation and started working on learning his native Klallam language. It's a language full of the sounds of water, of the river. "It was ours," Johnson says. "It was given to us through the spirit. Through the birds and the animals and the trees, and everything that nature has for us, you know. The wind and the rain, everything that has to do with nature. That is where the songs come from, too, the wind, the

This 1887 photo of the Elwha River (ʔéʔɬxʷə stúʔwiʔ) shows hunters in the canyon where the Lower Elwha dam was later constructed. The free-flowing river nourished a watershed alive with game, medicinal plants and herbs, and abundant runs of salmon that sustained the Lower Elwha Klallam people for generations. Bert Kellogg Collection, North Olympic Library System, ELWA RIVR 005.

rain, the trees, the sun, the birds, and the animals. Our language was given to us special, you know. It's our own. Our own. Something that we can call our own. Same as our way of worshiping."

The tribe's language was only one of the river's many gifts. The Elwha River was a thread binding a culture of twined needs, for one another and for a healthy, abundant, deeply known ecosystem, lived in intimately, with mastery and worship. The river nourished tribal relationships as well. Marriage and kinship ties ensured access to life-sustaining clam beds at the river's mouth, fishing spots all along it, and hunting areas in its watershed. The wealth of the Elwha River also formed the basis of trade networks with other tribes.

The river wound through every aspect of tribal members' lives: what they ate, what they wore, what they built, their art, worship, and healing arts. Even the tribe's name came from the river. During a big gathering at the river's mouth, Elder Beatrice Charles told the story of how the tribe received its name: "They ate salmon, clams, wild berries, and lots of good things from nature. Then they had a contest to see who was the strongest. They decided to see who could lift a big log to the top of a big house that they were building. 'Who can lift this big log?' they asked. All of the other tribes tried to lift the log. Each tribe chose its strongest men. None of them could lift the big log. Then it was time for the mighty Klallams. They remembered that logs float in the water. So they rolled the big log into the water. Then their strongest young men walked out into the water until it was up to their shoulders. Then they let the log float onto their shoulders and walked out of the water carrying the log on their shoulders. When they reached the longhouse, everyone was shouting at the same time. On the third time, they all lifted it up to the top. All of the other tribes thought that the mighty Klallams must be very strong to put the log up so high, and so smart to use the water to first get the log onto their shoulders. They shouted [our name], which means 'Strong People.' That is how our tribe received its name."

One of ten major rivers on the Olympic Peninsula, the Elwha River is 45 miles long and nourishes a watershed covering 321 miles, the fourth-largest on the peninsula. More than 80 percent of the watershed is in Olympic National Park. The Klallam people lived in villages all through the area and beyond, from the Hoko River to the west, to the Hamma Hamma River near present-day Port Townsend, and up the Elwha River deep into the mountains.

Fed by glaciers nourished by some of the heaviest snowfalls in the world on Mount Olympus, the river's clean, cold, clear waters are alive with oxygen and nutrients.

The Elwha flows in a long, sinuous curve of motion as liquid as the river's name. Its waters flash north from the Mountains That Look Like Reclining Lady, or Elwha River Range, nearly 8,000 feet above sea level, all the way to the Strait of Juan de Fuca. Vast swaths of towering forest stabilize its banks during soaking winter rains and filter the water.

Before the dams, natural processes drove and sustained this watershed. Fallen logs, standing trees, and boulders shaped the river's flow. Logjams sent the current surging in new directions and blocked flows that splashed over and around them, forcing the current to dig the deep holes salmon need for hiding and resting. Battlements of giant logjams, there for decades, also impounded the river's slow, quiet side channels. They provided refuge for young fish, especially when the river swelled with winter rain and spring runoff. Coho, chinook, chum, sockeye, and pink salmon used the river at different times throughout the year. Other seagoing fish, including steelhead trout, sturgeon, and smelt, also traveled up the Elwha River to spawn.

The river even shaped the surrounding coast with its transport of tons and tons of sediment rinsed from the mountains into the sea. The sand and gravel built not

Lower Elwha Klallam tribal member Joe Sampson fishes for salmon in the Elwha using a gaff hook, mid-1920s. Courtesy of Adeline Smith.

Joe Sampson takes a giant tyee from the Elwha River, mid-1920s. Courtesy of Lower Elwha Klallam Tribe.

only the salmon's spawning grounds in the river but beaches at the river mouth and the tide flats along the waterfront, alive with geoducks, oysters, mussels, and clams. Over thousands of years, the sediment also helped build the sheltering arm of the Ediz Hook that nestled the village of Tse-whit-zen at its base. Grain by grain, the tides formed the arm of the hook out of sediment washed down from the glaciered heights of Mount Olympus. Sands ground from igneous, sedimentary, and metamorphic rock were transported by the river on its journey from the interior of the Olympic Mountains to the Strait of Juan de Fuca. Washing east in the strait from the broad delta of the river, the sediments slowly built up the Ediz Hook, beginning some 9,000 years ago. Sea cliffs eroded by waves and tides also nourished the hook, which grew north and east, finally stabilizing about 2,000 years ago. More than three miles long, it is one of the largest sand spits anywhere in the United States and cradles one of the deepest natural harbors on the West Coast.

The effect of the hook can be read in the layers that make up the ancient beach berm at the Tse-whit-zen site.[1] The oldest layer is more coarse-grained and churned up, with its components poorly sorted. That betrays the more active, turbulent open-water environment of this beach line before the birth of the hook. The younger layers of sand are finer and laid down in a neatly sorted, settled surface that could form only within the shelter of the hook. The hook also allowed the formation of a tidal lagoon and marsh, located landward of a sand berm in the lee of the sand spit.

Native people began using this place as soon as it was formed some 2,700 years ago. Long before the time of Jesus, before the development of the English language, the Klallam people were using Tse-whit-zen as a seasonal camp. Once the shoreline settled down and stabilized about 1,000 years ago, people used it continually. Some thirty-seven radiocarbon dates taken at the site from charcoal, rock hearths, ochre processing pits, wooden posts, and refuse show only two gaps in human activity. Earthquakes may have occasionally disrupted occupation of the site, particularly between 1,500 and 1,000 years ago, when archaeology indicates inundation by water and structural collapse. Radiocarbon dates on archaeological deposits, in combination with the profile of the beach berm sands, show that the location of the village changed along with the landform. The villagers moved north, as the Elwha River and tides chewing at the sea cliffs grew the beach and sand spit into the harbor. The beach underlying the site finally stabilized, creating prime real estate for the hunter-gatherer society of the Klallam people.

The Elwha River not only helped create this landscape, it also fed the entire watershed that sustained Tse-whit-zen. Salmon have always been at the heart of the Klallam people's life on the Elwha River. Today the Lower Elwha Klallam still return the bones of the first salmon caught each year to the river, to make sure the salmon will tell the other Salmon People, who live in villages under the sea, that they were well treated and should come again next year. Johnson's grandfather could point to the places in this river where the lightning would strike, making big, deep holes where the largest salmon lived. "That is what made our river powerful, that lightning bolt," he said. "They also talked about the thunder and lightning, or X̌əmX̌əmcínəŋ. When thunder and lightning strike, that is what chases the salmon and the fish up our river. On different reservations I would hear them talk about our river; it had the biggest, hugest king salmon, our Lower Elwha River. And they were h-u-u-u-ge salmon we used to catch, that is what my grandpa used to tell me when I was young."

Whenever other tribes heard thunder booming, they knew the Klallams were around. Thunderbird followed them, and the Elwha was its home, in a cave far up above a high, high cliff. So high, rainbows danced back and forth across the river there, like a gate to the spirit world. "That is where the Thunderbird lived, in that area, and that is why our river is so powerful there," Johnson said. When Thunderbird flapped its wings as it flew up the canyon, it would chase the salmon up the Elwha. Its flash and boom would be the signal to the Klallam people that the salmon had returned. Only the largest salmon, one-hundred-pound tyee, could ascend to the upper reaches of the river, Thunderbird's realm, where the rock walls close in tight and squeeze the current into a powerful blast. The deep booming voice of the river there gave the Lower Elwha Klallams their unique power, a telepathic voice that could summon other people to their side, just by thinking about them.

In aboriginal times, the river was home to ten different seasonal runs of salmon that fed more than twenty-two species of wildlife as well as the Klallam people. Salmon returning to the river to spawn carried their wealth inland, to the forests of the watershed. After spawning, the salmon finned in the current, guarding their redds, or nests, in the river's gravel bed until death finally ended their vigil. Then

LEFT The remains of this sea otter (sc̓úm̓ ʔaʔ cə č̓aʔmús) dug from the Tse-whit-zen archaeological site show the abundance of animals available to the Klallam people for food and for making clothing, blankets, and tools. Courtesy Washington State Department of Transportation.

RIGHT The skill it took to sink a bone harpoon point into the spine of a swimming otter is hard to imagine. This piece of otter vertebrae was dug from the Tse-whit-zen village site. Courtesy Lower Elwha Klallam Tribe.

they loosened their grip in the current and drifted free, their bodies finally coming to rest at the riverbank. But even then their bodies were at work, gifting the land with nutrients gathered from the great pastures of the sea. The upstream migrations of the largest salmon brought a vast treasure of nutrients all the way into the upper reaches of the watershed and dispersed the wealth gathered from the sea throughout the food web of the Elwha ecosystem.

Even today, bears, bald eagles, raccoons, otters, shrews, deer mice, gray jays, dippers, and tiny winter wrens partake of the feast, notes biologist Jim Lichatowich. He sees parallels in the salmon's gift and the tribe's potlatch tradition, in which the richest members of the tribe earned status by bestowing lavish feasts and presents upon their guests. The salmon mentored the Klallam people, informing a culture that mirrored the ways of the Klallam's signature fish. Like the salmon, the Klallams showed their wealth by gifting and did not waste or hoard the largesse of the river, sea, mountains, and meadows that sustained their lives.

The Elwha River watershed was alive with a gourmet pantry of foods. The Lower Elwha Klallam people mastered the original diversified economy: They had something to eat in every season. With the earned luxury of abundant food stores, December and January meant they could take time off to enjoy long winters in residence at Tse-whit-zen. The winter ceremonial season included elaborate potlatches lasting a week or more, devoted to feasting, dancing, singing, and gift-giving.

Johnson's father was among the last to be born in a smokehouse along the Elwha. The Klallams lived in at least thirteen village sites up and down the river. The smokehouse was for the winter ceremonies, with songs and dances gifted by spirit power. No one knows for sure, but the smokehouse and the ceremonies were probably something like those used by the tribe's relatives today, at Esquimalt, across the Strait of Juan de Fuca in British Columbia. The smokehouse there is a simple, cedar-sided A-frame structure with risers inside along the walls. Tribal members keep two large fires burning continually on the earthen floor throughout the winter ceremonial season. Smoke and sparks ease through openings in the corrugated metal roof.

It was Johnson's father who taught him about the river's spiritual power. "He brought me to the creek every morning to bathe, like they did when they were in the smokehouse," Johnson said. "Every day they did that, in ceremony. It was to receive their power, whatever power they were seeking. And to pray each morning and to cleanse yourself every day in this holy water. And that is what he did with me, every day, until I was maybe out of grade school; then he finally quit making me go down to the creek every morning. It was an all-year-round thing, too. And it was to make you strong, not only in your body but in your mind and spirit. And I believe that's what helped me to survive everything that was to come. That was to help me in my own life." A mere dip wasn't enough. His father taught Johnson to go all the way under the snowmelt water. "He'd say, dunk under the water, because that is what he used to do. He'd dunk his whole body under the water, and he would come up and he would be screaming real loud, a powerful scream. I would be halfway out of breath. But I didn't scream."

And it was on the Elwha River, too, that the Klallam people say they were created, at a sacred place now drowned by the floodwaters of the dams. Many tribal members speak of stories passed down to them about their creation site, where there is a big, flat rock, with two holes in it containing water. The holes are shaped like a coil basket, and this is where the Creator would bathe the people and bless them. It was there that the people would go to learn about their future. If they put a hand in a hole and pulled out something like a shell, that meant they would be wealthy. If they pulled out a deer hair, it meant they would become good hunters. But before going to the creation site, tribal members bathed to cleanse themselves, physically and spiritually. They would go alone. They would fast and meditate, and then bathe in the cold, swift river.

Ed Sampson, born in 1901, lived nearly one hundred years. He passed on many

Lower Elwha Klallam tribal member Alan Bennett holds an anchor stone used by his ancestors at Tse-whit-zen. Bennett was one of many Lower Elwha Klallam youth who worked at the archaeological site. Courtesy Lower Elwha Klallam Tribe.

stories and teachings about the Elwha as a holy, sacred river, a place where some tribal members still seek their spirit power. Sampson explained that when you are clean, a spirit power will come to you. The spirit will give you a song, which brings the spirit power into force. When you return from your vision quest, you wait a year to bring out your song at the next potlatch. When the power comes to you, your family and friends help you sing your song, gifted by the spirit power. Erna Gunther, the anthropologist who compiled the only extensive ethnography of the Klallam people in 1927, goes on for pages in her report about the many sources of spirit power. The sun was merciful to orphans and helped them acquire wealth. The feeling of a spiderweb covering the face was one of the luckiest powers to receive; those who did would get everything they wanted. Spirit helpers brought hunters duck, elk, and deer. They helped women in fishing and digging clams. There were spirit helpers to find lost objects, make fish come to certain places, and give the power to see long distances. Other spirits helped men acquire many wives, or gave the power to find lost people, control the weather, or be formidable in war. Among the most powerful was the thunder spirit, and it was one of the hardest to obtain. When a war party started out, Gunther reported, all those with thunder power sang their songs. Then thunder and lightning would answer. Only then did the warriors know they would be successful. Spirit powers are a form of wealth and bring prestige, even today. Acquiring spirit power is a personal achievement, but it can benefit the whole tribe.

This pink point (yəčt) dug from the Tse-whit-zen site glows with color. Just the right size for taking small game, it would have been attached to a spear. Steve Ringman, courtesy *Seattle Times*.

Some Coast Salish children are still sent out at the time of puberty, and even younger, on vision quests to acquire a guardian spirit. But spirits don't come only when they are sought, or only to the young. Girls were sent out before adolescence and could get any spirit a man could. The stormiest time of the year was the right time.

Shells filled with red ochre, still used by tribal members today for painting the face and body for ceremonial adornment and spiritual protection, were found at Tse-whit-zen at the oldest known part of the site, dating back 2,700 years. The youngest

It took masterful skill to cut the notches in this bone harpoon point, held in the hand of a tribal member who had just plucked it from the ground at Tse-whit-zen. Courtesy John Loftus.

radiocarbon date at the village is from about 1860, the oldest from about 696 B.C. The oldest date was recorded from the rock hearth used to dry red ochre powder at the southernmost edge of the site, right where the oldest beach line used to be. Tribal members also found what may be a large dancehouse, or potlatch house, where feasts and winter dances would have been held.

Thousands of pieces of shell and animal bone from the site also document the rich food web that sustained the village. There were bits of bay-mussel shell, sea-urchin spines, clamshell hinges and rockfish teeth, the vertebrae of sole, and periwinkle shells. Bones of otters, elks, deer, whales, and birds. They all tell a story of what was in the environment of the ancient Klallam people, what they hunted for, what they fished for, and what they ate.

Post molds—the marks made by long-gone posts in the ground—show the outlines of drying racks, built on the beach for drying fish and clams. The outlines of smoke-houses, along with rock ovens, cooking hearths, and some 4,000 stone fish-cutting tools are testimony to the bounty that sustained this village. The rib of a whale and animal bones found everywhere also show that the Klallam people ate everything they could catch—and used every last bit of the carcasses. Bones and sinews were for tools, and the skins of deer and elk were used for everything from clothing to moccasins

Nephrite, a dense, heavy stone found in Canada, was a prized trade item sought by woodworkers at Tse-whit-zen. This adze would have been hafted to a handle and used for woodworking jobs ranging from hollowing out a feast bowl to constructing a canoe. Steve Ringman, courtesy *Seattle Times*.

and bags. Hides were also stretched and scraped until supple enough to make into the heads of drums. Deer hooves were crafted into rattles, which produce a penetrating sound still heard in traditional Indian ceremonies throughout Puget Sound country today. But it was not only the animals that nourished the tribe.

Jamie Valadez, a language instructor for the Lower Elwha Klallam Tribe, counts about 130 different species of plants traditionally used by her ancestors for food, beverages, flavorings, and medicines, including plants from the mountains, riverbanks, meadows, and even the sea. Early in the spring, the sweet, tender young shoots and greens of cow parsnip, fireweed, thimbleberry, salmonberry, western dock, and giant horsetail were harvested for their much-needed vitamins, especially vitamin C, which would have been in short supply in the winter. Later, when the sap started running, the Klallam people would eat the inner bark of western hemlock, Sitka spruce, black cottonwood, and red alder, peeling off the outer bark and scraping the edible part from the outside of the wood or from the inside of the sheets of bark.

The tribe's interdependence with the ecosystem organized the year into a seasonal round of activities, based on natural cycles of migration, abundance, and renewal. After the winter ceremonial time, spring, summer, and fall were for gathering and preserving food, with most tribal members dispersed to fish, pick berries, or hunt. By

Johnson Charles Sr. at Pysht Village, wearing blackface paint of the Klallam seowyn secret society. His son, Johnson Charles Jr., is one of the last living Klallams who was born in a smoke-house by the Elwha River. Courtesy Johnson Charles Jr.

late May and early June, fruits began to ripen in succession: salmonberries and wild strawberries, followed by red elderberries, huckleberries, gooseberries, and then currants and salal. Finally, in the late summer and fall, came the Pacific crab apples, high bush cranberries, bog and mountain cranberries, and evergreen huckleberries. Klallam people also created an array of tools and housewares from plants. Fir wood could be made into harpoon hafts, spoons, spear shafts, dip-net poles, fire tongs, and salmon weirs. Torches were cut from the pitchy heartwood. Fir pitch sealed the joints of harpoon heads, gaff hooks, fishhooks, and canoes.

The tribe used the hardwood of maple trees for fish clubs, ladles, dishes, and spoons. Maple saplings were made into split pole racks for cooking salmon over an open fire. Digging sticks for harvesting clams as well as spindle whorls, paddles, fishing lures, hairpins and combs, cattail-mat creasers, rattles, and adze handles were also made from maple. Red alder yields an orange-red dye that is still used today to color basket materials. Canoes, canoe bailers, masks, rattles, tool handles, and totem poles are all still painted with alder dye. Salmon and deer meat are still smoked over alder wood, which is also fashioned into serving platters and feast dishes. Western yew, tough as iron, was for bows, wedges, clubs, paddles, digging sticks, harpoon shafts, adze handles, and bows. No wood topped the cedar in importance. The clear, straight grain and nearly waterproof quality of the wood made it the material of choice for everything from house posts and planks to canoes and storage boxes. Today, Klallam people use cedar bark for making baskets, bags, hats, mats, capes, blankets, and dance regalia. Cedar boughs are also used for spiritual cleansing, whether to clear the floor of any bad feeling before a ceremony in a longhouse or to brush harmful spirits off a person, from head to toe.

Elders at Lower Elwha still remember the medicines their parents swore by, gathered along the banks of the river. Johnson Charles Jr. learned about them from his father. "There was one medicine he used to pick. It was kind of near where the water was," Johnson said. "He said it was good for everything. For your throat or a cold, it was just minty. I still use it whenever I can. The other thing he showed me, it is good for infection, anything that has to do with infection in your hand or arms or legs. They would put that medicine on there to keep it from getting infected. And another that my father used—he called it chittum bark—was wild cherry bark and crab apple bark. He kept a big tin pitcher of it in one of his cupboards, and I used to go drink it, and it was just bitter. People used to drink it, and they said it kept them from getting tuberculosis. I thought maybe that is why I didn't get tuberculosis. Because I was drinking that medicine."

And just as its side channels sheltered salmon during floods and storms, the Elwha River also offered refuge when diseases ravaged the tribe. Susie and Charlie Sampson took their son Ernie to live in isolation up the Elwha River at the Meadows, by Lake Mills on the eastern slope, where tribal members gathered medicinal plants. They lived in seclusion for eight years during the 1890s to escape tuberculosis and other diseases ravaging the village. People down below could see the smoke coming from their camp. It was the only way they knew the three were still alive, deep in the upper reaches of the Elwha.

The richness of the land and waters that sustained this culture would draw others—explorers and then settlers—seeking the same wealth that had sustained the Strong People for generations uncounted. It started with the Elwha River.

3

Calamity

IT WAS ABOUT TWO IN THE AFTERNOON WHEN THE CREW ABOARD THE *PRINCESA Real* first saw them: two canoes of Indians, offering salmonberries. Manuel Quimper, commander of the expedition, presented the Indians with two small pieces of iron in return. "I asked them if there was any fresh water in the bay," Quimper wrote in his journal of the expedition on July 21, 1790. "They answered by pointing to the place, to which I sent the armed canoe with empty casks. They returned at four in the afternoon with delicious water taken from a beautiful stream." The Elwha River.

Although European exploration of the Pacific coast was already well under way, Quimper was the first known to explore the Klallams' territory. He and his crew spent from June 15 to July 24, 1790, in Coast Salish waters in the Strait of Juan de Fuca, and he repeatedly met and traded with what must have been Klallam people, at New Dungeness, Port Discovery, Freshwater Bay, and Clallam Bay. Like so many others, Quimper was in search of *un fuego fatuo*—the mythical Northwest Passage—a quest that sent many an explorer beating his way up and down the Northwest coast. Quimper, unlike others, doubted he'd find the passage. Determined to make some use of

The first contact between European explorers and the Klallam people might have looked something like the moment depicted in this painting of the collision of two worlds. Bill Holm (American, b. 1925), *Mexicana and Sutil in Guemes Channel, June 11, 1792.* Acrylic; 18 x 28 inches. Collection of Dr. James Richardson; courtesy Bill Holm.

his trip, he departed from Nootka on May 31, 1790, on a short expedition down the strait. He was under severe time pressure, dispatched by his commander to be back at Nootka by August 15, even though it was believed the journey included a round-trip via the Northwest Passage to the Atlantic. "Quimper was only one of many commanders burdened with worthless instructions," the author Henry R. Wagner noted in his account of the voyage and translation of Quimper's journals, published in 1933.

The *Princesa Real* set forth with no chaplain or surgeon, with a crew of forty-one men in all, nine of them soldiers. She was a forty-three-foot-long sloop and carried four one-pound cannons and eight swivel guns, which were fired only once, during a dustup with the Native people at present-day Neah Bay. No one was killed. Quimper charted the northern and southern coasts of the strait, in the first known expedition to those waters by a European. Captain James Cook had come near but had not entered the strait in 1778. The Malaspina expedition followed Quimper into the strait in

1791, and the very next year, both the Bodega y Quadra and George Vancouver expeditions returned to Klallam territory. But Quimper was the first known to contact the Klallams in their home waters. And he reported the Indians friendly and eager to trade, repeatedly surrounding his sloop with canoes loaded with goods, and even at times paddling the explorers, under tow, to anchorage. Quimper's journals are a window into the lost world of a Coast Salish region of permanent winter villages, from which the residents moved seasonally, traveling usually by canoe to fishing, hunting, and gathering sites. The late ethnographer Wayne Suttles notes the villages were linked by ties of marriage, shared access to resources, and potlatches. Those intervillage ties made the entire region of the Strait of Georgia and Puget Sound basin a social and biological continuum, with a rich array of cultural expression and differences, including fourteen different languages in four distinct geographic regions.

One of Quimper's first recorded contacts with the Klallam people occurred at the western end of the Strait of Juan de Fuca, on a cloudy, squally July 4, at around six thirty in the morning. He was anchored about a half mile off the southern coast at present-day Tongue Point, at Salt Water State Park, west of Tse-whit-zen:

> Eight large canoes with fifteen and twenty Indians in each came alongside. They had been following us for more than two leagues. I succeeded in inducing them to come alongside through expressions of friendship and by showing them gifts which I made to them. These Indians by their suspicion showed manifestly that they had never seen a vessel even though I noted that hanging from their ears they wore some pieces of copper and beads. These I thought they had obtained in trade from the Indians at the entrance of the Strait. They also wore English, Portuguese and Chinese coins for earrings. At sunset, they returned to their settlement.[1]

The next day dawned "with floating clouds in the sky, the land misty and the wind freshish from the west," Quimper wrote. And the Indians were back again:

> At 7, many canoes of Indians came out with delicious and abundant fish and shellfish, among which were flounder, ray fish, salmon . . . sea bass, little dog fish, crabs and some venison. I obtained this in order to refresh the men, for cask hoops from two casks which I had knocked down. I presented the principal chiefs with some pieces of copper as a sign of friendship. They also traded some reed mats, some white painted woolen blankets, others mixed

The arrival of European explorers would detonate one of the largest demographic disasters in history: the transfer of diseases through trade and other contact. Detail from mural in the Smith Room, Suzzallo Library, University of Washington. Paul Gustin (American, 1886–1974) and John T. Jacobsen (American, d. 1998). Oil on canvas. Photo: Steve Ringman, courtesy *Seattle Times* and University of Washington Libraries.

with duck feathers, and some skins of bears, buffalo, deer and other animals un-tanned. Some were perfectly dressed, double, and with these, as they explained to us, they defended themselves from their enemies on the North coast. . . . At sunset the canoes went away, having passed almost all day alongside with much noisy display of pleasure evidenced by their singing demonstrations.[2]

Quimper missed the Tse-whit-zen village site. He did not follow the coast west from the Dungeness Spit but crossed the strait and came back to the south side again just west of the Ediz Hook, at Freshwater Bay, about ten miles west of present-day Port Angeles. But as he sailed the strait, Quimper noted the two rivers that bracketed Klallam villages along the southern shore, the Elwha and the Dungeness. Quimper described details of village life also documented by archaeological evidence at Tse-whit-zen, including the severed skulls of enemies, the use of red ochre paint, and the tribe's reliance on a diverse array of foods. Quimper's reaction to the appearance of the aboriginal people he encountered also offers a clue to a mentality that would allow some explorers to easily kill or rout the peoples they encountered. His puzzled reaction, while the first recorded, would not be the last, and it sets the tone for much of what is to come in Klallam-white relations:

> There are two rivers on whose banks or close by are the settlements of those who inhabit the bay. Fish are most plentiful, particularly large salmon, ray fish, flounder, sea bass, red snapper and anchovies. There are also the quadrupeds and birds already mentioned with the addition of geese, cranes and three kinds of ducks. The language of these natives differs from those on the Outer Coast. They recognize no superior chief and carry on continual warfare with those on the north side, thus accounting for the fact that the beaches are strewn with the harpooned heads of their enemies. They are affable, happy, of good stature and well formed but the different kinds of paint with which they disfigure their countenances make them horrible to behold. They pass their time in hunting, fishing and weaving baskets, reed mats and woolen cloaks, for wear and for trade with those from the outside. These pursuits prevent them from fishing for sea otters which nevertheless they have in great numbers.[3]

The salmon Quimper relished during his voyage also are testimony to the mighty salmon runs in the contact era. On July 25, at present-day Neah Bay, Quimper noted trading for "delicious fish, of 100 pounds or more in weight." By the time his journey was completed, Quimper had explored the southern shore of Vancouver Island and some of the northern shore of the Olympic Peninsula, mapping present-day Haro and Rosario Straits, and documented the existence of Admiralty Inlet. He also established the outline of the basin that is the eastern end of the Strait of Juan de Fuca but didn't go beyond it.

The arrival of the Europeans would mark the first recorded collision of the Native people of the Northwest with a truly alien world. Called the Cloud People by some of the Northwest tribes, because of their light eyes, or the Upside-down People, for their bald heads and hairy faces, the Europeans brought a calamity without precedent. The native people could not fight the invisible cargo that came with the newcomers and their trade goods: infectious diseases, to which the Indians had no resistance.

The source of the first outbreaks of disease among the Northwest tribes is still a matter of debate. But the Spaniards seem the most likely source, according to scholar Robert Boyd of Portland, Oregon, author of *The Coming of the Spirit of Pestilence*, the

Bea Charles (*left*) and Adeline Smith remember being told by their elders that there was a huge cemetery at Tse-whit-zen. Courtesy Steve Ringman, *Seattle Times*.

definitive work on the spread and effect of infectious diseases among the Northwest Coast peoples. Measles and, especially, smallpox so devastated the Native peoples of the coast that by the time white settlement began in earnest, their numbers had already been scythed. In the worst cases, the death toll by disease destroyed entire villages. Within a century, the precontact population of coastal peoples of the Northwest, conservatively estimated at more than 180,000 in the late 1700s, had been cut to an estimated 35,000 to 40,000.[4] The introduced diseases were a demographic disaster that shattered Native social and cultural systems and left the survivors traumatized by a terrible death force they did not understand. The diseases were borne on ships, trade goods, and even by Indian family members fleeing infected villages, not knowing they were carrying death to the relatives with whom they sought refuge. On the Northwest coast, the outbreaks of infectious diseases began in about the 1770s, maybe earlier, killing an estimated 80 percent of the coastal Indians in the first century of contact. When explorer George Vancouver traveled the waters between Vancouver Island and the mainland, he noted at Point Discovery, in 1792, human bones everywhere amid the grass, empty villages that should have been home to hundreds of people, and pockmarks on the faces of the Indians he met.

The spread of smallpox in the Pacific Northwest

From the late 1700's to 1863

The march of smallpox across the Northwest was relentless. Mark Nowlin, courtesy *Seattle Times*.

SMALLPOX EPIDEMIC(S)

The earliest documented evidence points to smallpox appearing in the Pacific Northwest in the late 1700s, followed by outbreaks throughout the 1800s.

■ Locations of late 1700s small-pox documented by early explorers, missionaries and anthropologists

APPROXIMATE RANGE OF EPIDEMICS (1800-63)

- 1800-01
- 1836-38
- 1853
- 1862-63

ALASKA

Sitka

U.S.

Fort Simpson

QUEEN CHARLOTTE ISLANDS

BRITISH COLUMBIA

Fort McLoughlin

C A N A D A

Strait of Georgia

VANCOUVER ISLAND

Fort Langley

U.S.

Juan de Fuca Strait

WASHINGTON

● Fort Nisqually

Fort Astor ●

Fort Vancouver

The Dalles

OREGON

N

CALIFORNIA   NEV.

Sources: "Handbook of North American Indians," Vol. 7, Northwest Coast, Wayne Suttles (Smithsonian Institution, 1990.); "The Coming of the Spirit of Pestilence," Robert Boyd (University of Washington Press, 1999.); "Pox Americana, The Great Smallpox Epidemic of 1775-82," Elizabeth A. Fenn (Hill and Wang, 2001.)

Boyd, in his landmark book, considers several theories as to how smallpox first came to Puget Sound and the Northwest coast. It could have been carried by Indians traveling across the Rocky Mountains to hunt bison on the plateau. Or it could have been carried by Indian traders, traveling by horse, who brought the disease across the Great Plains and the Columbia Plateau. But the most likely source, Boyd believes, is the Spanish explorers. They came in waves to the Northwest coast, beginning in the 1770s, journeying from Mexico to the Northwest, to claim it for Spain. Boyd has identified the 1775 expedition, led by Bruno Hezeta, commander of the *Santiago*, and Juan Francisco de la Bodega y Quadra, commander of the *Sonora*, as one possible source of the 1770s outbreak. That expedition landed and made contact with Indian people at Trinidad Bay in California, at Quinault in Washington, and at Sitka in Alaska. Clatsop tradition also strongly implicates the Spanish, in an account of survivors of a shipwreck who struggled ashore in the 1770s and may have brought the disease to the Northwest coast.[5]

Smallpox was a horrific disease, incubating undetected in its victims for up to eighteen days and then killing with devastating speed as pustules erupted on the flesh of the infected, until their bodies literally rotted in place. The variola virus, which caused the disease, was carried on exhaled droplets, usually propelled by a sneeze, or through contact with other bodily fluids and spread easily from one victim to the next. Once a sufferer was infected with the virus, nothing could be done to arrest or alleviate the sickness. The illness began with fever, headache, and body pains. Then a rash appeared, initially in red spots on the face, hands, and feet. Next, the rest of the body became dotted with red spots that quickly turned into raised lesions swelling with festering liquid. Pustules developed. In the few victims who survived, the pustules crusted over and formed lifelong, pitted scars. Victims would ooze, itch, and smell with the stench of the infection. Very often, they died within a month. Variola major killed an average of 30 percent of its victims. In the worst cases of confluent smallpox, lesions flowed together to form a solid mass and the patient lost slabs of festering skin. Variola minor, the less virulent form, killed about 1 percent of its victims. Infection rates were spectacular, with nearly 100 percent of tribal members sickened among closely knit, small, non-immune populations—so-called virgin soil epidemics. Traditional cures of the Native people, including cold baths, only hastened death in the weakened, fever-wracked sufferers.

Boyd's book relates the oral traditions of Native peoples that record the horror of disease, including "The Sun's Myth," collected from a Chinook informant named

Charles Cultee by Franz Boas in 1891. The myth describes the agony of an infected tribal member who returns to his town, only to spread the disease:

> *In vain he would try to stand, that one,*
> *see, something would pull his feet.*
> *His reason would become nothing,*
> *he would do it to his town,*
> *crush, crush, crush, crush;*
> *all his town he would destroy*
> *and he would destroy his relatives.*
> *he would recover:*
> *his town (is) nothing,*
> *the dead fill the ground.*
> *He would become*
> *"Qa! qa! qa! qa,"*
> *he would cry out.*
> *In vain he would try to bathe;*
> *in vain he would try to shake off what he wears, and his flesh would be pulled.*
> *Sometimes he would roll about on rocks;*
> *he would think,*
> *perhaps it will break apart;*
> *he would abandon hope.*
> *Now again he would cry out,*
> *and he wept.*[6]

Over the next decades, Indian peoples suffered and died again and again from diseases brought by Europeans. Boyd notes another smallpox epidemic, perhaps in 1800–1801, as well as influenza in 1836–37, measles in 1847–48, and smallpox yet again in 1862. The Klallams suffered an outbreak of smallpox in 1853, the same outbreak that wrought devastation to the west, at Neah Bay. The horror with which Indian people regarded the disease, and its penetration and reverberation in Indian culture, are expressed in "Small Pox Ship," by the late Klallam writer Mary Ann Lambert. In what may be a mix of myth and truth, she described the doomed voyage of a ship that bypassed the deadly Columbia River bar because of her crippled manpower: "Smallpox

Grave goods found at the Tse-whit-zen village site document trade links around the region and the world. This blue glass bead (qʷəyqʷi) was probably obtained in trade with Europeans in the mid-to-late 1700s. Such evidence confirming the time frame of some of the burials at Tse-whit-zen leads some archaeologists to believe that the site provides one of the few archaeological records of the smallpox epidemics that swept the Northwest. Steve Ringman, courtesy *Seattle Times*.

had broken out among the crew soon after leaving San Francisco, already some of the sailors had died," Lambert wrote. She assumed that the ship proceeded toward Puget Sound. Citing an "old Indian," she relates a macabre journey:

> Instead of disposing of their pox-infested garments and bedding by burning they were cast overboard and were carried by the currents to the very door of some of the Indian villages along the beaches. The first village contaminated by the blankets and straw mattresses was the Ozette Indian village. Not realizing these salvaged articles contained death for them, the Indians put them to use, and many quickly died. In a short time the village of 400 souls became a tomb, peopled by scores of dead and the fearful, desolate living. . . . By the time the smallpox ship reached and passed Dungeness Spit, she had become a funeral barge.[7]

This etched stone (nił cə xǝy̓ł) showing a shaman in cedar regalia is one of more than 850 found at Tse-whit-zen, the largest collection ever found anywhere in the Northwest, with no two alike. Some archaeologists wonder if a pile of these stones found in a refuse pit points to a village enraged at shamans who could not stop a terrible death force they did not understand. Courtesy Washington State Department of Transportation.

Smallpox ship or not, there is no dispute that in some areas of the Northwest coast, diseases wiped out entire villages before the Europeans themselves actually arrived. The diseases also disrupted Indian belief systems, as the mysterious death force took hold, defying the shamans, or medicine men, who traditionally provided protection.

Some archaeologists believe that Tse-whit-zen bears direct witness to the epidemics, in its burned house planks; carefully made stone tools left behind, as if dropped on the run; a possible mass grave, with one burial stacked atop another; and burned areas all over the village. And what about the piles of stones etched with the tribe's sacred teachings, yet heaped in a refuse pit? Were they discarded in anger? Fear? Disgust? Panic? What about the headless skeleton of a medicine man, buried with his telling sticks? Or the skeletons found buried facedown? The headless skeleton found buried holding one of his own neck bones? Were they scapegoats for a people enraged at healers who could no longer protect them? If the burials at Tse-whit-zen are linked to the epidemics, they would be one of the few archaeological records of the pestilence that swept through the Northwest. Under the terms of a treatment plan governing work at the site, the Lower Elwha Klallam Tribe did not allow archaeologists to date the bones of its ancestors dug from the ground. So archaeologists can't say for sure if they are linked to epidemics. Most of the burials date from two periods: 1,490–1,630 years ago and 260–500 years ago.[8]

Smallpox would have to be indirectly inferred from other evidence in the burials, because it does not leave a signature on the bones. There could be several explanations for the thick concentration of burials in one area of the village. The skeletons could be those of war captives, slaves, or others of low rank, whose remains would have been simply dumped.

Debate about whether the burials are the result of an epidemic is not yet settled. The layered skeletons may also represent burials laid to rest at different times. But epidemic is the most probable cause for some of the burials at the site, archaeologist Lynn Larson, principal investigator for the Tse-whit-zen site, found. She notes a combination of factors, including a lack of gifts with the burials; evidence of wave disturbance of the bones, perhaps showing that bodies were just left on the beach or only shallowly interred; the crowding of burials in one location; a range of all ages and sexes among the deceased; and the relative age of the landform in which they were found, probably prior to 1800 but after 1500. "The combined evidence points to an epidemic as the most probable causal factor," Larson wrote in her final report for the site.[9] Lower Elwha tribal members also believe smallpox explains the different ways in which their ancestors were buried at Tse-whit-zen.

In many burials at Tse-whit-zen, skeletons were found thickly dusted with red ochre and carefully placed within cedar boxes. The deceased were buried with gifts, tools, and favorite belongings for their journeys into the spirit world, along with etched stones depicting their lives and accomplishments. Skeletons were found arranged in a flexed position—knees to chin, hands to face—as in the womb, to leave the world in the same position in which they entered it. But this was not the case in what tribal members believe to be a mass grave, filled with smallpox victims. "They were placed on top of each other, they were placed embracing, as if husband and wife. We had witnessed a child and a mother embraced with each other," said Lower Elwha tribal chairwoman Frances Charles. "We had over 103 in one area and over 50 in another

This Chinese coin bears the reign date of the Qianlong (Ch'ien-lung) emperor (1736–1796) on one side and the mint mark of Yunnan province on the other. This coin and the others found buried in the crook of the arm of a medicine man document Tse-whit-zen's position as a crossroads of trade and culture. Courtesy Washington State Department of Transportation.

area where there was no preparation. It was something they had to do in a real hurry to protect themselves and their community."

The epidemics were an important turning point in Northwest history and the history of the Klallam people. Disease, accidentally transmitted by trade and other contact, not war, decimated the Indian population of the Northwest, Boyd noted. "The hurt is still there," Boyd said. "The bereavement through the generations is still there. The whole contact experience has done this, and it is just the first blow." The population of the Klallams was estimated to be around 3,200 before 1770. By the 1840s, census accounts tallied about 1,485 Klallam people, and there were only about 485 counted in 1880.

Settlers poured into the territory. The Klallam people would never be a majority in their homeland again. The United States Congress helped see to that. Under the Donation Land Claims Act, passed to encourage white settlement in 1850, Congress guaranteed tracts of land in Oregon Country (including present-day Washington) to any white male U.S. citizen eighteen or older. Each could claim 320 acres of Indian lands and take 320 acres for his wife. They had only to reside on the land and cultivate it for four years to take ownership. Indians could be pushed aside, and their protests ignored. Indians could not become citizens, so they did not qualify for ownership of their own homeland.

As the settlers staked their claims, pressure built for treaties that would grant them legal title to the Indians' land. By the time the Donation Land Claims Act expired in 1855, and before the treaties were signed, 529 people had filed claims on lands bordering Puget Sound, Hood Canal, and the Straits of Georgia and Juan de Fuca. Between 1778 and 1868, 367 treaties between Indians and the United States were signed and ratified. The first was in Delaware and the last with the Nez Perce. In Washington, the first treaty was signed with the Nisqually, so recently that the Treaty Tree, under which the document was signed, stood until it was claimed by a violent winter storm in 2006. Under this silvered snag, the Nisqually people in 1854 ceded 2.5 million acres. In six treaty councils in all, Washington's territorial governor Isaac Stevens terminated Indian rights to more than 64 million acres of land across the Pacific Northwest to the headwaters of the Missouri River. Tribal leaders signed the Treaty of Point No Point, ceding the Klallam, Chimakum, and Skokomish lands, on January 26, 1855, at a two-day treaty council convened on the northern tip of the Kitsap Peninsula. Stevens called the council on January 25. The treaty's provisions were translated from English into Chinook Jargon, a makeshift patois of some three hundred words of French, English, and Chinook origin.

The treaty makers were guided by several goals. In order to save the maximum amount of land for white development, they wanted to put multiple tribes together in as small an area as possible. Stevens worked from a model treaty document, little altered for his dealings in the Northwest. The treaty was already drawn up, and there was no thought that it could be only a basis for negotiation. Negotiation was not the idea. The idea was to make Indians into farmers by providing each person with a small homestead and to "civilize" the tribes by providing teachers, farmers, carpenters, and trades educators. Government representatives also wanted to save the treasury money by paying in commodities rather than cash.

Other goals included abolishing slavery within tribal cultures and stopping any trade across borders. The Lower Elwha Klallam, like other Coast Salish peoples, were targets of intertribal raids for slaves and goods, and they themselves attacked other tribes in retaliation. Slaves were also taken as captives in war. Put to work and seen as symbols of prestige and wealth, slaves could free themselves by marrying a free person. But the stain of slavery typically was difficult to erase, lasting through generations. Treaties with the U.S. government outlawed slavery among the Northwest tribes beginning in 1854, long before the Civil War was fought over whites' enslavement of blacks.

Treaty makers gained Indian assent by promising that Indians would be allowed to hunt, fish, and gather in their usual places. But the tribes' practice of holding land in common was to end. Stevens arrived by schooner on the afternoon of Wednesday, January 24. Indians had already begun to gather at the treaty grounds, despite classically wet and disagreeable Northwest January weather: "The weather was very stormy but the Indians having assembled during the night, it was decided to go on with the treaty," wrote George Gibbs, a lawyer who served as a member of Stevens's treaty commission. By the next morning, some 1,200 Klallam, Chemakum, and Skokomish Indians were gathered at the treaty grounds at Point No Point, Gibbs reported. Stevens began the proceedings with a sales pitch direct from Franklin Pierce, the president of the United States:

> My children—You call me your father. I too have a father who is your Great Father. That Great Father has sent me here today to pay you for your lands, to provide for your children, to see that you are fed and cared for. The Great Father wishes you to be happy. To be friends with each other. The Great Father wants you and the whites to be friends. He wants you to have a home of your own, to have a school where your little children can learn. He wants you to learn to farm, to learn to use tools, and also to have a doctor. Now all these things shall be written down in a paper. That paper shall be read to you. If the paper is good, you will sign it. And I will sign it. I have some gifts for you. Now sit quiet and the paper will be read.[10]

But his pitch apparently didn't have the desired effect—at least at first. Gibbs recorded the Indians' deep unease and resistance. Skokomish leader Che-lan-teh-tat said: "I wish to speak my mind as to selling the land. Great chief! What shall we eat if we do so? Our only food is berries, deer, and salmon. Where then shall we find these? I don't want to sign away all my land. Take half of it and let us keep the rest. I am afraid that I shall become destitute and perish for want of food. I don't like the place you have chosen for us to live on. I am not ready to sign the paper."[11] Stevens swept aside Che-lan-teh-tat's plea to keep half the Skokomish homeland, saying that if the Indians retained larger parcels, they would have to be confined within their borders. But if they agreed to remove to one smaller place, the Indians would keep their liberty to travel to fish "and work for the whites." The Indians were also assured that they "were not called upon to give up their old modes of living and places of seeking food, but only to confine their houses to one spot."

But the Indians' resistance continued. L'Hau-at-scha-uk, a Skokomish said: "I do not want to leave the mouth of the River. I do not want to leave my old home, and my burying ground. I am afraid I shall die if I do." Hool-hol-tan, or Jim, the first sub-chief to the Klallams, said: "I am not pleased with the idea of selling at all. I want you to hear what I have to say. All the Indians here have been afraid to talk, but I wish to speak and be listened to. I don't want to leave my land. It makes me sick to leave it. I don't want to go from where I was born. I am afraid of becoming destitute."[12]

Others said that the price, $60,000, was too low for their homeland, which stretched from the Hoko River to the west, all the way to the crest of the Cascade Range in the east, south to Olympia, and back north to the Strait of Juan de Fuca. Stevens responded that this land, replete with timber, salmon, and fertile valleys that white settlers were so eager to get, was poor land, worth little. Stevens returned to his sales pitch, laying it on thicker this time: "The Great Father wants to put you where you cannot be driven away. The Great Father, besides giving you a home will give you a school, protect you in taking fish, break up your land, give you clothes and seeds." Then, perhaps sensing trouble, Stevens called it a day. The council would reconvene in the morning. January 26 broke wet and blustery. The Indians returned to the treaty grounds, and when they did so, they were carrying white flags. Stevens tried again:

> I think the paper is good. Are you not my children and also children of the Great Father? What will I not do for my children and what will you not do for yours? Would you not die for them? This paper is such as a man would give to his children, and I will tell you why. Does not a father give his children a home? This paper gives you a home. This paper gives you a school. Does not a father send his children to school? It gives you mechanics and a doctor to teach and cure you. Is that not fatherly? This paper secures you fish. Does not a father give food to his children? Besides fish you can hunt, gather roots, and berries. Besides it says you will not drink whiskey and does not a father prevent his children from drinking fire water? Besides all this the paper says you shall be paid for your lands . . . I knew the Great Father was good to his children and did not wish to steal their lands.[13]

Nothing in Gibbs's account explains what happened next: The Indians changed their minds. Led by Chits-a-mah-han, also called the Duke of York, a Klallam leader beloved by whites for his propensity to dress in their clothes—and signal them of trouble brewing among his people—the Indians agreed to sign the treaty.

As he accepted the white flag from Chimakum chief Kul-kah-han, Stevens said: "I hope your heart will always be as white as your flag." With the last signature on the treaty, Stevens gave the signal, and the schooner fired a salute. Stevens and his entourage left, heading to Neah Bay for another round of treaty making. With one stroke that day, about 750,000 acres of tribal lands passed out of Indian hands, including 438,430 acres of Klallam territory. The second-deepest natural harbor on the West Coast at Tse-whit-zen and the Elwha, with its one-hundred-pound tyee—all were ceded away. The treaty required the Klallams to move far from their homeland along the Strait of Juan de Fuca to the Skokomish reservation, 3,840 acres on the arm of the Hood Canal. The treaty also gave the Great Father the right to move more tribes to the same reservation, should he choose.

Most Klallams refused to go. Legally, they were allowed to remain in their homeland, but it was no longer theirs. They could reside on lands not already owned by U.S. citizens, a class from which they were excluded. Or they could stay on the land of a citizen who allowed them to do so.

Mary Ann Lambert describes the melancholy exodus of Klallam people from present-day Port Townsend, east of Port Angeles on the Olympic Peninsula:

> The day soon arrived for the Indians to load their personal belongings into canoes and leave their beloved (home) forever. The side-wheeler *North Pacific* waited, anchored in the bay, for the twenty or more canoes she was to tow to the head of the Hood Canal. Only one Klallam remained behind, refusing to leave. "My parents and grandparents were born here on this very soil upon which I now stand," he said. "I was born a Klallam, not a Skokomish. I will die here, a Klallam." He stood alone on the beach and watched as the others paddled slowly toward the waiting ship. When the canoes reached the *North Pacific* they were tied to her stern, one canoe behind the other, and the ship departed. As the side-wheeler was about to round Marrowstone Point, the canoes' occupants, looking back at their ancestral homes, could see their village in flames, burning rapidly to the ground—by order of the Great White Father in Washington, D.C. The waters bounding the Skokomish Reservation were finally reached and the canoes were cut loose from the stern of the *North Pacific*. Sadly the Klallams paddled towards the beach, then sat dejectedly in their canoes, staring unhappily at the shore.[14]

Lambert notes that within five days, everyone had returned to the ashes of their village. Landless in their own territory, the Klallams soon learned that even the rights they had reserved to their hunting, fishing, and gathering places were not secure.

And a deal, it turned out, was not really a deal. Even the reservations, the remnants of vast aboriginal holdings retained by the tribes under the treaties, were not protected from further incursion by whites. Stevens had expressly promised, in return for the Indians' cession of their property in the Treaty of Point No Point, that no white would be allowed to reside on the reservation without the tribes' permission.

But in 1887, under the Dawes Act, reservation lands were allotted to tribal members in holdings of 160 acres per individual. Any "leftover" land was deemed surplus and was sold. The reward for accepting an allotment was citizenship, which was not provided to all Indians until 1924. Between 1887 and 1934, about 100 million acres, or two-thirds of communal Indian landholdings across the United States, passed into white hands. As a result, Indian homelands became checkerboards, with significant numbers of non-Indians owning land in the heart of the reservations. Many of these transactions were not true sales but acts of desperation committed by people without the cash to pay doctors or feed their families. Or they were outright thefts.

Ratification of the Treaty of Point No Point by the U.S. Senate came late, in 1859, and the annuity goods provided under the terms of the agreement were not what had been promised, in quantity or quality. The first distribution also was not made until 1861. No money was provided at the time of the treaty signing, but the government promised to pay $60,000 for the benefit of all three tribes, as determined by the president of the United States, over a twenty-five-year period. The unsuitability of the Skokomish reservation for the Klallam people, more than one hundred miles from their homeland and traditional hunting and gathering areas, was plain from the start.

Five years after the treaty signing, the Indian agent for Puget Sound, Michael T. Simmons, wrote: "The Clallams living on the Straits of Fuca should be allowed a reserve at Clallam Bay . . . my reason . . . is that these Indians reared on the wide waters of the Strait and the ocean, accustomed to taking the whale, the black-fish, and halibut, cannot content themselves or be made to remain except by force, on the narrow waters of Hood's Canal, where the reservation is situated."[15]

The Reverend Myron Eells, a missionary stationed at Skokomish, was not optimistic for the future of the Indians on the reservation, writing in 1873: "They are diminishing in number, and the most discouraging feature in relation to them is they have scarcely any children. Consequently as a nation, when this generation passes away, they will become almost extinct."[16]

But instead, the Klallams persisted, adapted, and survived. Not even half of them, about five hundred tribal members, ever came to Skokomish to receive their annuities. Most still lived in their traditional territory. They lived by fishing or working for farmers or in sawmills. The Indian Homestead Act, passed in 1884, allowed Indian people to claim homesteads if they renounced all tribal ties. About a dozen Klallam families acquired Indian homesteads in the lower Elwha Valley and around Freshwater Bay, according to an analysis by anthropologist Barbara Lane. The homesteads were contiguous, or nearly so, enabling Klallam families to retain some sense of community even after being forced from their original villages.

Contrary to the widely held belief that Indians could and would not farm, the Klallams adapted to their new circumstances and took up new occupations. By 1895, ten Indian homesteads, totaling 1,295 acres, were located in the lower Elwha Valley and vicinity of Freshwater Bay, Lane notes. Six of the homesteads were on the Elwha River. The tribe's ties were deep, not only to the river and the fish, but to the lands of the valley. Adeline Smith, born and raised by the Elwha River, spent her childhood on the homestead farm owned by her great-great-great-grandfather Hunter John, who took out homestead papers on the land in 1877.

"Those days were happy memories for me," Smith said. She and her niece Beatrice Charles are among the last speakers of their native language on the reservation and hold positions of prestige in the tribe. They are living links to the tribe's survival despite the epidemics, the time of dispossession from their homeland, and adaptation to their new circumstances. Smith has good memories of her childhood on the Elwha homestead: "You felt free. The farm that we had after my father died, my mother still ran it, and we had all sorts of animals, and we had two orchards, so everything was there for us to take." The family had about sixty acres on the flat where Smith grew up, and her father bought more property as well. Her mother had sheep, which she raised for their wool, dairy cows, a horse, turkey, ducks, and chickens. "We had everything," Smith said. "People had a hard time during the Depression, but we never felt it was bad as far as feeding the children. My mother used to say we were fortunate. They also planted plenty of vegetables, potatoes that I remember my mother sacking up to take to Tse-whit-zen to take to her friends and relatives there in exchange. We never bought; it was more like barter. They would give us fish, and my mother would give them vegetables and potatoes. That's the way people lived in those days."

Charles remembered gathering fruit from the orchard to trade, too. "We used to have to go out and pick different kinds of fruit—plums, apples. And we would trade them for sea fish at Tse-whit-zen, halibut and codfish and things like that. And we used to walk to the different beaches to get mussels and Chinese slippers as we called them. We used to walk to go and get them." And there were other ways to make a living. Adeline Smith's grandfather Joe Sampson would charge settlers twenty-five cents to cross the Elwha, on a barge pulled across the river with a cable.

Families didn't live in just one place. They moved around, using one another's houses to follow the work that needed to be done, whether haying or harvesting or drying fish. "They moved to where there was food, and to make a living," Smith said. "And I know that in those days also, if you had a house and you were living in a different place, if someone wanted to live there, they would ask permission, and usually the answer was yes. And in that way they respected each other." The Elwha River remained a mainstay, keeping the tribe alive with all five species of salmon.

Historical photos of Port Angeles in the early twentieth century also show Indian people still using the beach, which is crowded with their carved canoes and tents.

Settlers commonly believed that they were witnessing the last of the Indians, who would soon die out, a vanquished race. But the Klallams adapted and survived. Adeline Smith's grandfather Joe Sampson (*standing*) supported himself in the new money economy by running a ferry in the mid-1920s across the Elwha River and charging twenty-five cents per crossing. The ferry was hand-pulled across by cable. Courtesy Adeline Smith.

Haying time at the Sampson farm, ca. 1915. Here Ernest Sampson (*left*) works with Andrew Sampson (*center, standing*) to bring in the hay crop. All the homesteaders helped one another at harvest time. Courtesy Adeline Smith.

Others, called "spit Indians," continued to live on the Ediz Hook. Smith is one of the oldest living members of the Lower Elwha tribe. She remembered how her native tongue was used against her ancestors. "We were always considered—what would you say?—illiterate, because a lot of the old-timers didn't understand English," Smith said. "I am one of those that never spoke English because I was surrounded by elders that talked only their language. Until I went to school. Then we weren't supposed to talk our language."

Auntie Bea, as Charles is called on the reservation, hopes that rediscovery of Tse-whit-zen shows the true history of this tribe and the way it was dispossessed of the waterfront. "Sometimes I think what has happened has really opened the eyes of, say, the United States. Of what has happened before. They were as mean as the other countries in getting it. They weren't lily-white. They came and took the land away from us and treated us badly. At least they could have helped us. After all, taking it all, it was beautiful land, away from us," she said. "We were getting pushed off of the land. We had no say. We didn't become citizens of the United States until 1924. But this was our country. This was our land. But we couldn't say nothing about what was happening. My elders couldn't say nothing. It was a long fight before we got this land here [on the reservation]. You know, Indians knew where to live. Where it was easy. They lived on prime land. When the settlers came, they wanted that prime land, so they did everything they could to get my people off.

"I don't like to say what was done, because I have heard the history from my side of the family, from my own people, that the others don't want to hear about. They don't like to hear how they did it. They don't like to bring up the past because it isn't very pretty. We were told, like handing down from generation to generation, what happened, how they were chased out, how they were shot. They talked about the Elwha River and how it was red with blood when they were kicking the Indians out of there, shooing them off and sending them west across the river. My people knew it, how they slaughtered them to get this land, this valley where we are now."[17]

Smith said she knows many of the tribe's ancestors buried at Tse-whit-zen must have died of smallpox, because so many other tribal members nearby did, such as in Neah Bay, about an hour away at the farthest northwestern tip of the peninsula. "In Neah Bay, with smallpox, they were dying so fast nobody knew who was who. They were just wrapping them in a blanket, same way down here, that happened." The deaths of so many tribal members shaped the history of this tribe, and this town, profoundly, Smith said. Charles recounted that no reservation was set apart for the Klallam people on the Strait of Juan de Fuca, in part because President Abraham Lincoln had been told there were no Klallam people left. "We was supposed to have died." But Tim Pysht, Beatrice Charles's great-grandfather, who was born in the early 1880s and lived to be one hundred, made this prophecy: "The Klallam people will almost disappear, but they will come back once again and be a strong people."

Port Angeles still seems perplexed by the Indians who refused to die off. Local histories of the town usually give scant mention to the area's first residents. They are often consigned to a misty realm, usually with a combination of romanticism and insult not far from Quimper's original assessment. Consider this, on the origin of the Indian people of Port Angeles, written in 1983:

> From what remote place did he come? What ancient land spawned this mysterious creature whom early explorers found practicing strange customs and displaying even more peculiar dress. . . .
>
> Indians were the children of Babel, doomed forever to a primitive life as penance for their sins. . . . From an early explorer's standpoint, the Indians

and their magnificent land lay yawning and exposed like a giant pearl longing to be discovered.[18]

And just as their land was regarded as yearning to be taken for the white man's industry, so the culture of the Indians was depicted as in need of white guidance:

> He reminds us of a strong-willed teenager who wants to be given his head, who refuses to listen to the old man's advice, yet wants to know that the same old man is waiting patiently in the background to bail him out of any rash predicaments in which he plunges himself. . . . For isn't the Indian but a teenager in Western civilization? Actually rather little more than an infant by civilization's measure, for he was still cooking his fish over an open fire on the beach when the Civil War was fought. . . . Perhaps the white man has expected too much—too soon![19]

Sea captain Alexander Sampson was one of the first to stake his claim in the Klallams' homeland. Born in Duxbury, Massachusetts, Sampson, a trader, sailed his sloop into the west end of the Port Angeles Harbor in about 1856—some accounts place his arrival in 1858.[20] A master mariner who sailed full-rigged ships out of Gloucester, Massachusetts, Sampson used his sloop to trade with Indians and whites along the Strait of Juan de Fuca and Puget Sound.

It was on one of his trading trips that he saw the Port Angeles harbor. The deep harbor, sheltering sand spit of the Ediz Hook, and tidal lagoon just up from the beach caught his eye. He staked a homestead claim without delay, taking the 320 acres of land allowed under the Donation Land Claims Act, choosing the choicest parcel of flat land, right at the head of the bay, which included the saltwater lagoon. Sampson brought lumber on his sloop and began raising his house and barn, near where the Klallam had their cemetery. "They resented his location on the harbor, and at one point, while he was in the sloop, anchored in the harbor, they surrounded the boat in their canoes and started climbing aboard," Jessie C. Ayres wrote in the *Port Angeles Evening News* in a column published June 16, 1962. The two men were outnumbered, but fortunately a strong breeze came up, and the sloop outdistanced the canoes and sailed out of the harbor."

Sampson went to Old Indian Norman, one of the Klallams known to be friendly to whites, and convinced him to urge his tribesmen to cease hostilities. Sampson was able to build his house and prove up his claim, as long as he left the cemetery alone.

He lived in his white farmhouse between trading trips, or while on vacation from his job as a lighthouse keeper at Tatoosh, a job he kept for twenty-seven years. While encamped on the island, he would leave the farm at Tse-whit-zen in the care of an old shipmate, Jack Dunn. "They had rare celebrations when the captain was home, a huge bucket of hard candy, a wooden box of soda crackers, and a wheel of cheese to use as a foundation for the rum they drank," Ayres wrote.

For years, it went on like this, with Sampson, Dunn, a three-legged shepherd dog named Prince, and an old cow named Phebie. Sampson gave her a box of apples each Christmas. Sampson's claim lay entirely within the boundaries of the government reservation established by Lincoln for a military reserve and lighthouse in 1862. That created problems when the military reservation was thrown open to settlement almost thirty years later. Sampson refused to sell his claim and took his fight all the way to Washington, D.C., where forty acres of his homestead was protected by an act of Congress. He retained the land where his house and barn stood along with the cleared fields immediately surrounding them. The land survey was completed and transfer recorded in November 1891. The reserved, even silent and brusque sea captain, known for neat neckties improvised from narrow, fringed scarves—always mindfully kept out of his food while eating—held onto more than a quarter mile of frontage on the bay at its most important point. It was worth at least $2,500 per acre even then. "He was said to be the richest man in Clallam County," *The Beacon* of Port Angeles reported in his obituary on January 29, 1893. The land at Tse-whit-zen was the gem of Port Angeles. And it would not be long before this town, just awakening to its possibilities, would notice.

II
Amnesia

4

Conquering the Last Frontier

THOMAS ALDWELL ARRIVED IN PORT ANGELES ON A WOOD-BURNING BOAT, THE *George E. Starr*. How fitting. For no other industrialist would transform this frontier town from a place of self-sustaining natural bounty to an industrial zone with such zeal. The teetotalling son of the biggest brewer in Toronto, Aldwell arrived in Port Angeles in 1890 from Seattle, a town already too developed for his frontier ambitions. "Seattle and Port Townsend were both ideal places for an ambitious young man to stake out a claim. Free land, timber, water, promise was everywhere," Aldwell wrote in his autobiography, *Conquering the Last Frontier*. "But I felt a vague discontent . . . these towns were not the frontier any more. I wanted something ever newer, some place where only the potential existed, unrecognized perhaps by other men."

Well, not exactly. By the time he showed up, Port Angeles had already captured the eyes of schemers and dreamers pursuing what they saw as wide open country, free for the taking. For George Venable Smith, it started with the dream of forming a white utopia. A California lawyer, Smith had moved to Seattle in 1884. A year later, he became city attorney and found himself wrestling with "the Chinese problem," as it was called at the time. Smith became outspoken in his bigotry against the Chinese, whom he resented for staying in Seattle after they finished their work on the railroad. He led a group that didn't want the Chinese to take jobs that might otherwise be filled by white people. The group began to explore the notion of creating a one-race, white utopia. Smith envisioned a cooperative with free medical care, no taxes, and lifelong security. The idea of the Puget Sound Cooperative Colony was born.[1] Following anti-Chinese rallies in Seattle and Tacoma in 1885, Smith began advertising around the country for settlers. The colony purchased land just east of the Port Angeles town site, on Ennis Creek opposite a Klallam village. Hundreds of colonists arrived in 1887. *The Model Commonwealth*, the community's newspaper, waxed rhapsodic about the absence of the Chinese: Port Angeles was "blessed because it was as far removed from the vicious example as possible for those who have experienced the misery of having this degrading and debasing element in their midst."[2] Colonists built the area's first sawmill, office building, homes, schools, churches, and even an ornate opera house. But their vision would not last. The colony soon dissolved, the victim of infighting and a most un-utopian ending: lawsuits. But the town's growth had begun.

In 1885, mover and shaker Victor Smith was named customs collector for the Puget Sound district and managed to snag the customs port of entry and move it—temporarily—from Port Townsend to Port Angeles. He also convinced President Abraham Lincoln in 1862 to set aside 3,520 acres of land in Port Angeles, including a lighthouse on the Ediz Hook, as a federal government town-site reserve. Port Angeles was finally incorporated in 1890, the year Aldwell showed up. When he stepped off the steamer, Port Angeles had no paved road to the capital, no roads into the country, and about 1,300 people who got around by horse and canoe. The town's one newspaper advertised that it would accept ducks, chicken eggs, potatoes, butter, cabbage, hay, and grain as payment for subscriptions. Sixteen saloons were the hub of commerce, including thriving brothels. "I saw Port Angeles was a wild frontier town," Aldwell wrote. "If I was looking for undeveloped country, I certainly found it. . . . Between 200 and 300 Indians were living and camping on the beach in front of the town. Most of them had large canoes, hand-hewn from logs, and some practically lived in their canoes. They wore fancy costumes, especially the brides and grooms. The Indians made their living principally by fishing."[3]

And that is the last we hear about either Indians or fish in the more than three hundred pages of Aldwell's autobiography. He soon had other things on his mind. Aldwell looked at the Ediz Hook, cradling a deep, natural harbor, and saw the same prime real estate that had drawn first the Klallam people and then explorers, traders, and white settlers, including sea captain Sampson, to this spot. Like the others who had come before him, and who would come after him, Aldwell brought his own framework to his vision for this land. His nineteenth-century capitalist zeal fixed on the potential for wringing a new kind of wealth from this land. Not the wealth already there that had sustained this place for centuries but a wealth based on capital, industry, and payrolls and the transformation of this place from a natural economy to one he would control. "In my mind's eye I saw that harbor rimmed with vital industry with payrolls expanding, houses being built, and streets being laid. The raw material was here, raw material that called for the minds and hands of builders who would think of this as a home to make for their children and their grandchildren. I felt I had met a challenge to help build a happy and prosperous community and I decided to accept it. Whatever I would do in life was now tied to a ragged, sprawling, ambitious little town called Port Angeles." The same landscape that had drawn so many others drew him, too. "One thing about living along water as beautiful as the Strait of Juan de Fuca is that it keeps one thinking that the water itself has a magic to bring to some of its wealth to those who live near it. . . . There is something about belonging to a place. You want to control more and more of it, directly or indirectly . . . land was something one could work with, change, and develop."[4]

Aldwell set up shop in town, talking his way into a rent-free room with a chest of drawers and a mattress on the bare floor at a hotel on the main street. His first steps included gathering residents together and urging them to squat on the lots in the government reservation set aside by Lincoln, surrounding Sampson's claim. The wager paid off. By 1891, the federal government opened the reserve and gave the squatters the right to settle on and homestead two lots and thus acquire title to lots appraised at five dollars each. The rest were sold in 1894 at auction. By then, Aldwell was secretary of the town's chamber of commerce. He married and built a home on cə́łmət (Lake Crescent). He put in a five-hole golf course and brought in a piano all the way from Seattle so that his wife and daughters could practice their scales. There were trips to Europe for "the girls," as he called them, and for Aldwell, growing prominence in the local Republican Party and business organizations.

But Aldwell saved his biggest ambitions for the Elwha River. He vividly writes of the first time he saw the canyon where he would later build the Elwha Dam, with its clear spring reflecting the tracery of vine maples overhead. "The scintillating rays of sun were coming through the branches and sparkling on the water. My life had taken

OLYMPIC POWER COMPANYS WORKS AT 5.30 P.M.
NEAR PORT ANGELES WASH.
P. WISCHMEYER SEATTLE — P27
PUBLISHED BY MATHEWSON'S DRUG ST.

me to schools, to cities, to business, but suddenly that spring embodied all of life and beauty I thought I'd ever want. I didn't hesitate. Maybe I didn't even think. I wanted this place where I was as I'd never wanted anything before."5

Aldwell offered one hundred dollars above the going rate for the best claims at the time—three hundred dollars in all. There was no wagon trail to the site from Port Angeles, and no bridge over the Elwha. Aldwell packed everything in on his back, transferring loads to a raft or canoe, or sometimes swimming the river, to take possession of the site near the spring and prove up a claim. "I won't forget the effort I had getting a can of coal oil through the woods," he wrote. "I had to make frequent stops, and I'd lie on my back underneath some tree, looking at the sky." As he lay gazing skyward, he saw the beauty and abundance of a force of nature he believed should not be wasted a minute longer. Here was a wild river that in his view was just waiting to be improved by being harnessed for progress, its wasted free-flowing waters transformed into electricity. In 1894, Aldwell met up with a businessman interested

This photo, taken before 1912, shows construction workers at the Elwha Dam at quitting time. It was illegal to build this dam without a fish passage. But the developer, Thomas Aldwell, figured out a way around that with the help of Leslie Darwin, the state fish commissioner. P. Wischmeyer, Seattle. Bert Kellogg Collection, North Olympic Library System, ELWA DAMS-006.

The free-flowing Elwha River can be seen in this photo, taken before 1912, of the Elwha Dam under construction. Fish runs quickly began to dwindle after the dam was completed, restricting fish habitat to just five miles between the dam and the river's mouth. Bert Kellogg Collection of the North Olympic Library System, ELWA DAMS-008.

in developing a hydropower site, and the two struck a deal. It would take twelve years, but in secret, Aldwell and his partner stealthily acquired the land he would need for the dam and its three-mile reservoir above the canyon. While the spring enchanted Aldwell, it was the idea of a dam that possessed him.

> The property on the Elwha River always fascinated me, but it was not until I saw it as a source of electric power for Port Angeles and the whole Olympic Peninsula that it magnetized all my energies.
> . . . Suddenly the Elwha was no longer a wild stream crashing down to the Strait, the Elwha was peace, power and civilization.[6]

And a great source of cash. Aldwell smugly observed that because of their secrecy, he and his partner were able to buy the land for the dam site for a nominal price, and "for our purposes, it was naturally worth a great many times what we paid for it. Mine was a dream of power that would transform a city."

Port Angeles, Wash
Sept 12th 1911

Mr J. L. Riseland
State Fish Commissioner
Dear Sir.

There has been a complaint made here by the Cannery men, about the Dam on the Elwha River.

I have personally searched the Elwha River & Tributarys, above the Dam, & have been unable to find a single salmon, I have visited the Dam several times lately, was out there yesterday and there appear to be Thousands of Salmon at the foot of the Dam, where they are jumping continually trying to get up the flume I have watched them very close, and I am satisfied now, that they cannot get above the Dam.

I am enclosing herewith some Pictures taken by myself from the mouth of the Flume looking down the River and shows the fish after they had jumped into the Flume and were thrown out again,

The Elwha River being one of the principle Salmon Streams of Clallam County, and the big run of Silver Salmon just commencing to come into the River and if they do not get to their spawning Grounds, it will mean a very serious drawback to the fish industry of this County.

I would appreciate very much if you would let me know what action to take regarding this matter
I Remain,
Yours Etc
J. W. Pike Game Warden Clallam County

No one can take comfort in the thought that the builders who constructed the Elwha Dam without fish passage, and the state bureaucrats who allowed it, didn't know that it would hurt salmon runs. In this letter, written in 1911, Clallam County game warden J. W. Pike writes that he has personally searched the Elwha River and its tributaries above the Elwha Dam and was unable to find a single salmon. He warns that the fish runs would be destroyed if the salmon could not reach their spawning grounds. His letter was ignored. Today, Puget Sound chinook salmon, including the descendants of the fish Pike was searching for, are at risk of extinction. Courtesy Washington State Archives.

Aldwell formed his Olympic Power and Development Company in September 1910 and set about building a dam five miles from the river's mouth. Using capital secured in Chicago, Aldwell put some two hundred men to work with instructions to raise the dam one hundred feet high between the walls of the canyon. But instead of securing the dam on bedrock, the dam rested on gravel. It didn't take long for the Elwha River, a mighty mountain river, to shrug off the flimsy structure. After two years of construction, on October 31, 1912, the Elwha blew out the dam, by then nearly complete, to a depth of eighty feet. Indians at the Lower Elwha reservation today still tell stories of families sitting down to dinner, alerted by their dogs' barking and running for their lives to high ground. Dead fish were hanging in the trees. Incredibly, no one was killed. Undeterred, Aldwell ordered waste rock, evergreens, rocks, and gravel shoved into the dam to plug the holes and pilings rammed eighty feet into bedrock. He would force this unspoiled canyon, and this wild river, to accept his dam. On November 5, 1913, workers detonated the blasts to rebuild the dam. "It was raining, a real Washington rain that made all the leaves and trees look clean and washed," Aldwell wrote. "I was glad of the drops falling on my face because when I knew the work was soon to be done, I couldn't keep a tear or two from forming. . . . the muffled roar of the blasts was music."[7] The dam was finished by year's end. It had taken Aldwell twenty years in all to acquire the land for his dam, arrange the financing, and finally collar the Elwha.

But before the Elwha could become a river of cash, Aldwell had the state and its laws to deal with. Obstructing a fish run without providing fish passage was illegal in Washington even before statehood. Find the crumbling, bound volume of laws passed by the territorial legislature, shelved in the state archives at the Capitol in Olympia, and you can read for yourself the law passed February 11, 1890. There it is, printed on thick, creamy paper, right before the law prohibiting prize fighting and after the law to prevent deceptive marketing of dairy products. The law empowered fish commissioners to seek criminal prosecution, levy fines, and, if need be, modify or even dynamite obstructions over any stream "where food fish are wont to ascend." But the law was just a temporary inconvenience for Aldwell the dealmaker, who soon applied his skills to the state fisheries bureaucrats in Olympia. The game warden for Clallam County had already put his bosses on notice about the slaughter on the Elwha, where Aldwell was building his dam.

History is a funny thing. Sometimes, and in some places, it seems to speak more loudly than others. At the state archives, researchers can track down and actually hold the original documents that sealed this river's fate. You can smell the paper, look at the handwriting or the blows of a long-gone manual typewriter up close. Reflect on those marks made on the paper, on the Elwha River, its fish, and this region's history. One letter in the file, written by Clallam County game warden J. W. Pike, inked by hand in fine, flowing script, is not so much a letter as a silent scream, still piercing when read nearly a century later. "I have personally searched the Elwha River and tributaries above the dam and am unable to find a single salmon," Pike wrote, after inspecting the river's reaches because of complaints about the dam from cannery owners. "I have visited the dam several times lately, was out there yesterday and there appear to be thousands of salmon at the foot of the dam, where they are jumping continually trying to get up the flume. I have watched them very close, and I am satisfied now that they cannot get above the dam. . . . I would appreciate very much if you would let me know what actions to take regarding this matter."[8] But the state fish commissioner, J. L. Riseland, managed to ignore that letter as well as a barrage of publicity about the dam orchestrated by Aldwell during the first year of construction.

"Development of Olympic Power First Big Enterprise to Start Lifeblood of the Peninsula" was a typical headline in the *Port Angeles Daily News* in 1911. The *Seattle Times* and *Seattle Post-Intelligencer* slavered with equal enthusiasm at the prospect of the peninsula's first big hydropower dam. Nobody talked about fish. Or Indians. "We had the active, intelligent support of the press," Aldwell gloated in his book.

It wasn't until August 1913 that a new fish commissioner, Leslie Darwin, put Aldwell on notice that his dam was illegal. "Undoubtedly you are aware of the law which provides that you must construct a fishway and we will ask you to have the same ready to operate at the time you shut off the water at the dam," wrote Darwin. Aldwell couldn't have been too worried: Darwin signed his letter "Very respectfully."[9] Aldwell huffed back with a letter on August 15, signed with a bold hand. Didn't Darwin know he had already worked this all out with Darwin's predecessor? Aldwell wrote. With whom, Aldwell continued with barely concealed boredom, "we had thoroughly gone into this matter." They had, he assured the commissioner, agreed to an alternative arrangement: a fish hatchery, for which Aldwell would donate the site. And then comes the murder weapon that killed the Elwha tyee, written August 17, 1913, by Commissioner Darwin, misspellings, typos, and all. Darwin, so aptly named, decided who would win this contest of survival of the fittest. And it would not be the fish. In his letter to Aldwell, Darwin admitted he knew the dam was illegal: "No officer of the State has any right to waive one of the state's statutory requirements. Neither

No one has felt the loss of the great salmon runs of the Elwha like the river's first people, the Lower Elwha Klallam, who depend on the fish not only for their tables but for their spiritual well-being. Here Tribal Chairwoman Frances Charles's mother, Vera Charles, holds a big, freshly cleaned chinook salmon (sčánəxʷ), just caught in the Elwha River, 1920s. Courtesy Vera Charles.

Mr. Riseland as fish commissioner, nor myself are at liberty to say to you that you will not have to put a fishway over your dam," Darwin wrote. "The only possible way to avoid you having to do this would be for the state to select a hatchery site at the foot of your dam and to make use of your dam as its own obstruction for the purpose of taking fish for spawning purposes. The law gives to the state permission to obstruct streams for this purpose and I have no serious doubt that under the circumstances that we could join their obstruction onto yours and that you would thereby be relieved of the necessity of erecting a fishway."[10]

From then on, it was just a dreary matter of cutting the deal, trading the Elwha River's unique habitat, and the fish perfectly adapted to it over thousands of years, each a genetic gem, for a hatchery. Darwin gave the river away for a pittance: a site for the hatchery as well as a supervisor's residence, power for the operation of the hatchery and electric lights for the superintendent's house, and a concrete holding tank for the mighty tyee.

Even that was too much for Aldwell, who shot back on August 18 that "just looking at it right off the reel, it would appear that you were making a very heavy demand on us . . . it will be necessary for me to have the figures on this." Easily put back in his place, Darwin wrote Aldwell on August 21 like an anxious suitor, nagging him for his assent so Darwin could place orders for building materials. "I felt sure that when you thoroughly understood the situation that you would appreciate that our proposition was much better all around," Darwin wrote. "My plan forever eliminates bother in the future."[11]

By June 2, 1914, it was time for tough love, with Darwin writing stiffly, "I am sorry that you have not made any response to my last query to you relative to the hatchery at the foot of the Elwha dam. Unless I hear from you in some positive manner in five days, I shall issue an order for you to erect a fishway in accordance with the plans and specifications which I shall submit to you. It is out of the question for us to allow another fish run to beat its brains out against that dam."[12] That brought a letter from Aldwell the next day, promising, more or less, to get right on it. As author Bruce Brown points out in his singular book *Mountain in the Clouds*, even more was lost in this tawdry transaction than the Elwha. In trading a hatchery for habitat for wild fish—a policy later sanctioned by the legislature—the deal cut between the state and Aldwell set the precedent for nearly one hundred years of flawed fisheries policy in which salmon were expected to live without rivers. The state went on a hatchery bender that has yet to relent, building what would become one of the largest hatchery systems in the world. Hatcheries became reasons for building agency staff, plumping up department budgets, and creating political cover for development and overfishing that all but doomed wild salmon.

By 1922, the hatchery on the Elwha was abandoned. So few fish struggled back to the face of the dam that the department simply gave up. Aldwell had the last laugh. He never even deeded the hatchery site to the state, as promised, and paid only $2,500 toward the construction of a hatchery that failed within a decade. The magnificent salmon runs on the Elwha were sold out so one rich man could get richer. And the decisions made on that river set a course of destruction of wild salmon that is yet to be reversed. Today salmon are imperiled throughout the Puget Sound basin, with runs of wild salmon listed for protection under the Endangered Species Act from the Elwha River to the Cascade crest and south to the Oregon border, where the same sad story is repeated all the way to California.

The dams were not a gunshot to the head of an ecosystem but a botched hanging that left the victim to slowly twist. It wasn't just the placement of the dams that mattered. It was the cutting off of the great fish from the entire homeland that nurtured them, and which they nurtured in return with the gift of their very lives. With the damming of the Elwha, the tyee were limited to a fragment of their habitat, with only the lower five miles of the river left for their home. Restricted to a tiny remnant of their homeland, cut off from the natural systems that sustained them—just like the Elwha people themselves—the Elwha River salmon declined.

The region's natural abundance diminished gradually. Elders Beatrice Charles and Adeline Smith, born in 1919 and 1920, remembered how thick the fish were in the Elwha River even during their childhood. Charles sat on the couch in her trailer not far from the Elwha River on the reservation and reflected on the river she had known as a girl. Her memories of the fish were sharp and rich. "When we used to be playing around down there by the edges of the water and the salmon runs came in, you could just see them, glittering. Just schools of them going up. Some times they would just jump up in the air and we would holler and scream, we thought it was just the greatest," Charles said. "The Elwha River was always just so full of salmon— you see the schools going up, it was just black. No matter what season it was. Spring

Adeline Smith (front, wearing a coat), sits with her family at their homestead by the Elwha River, 1921. "There were thirteen or fourteen of us, and we would visit in the evening after dinner. We would sit and watch the fish go up the river," Smith said. The building behind them is for smoking and drying salmon and is where the children changed into their swimsuits. Courtesy Adeline Smith.

salmon, any species. It was loaded with it." Smith remembered that on summer evenings her family would gather on their homestead by the Elwha and watch the fish come up the river.

"The family, always if it was a nice day, they would all move down there and watch the fish go up." Charles, who in her childhood joined Smith for stays at her family homestead, got a soft look when she remembered those summer nights. "It was like a ritual." As the fish splashed, and the late summer evening light grew golden, Charles's father would take out the newspaper and read it aloud, translating it into Klallam for the elders. Meanwhile the kids would be playing, wading in the water, and swimming. "You couldn't keep us out of the river," she said.

Charles kept cooking pots down by the river especially for the pinks, "humpies," she called them. "I would catch a humpy salmon and I'd club it, and it would still be wiggling and I would be cutting it up and putting it in the pot and go boil it and eat it."

Smith laughed at the memory: "Oh, she was a real cannibal." But even then, their elders warned them about the demise of the salmon. "I'd hear the older people talk about it. They would say when the fish was going up, you know it was real plentiful, but they said after a while, there is going to be very few," Charles said. "They knew that the dam was going to destroy the salmon runs. They talked about it, and they felt bad that the white person built the dams just for the lights, they said. Of course, we never had electricity, so we didn't know." By 1916, the state declared fishing illegal for Indians outside their reservation. Despite the promise of the treaty of 1855, reserving the Klallams' right to continue to hunt and fish in their accustomed areas, suddenly the Indians had to steal their own food. The Lower Elwha Klallam people could not legally fish in their own homeland.

As Elwha tribal members were arrested for fishing in their homeland to feed their families, the newcomers held their first sportfishing salmon derbies on the Ediz Hook. The highliner hoisted a twenty-seven-pound six-ounce salmon, winning a 1934 six-cylinder Studebaker sedan. "We had to sneak to fish. That's what made me angry," Smith said. "The game warden was always down there, and they used to pick my dad up, and anyone else," Charles said. Smith remembered when her mother, who didn't speak English and hadn't gone to school, was nearly jailed over salmon. A hatchery employee told her that he was hooking salmon for eggs and the fish would be destroyed. So she took some of the fish and was butchering, hanging, and drying them when a game warden put a dollar bill in the pocket of her shirt and filed a complaint in town. He accused her of selling fish illegally. "Boy, that made me burn," Smith said. The hatchery employee—Smith still remembers his name some seventy years later—told of what was happening, hurried into town to keep her mother out of jail. Made into outlaws, the Elwhas resorted to dragging salmon on strings through tall grass, Smith said, so the fish would not be seen.

Just as hurtful to the Elwha people was the waste of their signature fish caused by dam operators, who jerked the Elwha River's water level up and down according to their need to generate power, with no thought of what it would do to the fish. Tribal members today live with vivid memories of shimmering pools of stranded salmon, left to die in puddles when the river level rose and fell as the dam was opened and closed to generate or shut off power. "The dam itself killed a lot of fish, a lot of salmon. By just opening and shutting and opening and shutting," Charles said. "Every Sunday they would shut the dam. And them little minnows were just all flipping around there, they were so thick. Thousands and thousands. They would just open it right up and it would overflow the riverbanks, and it would go onto the land where the road was. They would shut it up. Then it would leave pools of water, you know. Like I would say 'mud puddles' when I was a little kid. And they leave pools of water there, and there would be little minnows flipping around in there. And when the mud puddle would dry up, those fish would be dead. Just puddles and puddles and puddles all over. And you know they got trapped there." Charles and Smith and her brother would get lard buckets and try to rescue the baby salmon. "We'd be scooping the fish in there and be running them down to the river," Charles said. "Dumping them out and running back, looking for the puddles to find the fish. Scooping them back in there and run down to the river and put them back. They killed a lot of salmon," she said. Charles also remembered her family being reduced to gathering dead fish below the dam for the table.

The dam changed not only the flow of the river but the landscape it fed. The river's banks were twined with wild black raspberries and sweet strawberries Charles and Smith used to pick and bring home by the bucket to eat with saucers of milk. And they remember the medicinal plants, tangled thick by the riverbanks, and such an important part of life that no one in Smith's family had need for other medicines. All gone, under the floodwaters of the dam or lost to erosion. The impoundments—a second dam was added higher up the river in 1927—even changed the very shape of the shoreline, by choking back the sediment that fed the beaches and the Ediz Hook. Starved for sediment, shellfish beds rich with clams, oysters, and mussels were eroded into oblivion by the tides. Acres of land also washed away, land that used to be home to the Lower Elwha Klallam people. The salmon lost their home, too, as gravel, in which they used to dig their nests with thrashing tails, stayed trapped behind the dam. Big, bare river cobble was a poor substitute. And miles and miles of the best spawning habitat above the dam, built just five miles from the river's mouth, were walled off.

As the Elwha River salmon runs diminished, the Lower Elwha Klallam people, nourished for 10,000 years by the natural abundance of their homeland, needed money to feed themselves. "Before, we didn't have to have money to buy anything," Charles said. "They took away our salmon, our rights to fish. The settlers lived on the beach and we couldn't get our seafood because we would be trespassing. And they put up the dam and then diminished the salmon anyway. All that, we couldn't harvest anything. We had to learn that we had to have money to buy those things." Soon the Lower Elwha Klallam people had to turn on their own homeland to survive. "The only thing that our men could do to keep their families alive was to go and get that job cutting down the trees in this area," Charles said. "They couldn't go out to fish, they couldn't go out to hunt, they had to have a license to do this and that, and they had to have money. They took away our livelihood.

"I am asked that question, 'Well, your Indian men went out to help cut down the trees.' Yes. They had to. Because they had their families to think about and had to go and buy stuff when they didn't have to before. We learned about the mighty dollar. That you had to have that in order to survive again. That is what really irritates me. To see them guys log down their places, and they stack up those remnants of trees that they have felled and then they burn it. We never had to cut down a tree to make a fire. The only time they cut down a tree was to build a house or build a canoe. And they asked for that tree." The money economy also disrupted the tribe's web of social relationships and interdependence, held together by shared abundance. "Money wasn't a problem. It was barter," Charles said. "I've got this fish, and you give me that fish, or elk. Nine times out of ten, you were related to them. And they would trade berries and wild animals, and they would have the fish or the clams, and they would barter back and forth. Food was plentiful. All you had to do was go in the bay and fish for cod, flounders, any of those. You didn't want for anything. It was when the money came in, that mighty dollar. That was when things made a difference because they took control of everything."

On February 12, 1914, Aldwell threw the switch on the Elwha, and the town partied as the first kilowatts flowed. Governor Ernest Lister and other dignitaries from around the state attended a banquet and grand ball in Port Angeles. The power market in 1914 included lights for Port Angeles, Port Townsend, Bremerton, other small towns, and even the navy yard. Aldwell was in business. As for the Lower Elwha Klallam people, they were forced, like the fish, to subsidize the wealth of the newcomers with the sacrifice of their food, their homeland, even their very lives. "It was devastating to the people," Charles said. "Because the Creator gave us Indians the salmon. So we respected it. This was our way of life. And so that was taken away from us. And then besides, when they built the dam, all the spiritual places where our people used to go up. . . . The sacred grounds, that was all taken away from us. And so this dam has taken over the life of the Klallam people. It has taken away so much that you know that a white person can't understand how we Indians feel. You've got to be an Indian to have that feeling. Because it's in here," she said, pointing to her heart. "Not just in here," pointing to her head. Meanwhile, like a patient on the receiving end of a heart transplant, Port Angeles grew and thrived. And Aldwell was far from finished.

5

The Big Mill

WITH ALL THE ELECTRICITY TO BE WRUNG FROM THE MIGHTY ELWHA RIVER, Aldwell would need outlets for the juice from his dam. He looked to a member of the dam's board of directors and one of the dam's earliest financial backers: Michael Earles. Born in Genesee, Wisconsin, in 1852, Earles came west when he was thirty-five years old. He was, as the *Seattle Post-Intelligencer* wrote in his June 17, 1919, obituary, "typical of many in this community. The case of the young man of the East who comes west and grew up with the country—an infallible recipe for fortune in old age."

Earles was a busy man. He constructed the Hanford irrigation ditch east of the Cascades, developed coal mines at Bellingham, and held vast timberlands on the western end of the Olympic Peninsula. He didn't call them trees. Or forests. And certainly this place was not home—Earles lived in Seattle. This was timber, for cutting. Earles already had a sawmill in operation at Clallam Bay. Loggers towed most of the enormous firs from the rain-soaked forests down the Strait of Juan de Fuca, where company tugs pulled them in great log booms to Bellingham sawmills.

To increase his profits, Earles looked where so many others had for wealth: to the

harbor at Tse-whit-zen on the outskirts of downtown Port Angeles. Here was the place to build the largest sawmill of its day, capable of feeding a vast export market with ships snugging into the deep, natural harbor in the crook of the arm of the Ediz Hook. It was the only safe harbor on the West Coast north of San Francisco where vessels could sail into harbor without a pilot or assistance from a tugboat. Earles had already taken notice. In 1909, he approached the Clallam County commissioners with a proposition: He would build a large sawmill in Port Angeles to cut lumber primarily for export trade, and it would generate a fat payroll.

In return, he demanded a drastic reduction in taxes on his timberlands and a guarantee of nominal taxes on the mill he intended to build. But unlike the state fish commissioners, county officials demurred, saying such a payment was illegal. Earles got huffy and dropped the proposition. He laid blame for not building the mill at the feet of the county commissioners and vowed that as long as they were in office, he would not build a mill in Port Angeles. But a few years later, Earles was back. He had another deal in mind, this time for the citizens of Port Angeles.

If they would give him the land at the base of the hook for free, he would build the mill. Aldwell—seeing a major outlet, literally, for his electricity—got busy making

Pleased with their progress, tycoon Michael Earles (left) and local promoter M. J. Carrigan inspect the construction site of the Puget Sound Mills and Timber Company, 1913. The lumber mill opened in 1914 and was one of the largest of its kind in the world. Bert Kellogg Collection, North Olympic Library System, PTAN MILL-029.

the pitch to Port Angeles. He helped put together sixty local merchants who agreed to pool their resources and give Earles $33,150 to build the mill. The self-appointed committee members agreed to bind themselves to the sum set opposite their names in return for a sawmill with a capacity of 300,000 board feet per day that would employ approximately five hundred men. In the agreement signed November 2, 1912, Earles was guaranteed title to the fifty-acre waterfront site at the head of the bay, including Sampson's original homestead claim staked over the Tse-whit-zen burial ground. Aldwell would be one of the biggest donors, giving $3,000 toward the mill site to his friend Earles.

The state of Washington kicked in the near shore and tidelands—property of the people of the state—for $216.20 on February 25, 1913. The same piece of ground that had been at the heart of the wealth of this region since aboriginal times would now be the site of the town's largest employer and the bulwark of its industrial economy for the next several decades. Men in straw boaters and striped suits had figured out how to turn rain, trees, rivers, and waterfronts into cash. Port Angeles fairly strutted with confidence. "Talk to any old timer and, pinned down, he will admit that he loved every last bit of the whole rip snorting she-bang, not for anything it accomplished, but because it was the greatest industrial show in North America."[1]

Known for miles around simply as the Big Mill, the sawmill Earles built over the Tse-whit-zen site had no rival anywhere in the country and perhaps the world. The mill was built on pilings and fill, right over the Sampson land claim and the Tse-whit-zen village site, with its burial ground. Some of the pilings sunk by the builders were driven right through burial boxes. Hand-dug utility lines also plowed through the burial grounds. In the sensibility of the time, the remains, like the Elwha people themselves, were regarded as something to push out of the way. Elders on the Lower Elwha reservation today say the story of the desecration was passed on to them, with the instruction to never forget it. Smith and Charles learned of the cemetery from the late Sam Ulmer, one of the members of the first Lower Elwha tribal council who would help the tribe get its reservation in 1968.

"I was twelve and she was fifteen, and as soon as we would come in the house, he would say, 'Alright, you girls, sit down and I am going to tell you this, because you are the ones that are going to have to pass it down in the next generation," Charles said. "I really didn't believe him that her and I would be the ones doing it. But he told us about the cemetery in Tse-whit-zen, that it was there and that we were to remember it. And the stories that he told us, it was hard to really believe that it hap-

Some of the pilings used to construct the mill were driven right through Indian graves at Tse-whit-zen. The stones mark a burial site. Courtesy Lower Elwha Klallam Tribe.

OPPOSITE This company newsletter reflects the ethic of the day with regard to Indian burials as it recalls the building of the mill just west of the Tse-whit-zen village site. Courtesy Clallam County Historical Society.

pened. But when the mills were built in Tse-whit-zen, Port Angeles, they were just literally throwing the bodies around and covering the pipes that they were building for the mills. They didn't care. And that was what was told to us to remember. There was no feelings whatsoever by the people that were building the mills in there."

And it was a different time, legally. "We didn't have no protection in those days, either," Smith said. "They just did anything they wanted to."[2] In their account of the construction of the mill, Gretchen Kaehler and Stephanie Trudel note only one newspaper story about human remains found at the mill, in 1916.[3] That could be because finding Indian burials, which were not protected by non-Indian law or custom back then, was hardly regarded as news. It could also be because the mill was built on pilings, with a thick blanket of fill laid over the site, for drainage. All of that helped minimize disturbance of the ground, despite the massive scale of the Big Mill.[4] The Puget Sound Mills and Timber Company, built at a cost of $1.5 million, roared to life, with full operation under way by 1914. The mill devoured a spectacular 11 million to 14 million board feet of timber a month and had a monthly payroll of $50,000 to $60,000, not counting the men working in the woods. "Words fail to fully describe and explain the details of such a wonder," enthused H. H. Hill in the *Tribune-Times* of Port Angeles.[5] Between the mill and the logging company, the Big Mill employed some 1,000 men. Its cargo wharf on the harbor was busy with

CROWN-Z NEWS

Port Angeles, Washington, November 5, 1940

Newsprint Mill Observes 20th Anniversary

CROWDS VISIT BIG PAPER MILL FOR OPEN HOUSE

FIFTY GUIDES SHOWING GUESTS THROUGH NINE MAJOR DEPARTMENTS OF NEWSPRINT PLANT; JOURNEY TAKES 90 MINUTES.

It's Open House time at the Port Angeles division of Crown Zellerbach Corporation and throngs of Port Angeles and Clallam county folks are enjoying the 90-minute excursion through Western Washington's only newsprint mill as guests of the management and men.

The occasion marks the twentieth anniversary of the time when the Washington Pulp & Paper Corporation's newsprint mill started operation at the head of Port Angeles bay and began turning out between 55 and 60 tons of newsprint daily on one paper machine, the paper being made from groundwood and purchased sulphite pulp. Today the normal production from three paper machines is 350 tons in 24 hours, or 114,000 tons annually.

Visiting periods during the Open House are: Tuesday and Wednesday November 5 and 6, from 1 to 5 each afternoon and from 7 to 9 each evening.

The Open House committee includes: Raymond Austin, Robert Huff, William C. (Babe) Adams, George Hanson, A. George Johns, Winston Kidd, John Monser, Paul Neer, Brooks Payne, Arthur Severse, John Venables, Jack Webster, Thomas Hargreaves, Charles Hudson and Ed P. Read.

Fifty experienced guides are showing visitors through the entire mill, the following route being followed: Registration at office, thence to sawmill, filter plant, sulphite mill, groundwood mill, paper machines and beater rooms, finishing room, acid plant and power plant.

In addition to seeing the route taken by hemlock, white fir and spruce logs until their fibres become white newsprint paper, visitors are being shown a large number of exhibits prepared by the committee and men of the mill. In the sawmill is being shown a number of saws and other sawmill gear, and huge cuts of spruce and hemlock are exhibited. In the filter room is a first aid and safety equipment exhibition. Different materials used in pulp manufacture are being exhibited and explained in the sulphite and groundwood mills. In the machine room will be seen exhibits of paper machine felts, greases, oils, carrier rope, etc. The maintenance department is showing fire fighting equipment.

One of the most interesting shows along the whole route is the finished paper products display brought to

(Continued to Page Four)

WASH PULP HAS A BIRTHDAY

1920-1940

WELCOME TO OPEN HOUSE VISITORS

☆ ☆ TWENTY YEAR VETERANS ☆ ☆

GEORGE COWLING,
Power Line Foreman.
LEON L. DUPUIS,
General Superintendent.
WILLIAM EDWARDS,
Assistant Superintendent.
E. H. VICARY,
Supervising Engineer.
JAMES HICKEY,
Boom Foreman.
DAN PROVO,
Shift Superintendent.
ARTHUR A. SEVERSE,
Shift Superintendent.
JOHN SOMERS,
Finishing Foreman.
CHARLES HUDSON,
Pipe Foreman.
JAMES JACKSON,
Pipefitter.
GEORGE JOHNS,
Beater Room Foreman.

WALTER LAFEMAN,
Jigger Boss.
PAUL LAMOUREUX,
Back Tender No. 3.
PHIL MORIO,
Machine Tender No. 3.
GEORGE OSTENSON,
Machine Tender No. 3.
OTTO PETIT,
Yard.
CLAUDE RIVETTS,
Machine Tender No. 2.
C. L. SPICER,
Machine Tender No. 2.
LESLIE TOBIAS,
Grinderman.
JACK WEBSTER,
Painter Boss.
* * *
'C. "BILLY" WILLIAMSON,
Master Mechanic, deceased.

SQUATTERS AND BONES OF INDIANS BOTHER BUILDERS

NEWSPAPER FILES REVEAL PROGRESS OF NEWSPRINT MILL CONSTRUCTION; FIRST PILE DRIVEN MARCH 20, 1920; FIRST PAPER MADE DECEMBER 14.

Fifteen squatter families were shooed away and hundreds of Indian bones disturbed just twenty years ago last spring when ground was broken and excavations made for foundations of the Washington Pulp & Paper Corporation's newsprint mill on the base of Ediz Hook Spit. Old timers tell of at least one Indian massacre on the site of the mill in the old days when the Clallams and the Chimseans were enemies, but one of the Kuppler brothers who constructed first units of the mill thought for a time there might be a 1920 massacre as one irate woman squatter challenged his right to remove her shanty until shown the company actually owned the property. She was of the opinion she was squatting on government property.

Twenty year files of the Evening News chronicle the advent and progress of the mill. While rumors had traveled thick and fast about big companies buying the Whalen paper machinery which had been stored on Ediz Hook, it was on January 14, 1920 that a headline, "Work On New Paper Mill To Start Soon; Officials Are Here," was given prominence. The article said: "It was stated late this afternoon from authoritative sources that the Washington Pulp & Paper Company will let the contract for the construction of their giant pulp and paper mill here to the contractor who can guarantee the best construction in the shortest time possible. Mr. E. M. Mills, of Peabody-Houghtelling Company, A. V. Simonds, construction engineer, George F. Whalen, J. F. Carroll and P. D. Nims were on the ground today."

The next edition of the paper carried an imploring editorial for people to build. "Where Will We House All The Newcomers?" was the headline.

On January 26 it was announced Christ Kuppler's Sons had been awarded the contract for the first four buildings and Owens Brothers the contract for pile driving. The next day Dick Owens announced he would "have a crew of 30 men at work in a short time."

Then, on January 19, came a front page interview in the News with M. R. Higgins, of the Zellerbach Paper Company of San Francisco, who said of the new paper mill: "This is no prospect, this is

(Continued to Page Four)

MILL. PORT ANGELES

as many as six vessels at a time, taking lumber to all points of the globe.

It took the hides of 350 steers to make the seven-foot-wide belt for the main shaft of the mill. The Big Mill covered fifty acres and would be the city's largest employer for the next twenty years. It was the most technologically advanced mill of its day. One of the few so-called long mills in existence, it could handle timbers 150 feet in length, or, put another way, fifteen stories tall. The mill was a city in itself. It had a company store that issued its own money—tin coins redeemable only at the store, used as an advance on employee paychecks. Port Angeles suddenly had it all: proximity to seemingly endless timber, hydropower, and an industrial-scale mill feeding markets around the world. Heady stuff in a state with the motto "Alki," Chinook Jargon for "by and by." The motto is inscribed on the state seal, with its scene of a forest giving way, through effort and enterprise, to a glorious city. Town boosters, led by Aldwell, had found a way to mortgage the Northwest's rain and trees for investment capital from the East and to lure industrialists like Earles. He brought his big-city tastes with him.

Not content to build just the sawmill, Earles turned his attention to the Sol Duc hot springs, once the private realm of Klallam vision quests, for construction of an upscale resort. No longer a private place for praying and seeking spirit power, suddenly Sol Duc was to become a resort for the region's swank crowd. Earles clearly had a thing for big: The resort opened May 15, 1912, and was said to be the largest of its kind in the world. Built entirely of wood, the main lodge was 160 feet high with 165 bedrooms. Some two hundred workers cut 750,000 cedar shingles for the roof. Each room had a balcony, hot and cold water, telephones, and steam heat. Many had private baths. Dress was formal for dinner, according to *Jimmy Come Lately*, a history of Clallam County. The guests' chauffeurs, personal maids, and governesses were served their meals in a separate dining room. There were golf links, tennis courts, croquet grounds, bowling alleys, a gallery for musicians in the lobby, a theater, and billiard and card rooms. And then there were the baths. The resort advertised 130–degree bubbling hot springs, Turkish massages, and private masseuses to see to the guests' relaxation. The resort became a fashionable destination for Seattle's upscale set, who traveled by boat from Colman Dock to Port Angeles. There they would board big red Stanley Steamer automobile stages and ride the nearly twenty miles to Lake Crescent. Then came another boat ride, twelve miles across the lake. Then a stage coach ride, for the last fifteen miles to the resort. The Sol Duc was a popular place: More than 10,000 guests visited in the resort's peak year. But its splendor was short-lived. A defective flue spewed sparks onto the roof, igniting its hundreds of thousands of dry, split-cedar shingles.

If we are to believe *Jimmy Come Lately*, the ensuing fire was so hot that the resort's sterling silver flatware fused into a single lump and the hotel's organ got stuck playing Beethoven's Funeral March throughout the blaze, which burned the hotel to ashes. Only some twenty guests and forty-five employees were in the hotel at the time and no one was hurt.[6]

Even with that disaster, the peninsula's identity as a place of superlatives—the biggest trees, the largest dam on the peninsula, the largest sawmill just about anywhere—was secure. But it still was not enough for Aldwell. "The waterfront continued to bother me," he wrote in his autobiography. "The tide came in and went out over the lots and a vast area of property seemed to have no usefulness."[7] He'd see to that, too. Aldwell urged total development of the waterfront, with a plan to fill twenty-one more acres and create more industrial land, to lure investors. "If we do not, they will go to other places and thus transfer to those fortunate places the God-given natural wealth of our country through our own neglect to care for our birthright. All the approaches to the highways of the seas, just like the highways on the land, must be built and kept open for the commerce of our industries and our citizens. This has proved more than a slogan; it has been a guide for action."[8] Aldwell was president of the Port of Port Angeles from 1925 through 1933 and in that position oversaw the total transformation of the waterfront. "I participated in every bucket of fill, every bit of rip rapping along the waterfront, every industry that located here . . . splendid work. It [the port] now owns sixty acres of filled industrial and ten acres of unfilled lands and 6,000 linear feet of waterfront."[9]

For the Lower Elwha Klallam Tribe, the loss of the beaches, tidelands, and the Ediz Hook to development, private-property owners, and pollution meant destruction not only of their village sites and burial grounds but of one of their most important food sources. With their gleaming silver bodies, leaping acrobatics, and dramatic life story, salmon get all the press. But shellfish, those reclusive, modest dwellers of the tidelands, offering only the occasional squirt for drama, were invaluable foods. With more than 3,000 miles of coastline, western Washington during aboriginal times offered a dazzling array of tidelands and nearshore habitats: rocky shores, sand and mud beaches, gravel strands, and sheltered bays.

And they were packed with intertidal delights. Clams, cockles, mussels, oysters. Scallops, limpets, snails, chitons. Crabs, shrimp, barnacles, octopus. Squid, sea urchin, and sea chum. All were used by Indian people for food. Shell middens and other archaeological evidence show that shellfish were important food sources for Native peoples of the Northwest coast for at least the past 2,500 years and that shellfish were used at least as far back as 5,000 years before the arrival of non-natives. The huge quantities of oysters and clams in the sheltered inner waters of Puget Sound reflect the integrity of the habitats that once existed from the mountains to the sea. Nutrients and sediments washed to the shore by the Elwha River, before Aldwell's dam, nourished beaches and a nearshore environment teeming with life.

Shellfish were harvested year-round, with major gathering expeditions undertaken in spring and summer to collect shellfish and cure the catch for winter stores. People from upriver villages would visit the coasts, and people from mainland villages would travel to the islands in Puget Sound to dig at favorite beaches. Shellfish were eaten at daily meals. They were a favorite at feasts and made great snacks. Dried shellfish strung on cordage spun from nettles and other plants were worn around the neck by travelers and hunters. Lightweight and nutritious, they were the road food of the aboriginal world. Shellfish were also used as fish bait, and the shells themselves had dozens of uses: dippers, cups, knives, spoons, harpoon points, rattles, tweezers, and lances. They were used for jewelry and decoration for wooden objects, from masks to boxes. People also used shells for toys, money, paint boxes, and medicine. Strings of dried clams and strings of shells were traded over long distances, into the interior of Washington and beyond. Shellfish were often placed in open-worked baskets used not only for carrying but as ingenious live tanks. Harvesters would place the baskets in the tidewater as they worked, allowing the shellfish to clean themselves and keeping them alive until the harvesters were ready to go home.

Anthropologist Barbara Lane points out that non-natives could easily overlook the importance of shellfish to western Washington tribes:

> The first Europeans to visit the area were impressed by the wealth of salmon they observed filling the streams and hurtling themselves over rapids. It was easy for them to overlook or be less impressed with the abundant shellfish. . . . A beach loaded with shellfish does not appear radically different from a beach without shellfish. A salmon run is visually more impressive to a non-native than is a bed of clams. Even dried stores of salmon in a house are more impressive and visible than stores of dried shellfish. Weirs, reef nets and harpoons are technologically more interesting gear than digging sticks.[10]

Lane also points out the special role shellfish played in western Washington as non-Indians pushed the tribes from their homeland. Shellfish were important crisis foods. People on the coast who were left alone, weakened, unable to travel because of disease, dislocation, or other disaster, or unable to fish because of regulatory restrictions, could always find something to eat by digging shellfish. When non-Indian settlers and government officials burned their villages, bulldozed their homes, and destroyed their winter stores of food and gardens, families could restock some of their larders from the beach.

Reliably accessible, rich in protein, fat, iron, zinc and magnesium, portable, and easily digestible, shellfish were survival food for a people forced to live underground, and on the run. And the Klallam people, already pushed west toward the Ediz Hook by the Big Mill, were about to be displaced again, this time for a pulp mill. Forest industry chemists had discovered techniques for turning hemlock into newsprint and cellulose. Suddenly, Port Angeles had a whole new market for trees unsuitable for sawmills. Pulp and paper would turn abundant western hemlock and other pulp woods in the rainforest, previously mostly ignored by loggers cutting Douglas fir, into jobs.

Aldwell, still seeking markets for power from the Elwha Dam, once again got busy. And he had a ready partner in the U.S. Forest Service. While industrialists like

Aldwell beat the drum for Port Angeles, talking up the town to potential investors and tirelessly shaking down the boardrooms of Chicago, San Francisco, and Seattle for capital, the U.S. Forest Service was only too happy to supply letters for would-be investors, assuring a virtually unlimited supply of timber on the peninsula. This was no different from other federal government agencies, such as the Bureau of Reclamation, that saw themselves as partners in the development of the West. The bureau's motto "Total Use for Greater Wealth" summed up its agenda. Aldwell targeted the Zellerbach Paper Company in San Francisco, bearing a letter in his pocket from the U.S. Forest Service attesting that there was more timber suitable for pulp and paper-making in Port Angeles than anywhere else in America—some 400 million board feet per year for starters, with more to come. He also was able to offer power for the mill from the Elwha River, helping to seal the deal. The company committed to building a pulp plant just west of Earles's Big Mill, at the base of the Ediz Hook.

That meant more displacement for Klallam families. "Squatter City of Port Angeles

This photograph, believed to be from about 1900, shows residences on the Ediz Hook before pulp mills and, later, a U.S. Coast Guard station were built on the land. Courtesy Clallam County Historical Society.

Gradually Passing, Coming of New Industries Forcing Squatters from Ediz Hook Spit. Twelve Now Living on Ground to Be Used by New Pulp Mill and Are Ordered to Move" was the headline in the *Port Angeles Daily News* on January 30, 1920. The story by William D. Welsh reported:

> Just as the pioneers clearing lands in the forests drove the Indians to seek other hunting grounds, so is the progress of Port Angeles as an industrial center driving the squatters from the government reservation on Ediz Hook Spit, forcing them to seek homes in the city, and it will not be long at the present rate until the last squatter will be forced to move. Even since Lincoln's order made it possible for the town site at Port Angles to be laid out, there has been squatters' shacks on the spit. Salmon trollers, devil fish trappers and beachcombers for years have resided over there. With the coming of the Puget Sound Mills & Timber Company a great number were

forced to move further into the spit. . . . So the squatter city of little Port Angeles is gradually passing. With it goes many stories, many tragedies, many tales of suffering and many hidden mysteries of the old days . . . they will have to move into the electric light and bathtub zone shortly. Industry and progressiveness must be served.

Like the earlier Big Mill, the Crown Z newsprint mill was built over Klallam graves. And it was no secret to anyone that pilings for the mills were driven right through Indian burials: "Fifteen squatter families were shooed away and hundreds of Indian bones disturbed just twenty years ago last spring when ground was broken and excavations made for foundations of the Washington Pulp and Paper Corporation newsprint mill on the base of the Ediz Hook," the company newspaper reported. "Old timers tell of at least one Indian massacre on the site of the mill in the old days when the Clallams and the Chimseans were enemies, but one of the Kuppler brothers who constructed the first units of the mill thought for a time there might be a 1920 massacre as one irate woman squatter challenged his right to remove her shanty until shown the company actually owned the property."[11]

The first pile was driven March 20, 1920, and by December, 14, 1920, the first two reels of standard newsprint rolled off the line. The mill was in full production in 1921, turning out 131,000 tons of paper from three machines that could make 1,014 miles of paper daily. With 620 employees in the mill and another 190 in the woods feeding the mill, the total payroll was more than $3 million. The town was booming, especially on the waterfront village site of Tse-whit-zen and the Ediz Hook.

Describing Port Angeles of the 1920s, John McCallum and Lorraine Wilcox Ross wrote in *Port Angeles, USA*: "Where once the wild strawberries and celery grew and the Indians came to bury their dead in little cedar huts, the spit is now the busiest and most versatile three miles of land imaginable."[12] There were salmon derbies, skin-diving meets, the lighthouse, and even the first ever documented swim across the strait. Tugs were pulling log rafts into town, and boom men walked the logs in a harbor frosted with wood. Deliveries of sulfur to the paper mill came in by railroad car. The Crown Zellerbach Corporation soon purchased Aldwell's dam on the Elwha as well as the transmission lines and power plant. Crown Z then built a second hydroelectric project on the Elwha, Glines Canyon Dam. The upper dam came online in 1927 and was even bigger than the Elwha Dam. More than 200 feet high, it, too, was built without a fish passage. Crown Z ran the dams for the mill's electrical power

supply, periodically shutting off the flow through the power plant as needed for industrial production. The company gave no thought to how that would affect fish or people downstream. That the needs of industry totally dominated in Port Angeles shows in today's street names such as Lower Dam Road, Crown Z Water Road, and more.

The Klallam people were meanwhile pushed into a smaller and smaller remnant of their homeland as Port Angeles continued to expand. Even their language reflected the change. By 1921, Klallam place-names for their local community included not only "Place of Creation" and "Lots of Clams" but "Where Big Sawmill Is Going Up to the Lagoon," "Where Went When Driven from Elwha," and "Power Plant."

Newspaper headlines documented the rout on the waterfront as the town continued to boom. The *Port Angeles Daily News* ran this banner headline on Tuesday, September 17, 1929: "Squatter Shacks Doomed Torch Will Be Applied to 36 Small Cabins." The newspaper reported:

> Thirty six squatter shacks on the navy reservation part of the Ediz Hook will be burned as soon as the first fall rains dampen the driftwood and grass to keep the blaze from spreading to legitimate buildings. And some 30 or 40 squatters are not any too pleased about the matter. In fact they have

As their world changed, the Klallam people formed a tribal council to contend with the newcomers. The first tribal council in 1925 represented all three bands of the Klallam people: Elwha, Jamestown S'Klallam, and Port Gamble S'Klallam. The council included Tim Pysht, born in 1825, who, in 1855, was the first runner to reach Lower Elwha with the news that the Treaty of Point No Point had been signed. *Left to right, front row:* Tim Pysht, Joe Anderson, Sam Ulmer, Charlie Hopi, and Bennie George. *Back row:* Ernest Sampson, Joe Allen, David Prince, Bill Hall, and Lester Jackson. Sampson was the youngest and, as he knew how to read and write English, translated for the rest of the council. Courtesy Adeline Smith.

torn down most of the signs placed on empty shacks declaring it was the government's intention to destroy the hovels and maintain a stolid silence when asked what their program will be when the torch is applied.

Yet the Klallam people still hung on. Anthropologist Karen James interviewed Lower Elwha tribal member Oscar Charles Sr. in 1995. She writes that he was born at the Ediz Hook in 1933. He recalled watching his father and grandfather roll their canoes on logs from the upper beach to the salt water. They and other Klallam men made their own jigs and fished with hand lines from their canoes for halibut and salmon in the waters off the hook.

Charles and others stated that during the 1920s and 1930s, Klallam families and individuals were still clinging to the old village sites at Ennis Creek and at Hollywood Beach, near the foot of Lincoln Street, on the eastern end of the bay. Others lived at the western end of the bay, on the bluff above Boat Haven and around the Merrill and Ring Timber Company mill, built on the site of the Big Mill, which closed in 1929.

More families lived along Marine Drive and along the inside shoreline of the Ediz Hook. At least one family lived in a houseboat on pontoons. Many of these families also had homes in other areas, including Freshwater Bay and pəšct (Place Where Wind Blows All the Time), or Pysht. They moved back and forth between these places, as

Gathering firewood along the bluffs of the Elwha River, 1920s. With their traditional economy destroyed by displacement and industrialization, tribal members turned to all kinds of new work to make a living, including gathering wood to sell to restaurants in town. Many tribal members also worked on logging crews and in the mills built atop their former village sites. Courtesy Adeline Smith.

family needs, food gathering, and farm harvest demanded. Pushed off the waterfront, some made successful farms at Pysht and in the Elwha River Valley. The Klallam people did not give up or die off, as so many expected. They adapted, found ways to make a living in the job-and-wage economy of the newcomers, and survived.

Beatrice Charles vividly remembers her life as a nine-year-old on her family's homestead at Pysht in 1928. The children would get up with the sun and wash their faces with water they had carried in the night before. The toilet was an outhouse. For breakfast, they had oatmeal mush with canned milk and wild tea, usually blackberry, or swamp tea made from medicinal plants. Lunches were packed with sandwiches of peanut butter and homemade blackberry or thimbleberry jam. Sometimes there was homemade bread or biscuits. Dessert was an apple or an orange. Drinking water came from the school tap.

The children would walk the two miles to school, or if it was a good day, they used the canoe. Their class was in a two-room schoolhouse, with more than twenty kids per room. It was a long day, from nine to four, with time for playing outside if the weather was good or in the basement. Indian children were forbidden to speak their own language. If they did, the teachers would slap their hands or wrists with a ruler, give them detention after school, or keep them in during recess. And they might have to write an apology on the chalkboard or on paper one hundred times.

All the children walked home together. At home, they changed their clothes and did their chores or babysat the younger children while their mothers worked. Adults ate dinner first, and there was a second setting for the kids. Dinner was usually dried or fresh fish, clams or fritters, and potatoes. Almost everything they ate was from the land and beaches. Before it got dark, the children would bring in water from a hand pump for the next day, and the boys would bring in firewood. "Everything was done and cleaned up; then they would sit at their great-grandfather's feet and hand him kindling, which he whittled into flowers and told stories, traditions, and sang songs," Charles remembered in an oral history recorded by the tribe. "The stories always had meaning to them." Kids would go to bed around eight. They would wash their faces, brush their teeth, and, on certain days of the week, wash their hair with rainwater. They slept on feather mattresses. Charles would jump in the middle of the mattress so that it went around her and then cover herself with blankets. "Like a cocoon," she said.

Every Saturday was the day to bathe, after breakfast. The boys would carry in water to be warmed in a big aluminum tub on a woodstove. "This was a treat," Charles remembered. On Saturdays, too, the family sometimes went by boat to Port Angeles to buy food by the case: mostly crackers, oranges, apples, sugar, flour, salt, pepper, corned beef, and rice. Great-grandfather would get treats for the kids: gum, candy, and Cracker Jacks. Charles's father would cut wood, and she would wheelbarrow it to the house. They didn't call doctors, relying instead on their own remedies.

Some of the Klallam homesteads were held by Indian families who had obtained title to their lands. But others were held informally. And some homesteads were lost, despite the efforts of Indian families to hold onto them. The reasons were many, from illness to outright chicanery. Elders at Lower Elwha today vividly recall the day Pysht Village was bulldozed. In June 1992, Edward C. Sampson told the story of the destruction of the Klallam village at Pysht in about 1930. His oral history, given in Klallam, was translated by Charles, Smith, and Timothy Montler, a linguist who has worked with the Lower Elwha for years to keep the Klallam language alive.

According to the transcript, Sampson said:

When we were at the village of Pysht working on the logging, the logging jobs ended. And there was no more work there again. And so we left our homes and moved to Port Angeles. Then the logging bosses tore down our houses. Our houses were torn down and burned to nothing. There was nothing left of the Indian homes. Everything, our belongings that were

This couple is about to take a net, held in the hands of the man standing at center, and go out to fish from their canoe. Taken in about 1921 at Pysht, this photo also shows the tower used to load logs for towing on the water to the Big Mill at Port Angeles. Courtesy Adeline Smith.

inside the houses, everything that was inside and didn't get taken out, that wasn't brought to Port Angeles. All our belongings, water buckets, beds, dishes, everything we owned. Our belongings and everything inside was torn down by the bulldozer. Everything we owned. We weren't told by the logging bosses about our houses being torn down. It was their own idea. We didn't know what they were going to do. That's the way it is. We Indians have been treated badly by the white man. Pysht was a very nice Indian village. That was our home. It was where we were from. It was our land. And it was taken away by the white man, evil white men.[13]

Beatrice Charles also lost her family's thirty-six-acre homestead at Pysht. Her family had never taken formal title to the home. That was something whites did. Not Indians.

"You surveyed, you say this is mine, and you got the paper to prove it. Indians didn't have things like that," Charles explained. "That was their village, that was their home. They didn't think they had to take papers out," Charles said of her family. "That was the reason Merrill and Ring did take papers out, and that included the village, and see, the Indians didn't know, and they still thought that was their home. I was born in Pysht," she continued. "My great-grandmother and her grandma were buried in Pysht." Like Sampson, Charles said the family homes at Pysht were bulldozed by the logging company—she names it, Merrill and Ring—without warning while the families were away at Jamestown. Both girls were at boarding school by then, at Chemawa, in Oregon.

"I was away at school, but my great-grandfather Tim Pysht had a house there," Charles said. "And there were about eight houses there and there was about four of them that was bought new." Built from lumber bought from Merrill and Ring.

"When the tides came up in the wintertime, the tides came right to your front door, so you had board-walks. Made out of those thick planks they made at the mills. But in the summertime it was just beautiful. I really loved that place."

Smith also confirmed the destruction. "All of them were destroyed," she said of the houses. "They didn't give them warning or anything. That is the one that hurts me the most. Pysht Village. They waited until most of the Indians went away to visit in Jamestown, and when they got back, they didn't have no house. They bulldozed it down." The two said they have wanted to find their family graves at the village site, but it has been logged twice by Merrill and Ring. And the company will not allow them on the land without an escort. "We don't know where it is," Beatrice Charles said of the family cemetery. "Because Merrill and Ring logged over it twice and prob-ably destroyed it. We have been looking for it, and every time we go in there we have to get permission from Merrill and Ring to go and look at our own village," Smith

Tim Pysht at Bea Charles's family homestead in Pysht. The sharpening stone in the foreground was for the butchering knife for fish. The gate in the doorway was to keep Bea's little brother, then an infant, from crawling out. The house was built on stilts because high tides in winter would come nearly to the door. This house and others were bulldozed without warning by a logging company while the families were away, a wound that still festers. Tim Pysht, Bea Charles's great-grandfather, had this prophecy, Charles said: "The Klallam people would almost fade away, but we would come back strong." Courtesy Adeline Smith.

said. "We are never in there by ourselves. The man is always there to know what you are doing. My two older sisters knew where it was, and they were able to walk in in 1951, but they would not let them in there."[14]

Smith's family also lost their homestead on the Elwha River. The city of Port Angeles coveted her family's land for a pipeline that would suck water out of the Elwha to slake the thirst of the mills going up on the waterfront. "The City of Port Angeles wanted water, and they chose our place, and they were after it," Adeline said. "We were all against it because my mother liked that place; everybody liked that place, and they wouldn't sell. Finally it came down to . . . I believe it was 1929, and they said you either sell and take the $1,100 or else we are going to condemn it. So my mother just let it go. We were going to lose out on it, so we might as well take the money—$1,100 for sixty-seven acres. The ditch line went right through the middle. It just ruined the farm. They had a tunnel there, and they told my mother they were only going to use twenty feet to get the water into the pipe for Port Angeles. When I think about it, it makes me sick," Smith said. "It makes me sick the way they destroyed it."

Fire, as the residents of the Ediz Hook had learned, also worked for clearing Indian people out of the way. By the 1930s, Hollywood Beach, for centuries the gathering site for the Klallam people, was regarded as a slum by county health department officials, who declared the settlement both a health and a fire hazard and ordered the community burned in 1942. It would not be until 1968—113 years after the Treaty of Point No Point was signed—that the Lower Elwha would have a reservation in their own homeland.

In 1936 and 1937, the United States began buying lands in trust for the Klallam under the terms of the federal Indian Reorganization Act of 1934. Nationally, the act was the beginning of a trend toward recognition of Native treaty rights and marked a return to earlier policies supporting protection of Indians lands. The act ended the policy of allotments under which the Native land base was cut from 156 million acres in 1881 to about 48 million in 1934.

The lands transferred under the act eventually became the Elwha and Port Gamble reservations and were settled by several Klallam families, including some of the people who had been living on the Ediz Hook and in other areas of Port Angeles. A total of 372 acres was purchased by the federal government in 1936–37 at the mouth of the Elwha along with about a mile of beach along the Strait of Juan de Fuca.

The waterfront that had been at the center of the Klallam people's livelihood was devoured by one industrial development after another through the rest of the century.

Earles's Big Mill ran until 1929. He had sold it by then to the Charles Nelson Company, making his fortune. The mill was finally destroyed in a fire set by a Seattle demolition company in 1940, which was big news in this town: "A landmark on the Port Angeles industrial waterfront for more than twenty-five years and the first large industry in Port Angeles, the old Charles Nelson Mill is rapidly disappearing."[15] Wrecking crews destroyed the remnants of the plant's sawmill building, and the fire set by demolition crews drew thousands of spectators.

The site would be used by a series of industries for more than sixty years, but many of those developments reused existing structures and improvements rather than digging up the ground anew. They also used large portions of the ground for lumber storage, Kaehler and Trudel noted. That resulted in less disturbance of the site than would seem possible after decades of industrial use and even inadvertently protected it. Olympic Shipbuilders, Inc., was among the next to use the site in 1942 and 1943, building a shipyard to construct the *Red Alder* and other wooden barges intended for the war effort. The barges had no power of their own and were to be towed in groups of three or four by oceangoing tugs. But the vessels proved impossible to steer, and none saw service.

Beginning in 1956, the Merrill and Ring Timber Company operated a sawmill at the site. Later, the Port of Port Angeles would also use the site, for a chip yard and log storage. The western end of town had become a place with a waterfront where you could not see the water because of the industrial buildings that walled off the strait. The ancient beach lines were long buried under fill, the tidelands poked full of pilings covered with fill, paving, and concrete. The natural shape of the shoreline became difficult even to remember; it was certainly no longer a place to live or gather food. The Klallams found work in the cash economy in order to survive. Often, the men worked in the very mills that had displaced their food supply, powered by the dams that had killed the salmon.

At the state level, it would not be until February 12, 1974, with the decision by federal judge George Boldt in *United States v. Washington*, affirming fishing rights for western Washington tribes, that assertion of tribal treaty rights would begin a slow shake-up of the status quo in Washington. The Boldt decision launched an era in which the promises of the treaties are taken seriously. In Washington, sharing the catch and the responsibility for management of the fisheries has been both a milestone and a metaphor for sharing power between state agencies and tribes. The bloom of economic development in Indian Country from casino gambling is one more fruit of the sort of government-to-government negotiations initiated since the Boldt decision. The money tribal governments earn from casinos is in turn paying for the infrastructures of modern tribal governments and cultural preservation.

Indian burials and cultural property didn't receive federal protection until passage of the Native American Graves Protection and Repatriation Act in 1990. But the act is limited in scope. It applies only to federal lands and cultural items held in collections that receive federal funds. The National Historic Preservation Act requires governments to consult with tribes before taking actions that affect cultural property, but it does not require preservation.

The long era of violence against the tribes had also taken its toll. Elders on the reservation today say their parents didn't pass on their language and culture to them, because they didn't want to see their children suffer as they and their grandparents had, when they were beaten in school for speaking their language. Many Indian parents had come to believe that what their children needed most of all in a place that could no longer feed them was to learn how to make money. Lower Elwha elder Al Charles Sr., sixty-two, remembers that his parents spoke Klallam but culture took a backseat. "They wanted you to succeed in school and get a good job. Back in the day, money didn't mean anything. But they realized you have to have money now to survive in this world." He served in the U.S. Marine Corps, worked in the woods, in the Seattle shipyards, and in the ITT Rayonier mill built over the Klallams' village at Yennis until the mill closed. He remembers how his father, born in 1910, used to take a ride out to the Ediz Hook and just sit there in the car, looking back across the water, at the land, and at his past. "That's where their roots were."

Elder Johnson Charles Jr. becomes bitter when he talks about the language his father did not pass on to him. The smokehouses on the Elwha River used for the sacred ceremonies, the use of medicinal plants that grew there, all died with his father's generation. "Everything was just taken away. The language. The smokehouse. Drumming. Everything was taken away, so he probably didn't feel the need for me to even learn," Charles Jr. said. "The language, I was really angry about that. It is like taking my tongue out." He left the reservation to survive, working as a logger in the woods.

Beatrice Charles and Adeline Smith went to Seattle to become maids. Getting work in Port Angeles was unthinkable. "You learned to get along. I did. For a while when I was growing up, if you didn't look Indian, you never admitted it," Smith said. "The minute they knew you were Indian, you'd never get a job." She remembered that her best years in school were at the Indian boarding school at Chemawa, near

Salem, Oregon. "I learned how to be a seamstress and work in the laundry." When they were there, Chemawa was the largest boarding school in the Northwest, with 903 students by 1920, from ninety different tribes, nearly a third from Alaska. Both girls were orphans and had to go to work while they were still in their teens, killing their hopes of graduation. They went to Seattle together. Charles got a job helping a mother weakened by a heart attack who had a developmentally disabled son. She was paid twelve dollars a month. Smith took care of three children in Ballard, one of them mentally disabled. She lived in Seattle on and off for some forty years and didn't move back to the reservation until 1983. Charles lived in Canada, on Vancouver Island, but then came back to the reservation in 1963. When they returned, they found that Port Angeles was a place of two cultures that did not mix. The tribe's history on this land was buried by 150 years of disease, dispossession, industrial development, forced assimilation, and attempted annihilation. Within the tribe, a cultural gap had opened. This town, this state, and this tribe would soon fall into it together.

6

Collective Amnesia

THERE WERE BITS OF RUBBLE LYING AROUND, STRETCHES OF PAVING LEADING to nowhere, the shells of outbuildings. Owned by the Port of Port Angeles, this waterfront property was flat, scarified, with weeds poking up between seams of broken concrete paving. Battlements of logs were stacked at the tide line, which had long ago been riprapped and filled beyond recognition. By the time the Washington State Department of Transportation took a look at it in 2002, the site was known primarily by the jobs it had generated. It was the Earles Mill site in 1912. The Charles Nelson Mill in 1914. Olympic Shipbuilders, Inc., during the Second World War. Then the Merrill and Ring Timber Company and, most recently, the Daishowa site, named for the paper plant next door.

At that point, the Department of Transportation was looking at a dry dock in Tacoma, Washington, where it could build replacement pontoons for the Hood Canal Bridge. For this was no ordinary bridge. The Hood Canal span was a floating bridge, with the roadway supported in the water by giant concrete pontoons. The state needed a big, industrial-size dry dock, where it could build a lot of large replacement pontoons all at once rather than in stages. Then it would tow the pontoons through open water to the bridge to make the repairs.

The department knew at least as far back as 1997 that the Hood Canal Bridge was falling apart and that it would need to replace the bridge's eastern half. By the winter of 2002, chunks of concrete were calving off the bridge as salt water worked its way into the structure. This vital link, carrying an average of 20,000 vehicles daily during the week and 25,000 on weekends, was in urgent need of repair.

Corrosion and deterioration were causing the concrete to split and chip. The draw span would jam in the open position or not open completely. Risk of critical damage from a major storm was reason enough to replace the eastern half of the bridge, a panel of experts declared in 1997. For state transportation planners, the idea of a bridge collapse was no idle possibility. The western half of the Hood Canal Bridge had sunk in a storm with wind gusts of up to 120 miles an hour and sustained winds of 85 miles an hour in February 1979. And another floating bridge, linking Seattle and its eastside suburbs, had sunk into Lake Washington on November 25, 1990. During a $35.6 million renovation, a contractor had mistakenly left open hatches atop the pontoons that floated the bridge. The pontoons filled with water during a winter storm, and the bridge sank with slow-motion drama as TV cameras rolled. No state highway engineer ever wanted to see anything like that again.

Already warned that the eastern half of the Hood Canal Bridge was at risk, the department's engineers didn't want to take any chances. Tidal swings of 16.5 feet battered the aging structure, tethered by cables and anchors in as much as 340 feet of salt water. The bridge could be vulnerable in a severe, sustained storm from the southwest, engineers warned. "When our bridge engineer says, 'This is going; you need to take care of this,' you bet people listen," said Randy Hain, former administrator for the Washington State Department of Transportation's Olympic Region. Replacement was recommended by 2006. Retrofits would be a costlier and less satisfactory fix. The need to get to work was urgent, as a matter not only of schedule and budget but of life and safety. But to do the repairs, the department needed a place where it could construct fourteen pontoons and twenty anchors for the eastern half of the span.

The pontoons would be immense: more than four times the length of the average blue whale and about forty-two times its weight. The concrete anchors would also be gargantuan, nearly three stories tall and nearly twice the weight of a semi. But finding a spot in which to efficiently construct so many enormous concrete pontoons and anchors, and then float them out to open water for transport, proved difficult.

Urban development had already devoured many dry dock sites in the Puget Sound region—including one filled and paved for an Indian casino. The dry dock the department was assessing in Tacoma was soon deemed too small to get the job done quickly enough without raising the hackles of federal regulators. Department officials worried about mooring the completed pontoons and anchors near shore, awaiting transport. That, regulators warned, might harm salmon, a protected species, by shading their habitat. Still on the hunt for a site, department engineers conducted a tour of the Hood Canal Bridge for local legislators in June 2002, to explain the need for the project. Larry Williams, a city councilman for Port Angeles, went along. He remembers that day well. It was a rainy, blustery afternoon. Williams and other local officials clapped hard hats on their heads and went below the roadway deck to examine the bridge structure.

"We were amazed to see pieces of exposed rebar and pieces of concrete," Williams said. "At that point we were glad we were wearing hard hats. We started looking around at what else was going to pop off as we stood there. I took a large piece of concrete home as a souvenir. The entire surface was encrusted with salt—that is how badly salt had penetrated the bridge. The sense of emergency was there." It was then Williams realized that the port's parcel of waterfront land, long a center of wealth for the area and available for use, might have a new job to do. He walked over to the department's engineers. "After everyone else left, I asked them to give Port Angeles some consideration," Williams said. "I figured we would get a little state funds up here for our timber community. They are looking for a spot, and we have a flat one. They came up and their jaws dropped open. It was, 'We have reached the promised land.'"

Hain remembers the come-on the state transportation department got from the city of Port Angeles. "It's not like DoT went up there looking," Hain said. "It was the city, saying, 'Come up here and build this. We've got a great site for you.'" The city initially offered the site for lease, but the department quickly decided to buy it instead. It was the size of the site—more than twenty acres, right on the water—that caught the department's eye. For it had not only the Hood Canal Bridge to fix but a far larger repair project looming in the future: the floating bridge carrying State Route 520 across Lake Washington, which connects Seattle with its eastern suburbs.

Here in Port Angeles, there was plenty of flat, industrial land for construction of all the pontoons and anchors. And the site's location, right on a deep, natural harbor, meant that the department, so far unable to find a suitable dry dock, could dig the gigantic hole it needed for its own facility. Then it could use the dry dock, over time, to build the pontoons to fix not only the Hood Canal Bridge but the SR 520 bridge in the future. "We could really collapse all these efficiencies into one site," Hain said. The city was equally interested. The department's project promised to create one hundred jobs over fifteen months of construction, then scheduled to begin in June 2003. Work would go on twenty-four hours a day as the 10.5-acre pit for the dry dock was dug and paved. The department planned a dry dock big enough to moor four battleships side by side, with room to spare. The dry dock would hold 68 million gallons of water, floating the pontoons in a pit so big and so deep that it would take three days to fill with water pumped from the harbor. The upper end of the dock would be 18 feet deep, in order to hold vessels with up to a 16-foot draft. The lower dock would be much deeper, at 43.5 feet, to handle vessels with up to a 21-foot draft. The sea gate, which would hold back the tide, would be massive: 100 feet long and 43.5 feet high. Some 200,000 cubic yards of material would be dug from the site in all, enough to cover a football field 113 feet deep.[1]

Williams called several city officials after the tour and said, "Get on top of this." The city soon showed the department an engineer's dream. Here was a large piece of flat land, already zoned for heavy industrial use, right on a deep, protected harbor. There were no endangered species showstoppers. And Hain remembers this: No one said anything about Indians. Or history. Or burials. Or waterfront villages. No one. Not one person with the port or with the city. "At no time, in any of the discussions, did anyone say anything about 'Did you know?' And we didn't ask him," Hain said. But the tribe's early use of the waterfront was hardly a secret in Port Angeles, city councilman Williams said.

"We had just done a lot of work on sidewalk replacements. The city is built on fill, and in the pre- and post-construction photos, you can see where there were old houses. In turn-of-the-century photos, you can see there were gatherings. I don't know if anyone realized the extent of the encampment that was down there." A resident of Port Angeles since 1986, Williams said, "I had no idea, no background, no sense of the real history. No front-level consciousness or cognition of the implications of the history on modern-day activity. The closest parallel I can figure to that is, why in the world would we continue to build houses around Mount Rainier [a massive volcano south of Seattle]?" "That's an obvious 'hello' also. But just because we are staring right at it doesn't mean we recognize it."

The Department of Transportation, which had been considering the Port Angeles site since that June field trip in 2002, waited until October 2002 to send its first letter to the Lower Elwha Klallam Tribe, asking for comment on the project. By then, the tribe was still playing catch-up. Its first contact about the project had come not from the state but through the "moccasin telegraph." The Makah tribe, neighbors to the west, had faxed the Lower Elwha a copy of the inquiry it had received from the department earlier in the year. The department was looking at a spot on the Makah reservation at Neah Bay, an hour and a half down the road, for its project. The department had quickly rejected the idea. Neah Bay, which could be reached only by a spaghetti tangle of two-lane roads, was too remote, and its relentless rain, driving in off the Pacific in sheets, would bugger up the work.

Dennis Sullivan, Lower Elwha Klallam tribal chairman at the time, was unaware that city officials and business leaders had been pushing since June to bring the project to Port Angeles. Tribal members weren't at those meetings, or in on those phone calls, or at those lunches. Tribal members didn't go on the tour of the failing Hood Canal Bridge. Mostly, they didn't attend the meetings of the local chamber of commerce, the economic development council, or the city council. And despite their name, the Strong People, many of the locals in this city had always found it easy to bypass the Lower Elwha Klallam. A small tribe with a high unemployment rate, the Lower Elwha had come a long way since gaining federal recognition. But they had not shared in the renaissance in Indian Country enjoyed by some of the wealthier tribes closer to Seattle who operated large casinos. They had no cultural resource or repatriation program, and nothing like the batteries of lawyers, staff archaeologists, planners, and cultural resource specialists employed by bigger, wealthier tribes.

When the department's letter arrived in October, requesting the tribe's input, it was late in the game, with momentum at the agency and among city officials already smoking in favor of the Port Angeles site. The department approached consultation with the tribe as a bureaucratic formality. One more box to check. And the tribe responded in kind. Tribal officials were already overwhelmed by other priorities, including the scheduled takedown of the Elwha River dams, the largest dam-removal project anywhere in North America. After a campaign launched by the tribe more than twenty years earlier, preparations for dam removal finally were under way,

Yet another developer's industrial project proposed for property on the Port Angeles waterfront did not make the urgency cut for tribal officials. Especially when the state and the city did so little to engage them. "Consultation isn't where you make a phone call and say, 'We are going to do this, we are sending a fax, we are going to be in this area, do you have anything to say,'" said Frances Charles, who was on the council when the project was first proposed and was later named tribal chairwoman. "You go to that tribe, you find out who the individuals are you need to talk with, you go over the plans in person, you get the history and don't ignore it or take shortcuts and say 'There's nothing there' or 'They don't know.' You have to actually come down and visit, with something in detail, so our elders would have an idea, know by photographs what they are looking at. With photos you can visualize better than with a map. They need to adapt to the ways of the culture, be able to provide the adequate information to the elders. I know that didn't happen. And if something is not adequate, you can't just dismiss it. Don't ignore it. Go into depth. Don't take a chance of taking a loss, like they did. Not once did they come down to Lower Elwha. They took the shortcut on this one."

On the same day in October that its letter went out to the tribe, the department hired one of its on-call archaeological consultants, Glenn Hartmann of Western Shore Heritage Services of Bainbridge Island, to take a look at the site. In its letter to the archaeologist, sent October 21, 2002, the department made it clear it was in a hurry. "The project is being fast tracked and we encourage you to accomplish this task with urgency," the letter said. The agency asked Hartmann to do a routine, $6,285 survey, including $1,660 for fieldwork. It allotted five days for field research, with the stipulation to ask first before taking more time. Hartmann didn't go to the site himself but sent one of his staff archaeologists, Lara Rooke, instead. Even as she worked in the muddy flats of the site, using an auger to drill for signs of archaeology, the business community of Port Angeles packed a public hearing on the project. This is a town where bones were unearthed when the local hospital was built. They found bones when they built the paper mill at the Ediz Hook and when they modernized the plant. They found bones when they built the opera house downtown and when they built the Commercial Hotel. They found bones when they ran the Milwaukee railroad tracks through the east end of town. They found bones when they built the Big Mill on the west end. And they found bones when they constructed the Rayonier plant, right over another Klallam village. But nobody talked about bones at the meeting. Speaker after speaker, including many elected officials, endorsed the dry dock project.

The archaeologist worked for four days, with hard rain soaking the site half the time. On the first day, she discovered she had the wrong bit for the work and lost half a day when the auger broke. The wet conditions made for sloppy core samples, and she didn't screen the dirt that came out with the auger. By day three, much of the site was under water. The drilling rig—supplied by the department—broke down again and was out of commission another half a day. An entire transect of the site was missed because concrete paving, water, and downed wires made digging impossible. About a third of the site in all was off-limits for sampling because it was covered with paving. The department gave no instruction as to how the work should be done. There was no directive to locate the ancient beach line, buried below the fill dirt, and look there as the most likely place for signs of a village or burial ground. The department did leave a door open for further exploration of the site, at the consultant's discretion, by defining the area potentially affected by the project as "any areas of concern noted by the appropriate tribes." But Hartmann's firm never made contact with the Lower Elwha Klallam. The department had requested "coordination with appropriate tribal representatives" but did not specify what that must, at a minimum, include.

"Were we aggressive about it? No," said Hartmann about contacting the tribe. But he said the tribe also could have taken a more proactive role in making sure its cultural sites were protected. "Anyone who thinks I'm going to develop an interactive relationship with the elders, there is not enough time in the day," Hartmann said. "Tribal people have a certain distrust of archaeologists. They don't want us digging up burials. But we should have instant ability to recognize human remains and know where they are? Guess what, guys, we are not interested in burial grounds, and to expect me to know their inner workings when it is information I'll never use—it's like me asking you to know the inner workings of Wall Street when you are going to stay on the reservation."

The field survey found no evidence of a site. Hartmann said he was a bit surprised. After all, archaeologists, anthropologists, historians, and others had written repeatedly of Klallam villages on the waterfront, in the same general area, including Tse-whit-zen. An 1853 survey map located not one but three Indian villages in the area. A competing archaeological firm had already prepared a detailed report in March 1991 on the paper-mill site next door, directly to the west. That report described Tse-whit-zen village, its approximate location at the base of the Ediz Hook, and its large size and importance. "Around 2,000 years ago, the west end of the Ediz Hook was probably one of the most productive, optimum settings for hunter-gatherer settlement along the entire northern Washington Strait of Juan de Fuca shoreline," the report noted. "The village was not far from the lagoon outlet and the base of the Ediz Hook."[2]

The archaeologists went on for pages about the large cemetery associated with the village. And they noted that its importance lived on in the memories of contemporary elders interviewed at the Lower Elwha Klallam Tribe: Beatrice Charles and Adeline Smith. The report detailed burial methods at the cemetery and the grave goods that would likely be encountered if the graves were disturbed:

> The cemetery associated with Tse-whit-zen was located, at least at some point in the history of the village, in the location of the mill complex although the precise location is not known. Alexander Sampson first encountered the Ediz Hook cemetery in 1856, when he claimed homestead acreage that included the village site and cemetery. . . . The cemetery again became a focus when the Washington Pulp and Paper Corporation excavated the footings for the pilings of their mill in 1920. At that time, hundreds of Indian bones were disturbed . . . when ground was broken for the foundations. . . . Contemporary Klallam tribal members who are now part of the Lower Elwha Klallam community think of the Ediz Hook cemetery as the "big cemetery" and that it may have been the cemetery for villages other than Tse-whit-zen.

The report's authors attributed this knowledge to Beatrice Charles and Adeline Smith, interviewed back in 1991.

There was more in the report, about the structures likely to be found at the village and the archaeological evidence, probably still there, of a sophisticated hunter-gatherer society dating back at least 2,000 years. The report noted that the site overlaid the village of Tse-whit-zen and a burial ground, which continued directly to the east—the very spot the department was looking to purchase. And despite all the disturbance of the ground in many years of industrial use, the archaeologists warned there probably still were intact archaeological deposits under the fill. The archaeologists observed that any find here would likely be significant, worthy of placement on the National Register of Historic Places. Dig here *at all*, to any depth, and there had better be an archaeologist present, they cautioned, because there is such a high likelihood for hunter-gatherer occupations to have occurred.

Because an historic Klallam cemetery has been identified on the property and the mill property is one of the most likely locations on the south shoreline of the Strait of Juan de Fuca for hunter-gatherer occupations, we conclude that nearly any intact cultural resources which remain here may be significant. . . . We also believe that it is possible that cultural resources may be present in areas that have not been completely disturbed.[3]

The report Hartmann prepared for the department wasn't nearly as long or detailed. It, too, noted the historic presence of the cemetery and the village but not with the same sense of imminent discovery for anyone disturbing the ground in the area—at all. His report sent a mixed message. Hartmann called the site a high-probability area because of the historical record of Indian settlement there. But because the field survey turned up no evidence of it, he deemed a discovery "unlikely." He recommended the standard fallback position of archaeologists everywhere: have a monitor on-site during construction, just in case.

Hartmann said he didn't feel rushed in the survey or that he should have called for a deep-site analysis of the ancient beach line. "It's not standard practice, and how in the world would you have justified the cost?" But he did feel uneasy about the survey results, uneasy enough to look for a colleague to cover for him in August 2003, when he was away on vacation and the department was breaking ground at the site. Arranging a backup like that was something he had never done in his thirty-year career. "I really did have a concern archaeology might be there, because of the limited nature of the survey," Hartmann said. "It struck me, there's the 1853 map—you know something is there. There was the lagoon there, and mostly, to me, it was the idea that you had this village site in close proximity. To not see anything there? But given the industrial use of the place, and all the fill, I didn't find it to be totally unsettling. You are kind of caught. You have historic documentation that says something is there, and ethnography of a more general nature. Those become yellow caution lights—take some care here. I'd said to my client there is supposed to be a village site in the area and a landform where burials were recorded in the 1920s. At the end of the day, it's worth remembering this didn't happen in a vacuum. That report was reviewed by the city, the tribe, and the state historic preservation officer, and no one said anything."

The state historic preservation agency missed the site, just like everyone else.

Based on its review of Hartmann's report, Robert G. Whitlam, archaeologist with the state Office of Archaeology and Historic Preservation, wrote on January 14, 2003: "We concur with your findings that no historic properties are in the area. . . . Thus, no historic properties are affected." The agency did not visit the site, did no independent evaluation, and made no request for further information. Like Hartmann, the agency cleared the Department of Transportation to proceed with construction, with the safeguard stipulation that an archaeologist monitor the site during construction, just in case. "It comes down to one state archaeologist reviews more than 5,000 projects in a year," said Allyson Brooks, director of the Office of Archaeology and Historic Preservation. "How many would you have to do in a day to visit the sites?"

The transportation department didn't question Hartmann's survey either. Far from it. The department had already announced in a press release issued November 20, 2002, that it, with the endorsement of then-governor Gary Locke, had selected the Port Angeles site. The press release quoted Locke's prepared statement, saying that the project would "result in 100 jobs for Port Angeles and provide a shot in the arm for the area economy." The department issued that release just five days after Hartmann's archaeologist pulled the auger out of the ground. It hadn't even waited to hear the results of the cultural resources survey. In retrospect, Hain said, the department's mistakes are obvious. "Hindsight is twenty-twenty," he said. "Instead of simply sending the tribe a letter, we should have gone out and introduced ourselves and asked, 'What about your elders? We should take them down to the site and see if it jogs their memory.' Did we think about that? Absolutely not. We made that mistake. And I've heard stories about 'Just wait until they get into that,' not only from the tribe, but other people who probably knew about this. Why didn't those people come forward and say, 'Did you know about this?' It sure makes you feel stupid. I didn't hear it often, but I'd think, 'Oh you dope, why didn't you go find that out?' But it is not the kind of thing you think to ask. I am not a geologist or an archaeologist. And the department didn't have much waterside history. We hadn't done enough of this kind of work in the past."

The department's problems started with its schedule. Archaeological review for major projects is preferably done a year or two in advance of construction, so that if significant archaeological or cultural materials are found, the department can make alternative plans. But construction of the dry dock was on a rushed schedule to meet a date the agency had already set for closing the bridge to traffic, towing the anchors and pontoons to the bridge site, and beginning repairs. Those plans, in addition to arrangements to provide alternative ferry service during the repairs, had put hard edges on every other date in the project, including the start of construction of the dry dock.

Environmental permits for the dry dock were also processed under a pilot expedited review process, since abandoned. The proposal was never reviewed through the more elaborate process of an environmental impact statement. Instead, the Hood Canal Bridge project was a demonstration project under the new process, which was intended to speed up environmental permitting review in part by bringing participants from various agencies together at one table for discussion of the project. But historic preservation and cultural resource specialists weren't part of the team. That exclusion was a reflection, in part, of priorities in Washington State. Salmon, listed for federal protection in Puget Sound under the Endangered Species Act, were the chief concern in major land-use projects and a dreaded potential slowdown in any permitting process.

"No one is thinking about Indians. Everyone is thinking about salmon," said former transportation secretary Douglas B. MacDonald. Nobody at the city or the port brought up Indians either. Seeing requires looking, and nobody was. "'How could you possibly have missed this?' is one of the questions the world is fairly going to ask," MacDonald said. "It's much more than just a question of blaming the archaeologist. The really interesting thing to reflect on is the collective amnesia about what was at that site. I don't think the Port of Port Angeles had a clue, or gave it a moment's thought, and the collective amnesia about that site was a really important part of the question of 'Why did we miss this?' Not only does it tell the history of the contact but also the history of the forgetting, and it is not that many generations ago. The collective amnesia is so profound that no one even asked the question, and that goes to the collective disconnect in the Port Angeles community."

The department filed its request for a permit to build the project with the city of Port Angeles on Christmas Eve, 2002. Port Angeles assistant city planner Scott Johns found Hartmann's report reassuring as he reviewed the permit application. Just four years into his job, he was well aware of the big push in town to get the dry dock project permitted and built in Port Angeles. "We were being as unobstructionist as possible. It was, 'Don't stand in the way of this, so in your permitting don't look too close. We want this to happen,'" Johns said. "But from my perspective it was very thorough. We analyzed it to death, in so many ways. Calculating the cubic feet of soil that would be dug, counting how many trucks. Will they be working at night? What about back-up alarms? That will bother people. Is there enough parking for

Taken in 1884, this earliest known photo of the Port Angeles area shows the base of the Ediz Hook, where a major paper mill would later be built. A wagon road that came down the hill is on the left. At the dock, boats landed to load cordwood and unload supplies. Just outside the picture to the right was a Klallam Indian village and longhouse, the Tse-whit-zen site, where the transportation depart-ment would locate its dry dock project. Courtesy North Olympic Library System, Bert Kellogg Collection, Ediz Hook-PTAN VIEW-001.

employees? Bright lights? That will ruin people's views at night."

The state had already done its environmental assessment and declared that the project would have no significant impact. Completed before the Port Angeles site was even selected, the assessment was updated for the city permit application with a checklist of resources deemed unaffected by the project. "Archaeology didn't seem to be an issue," Johns said. City code requires surveying with the tribe any potential development site in town that could disturb cultural materials. But that could be waived if a survey had already been done and a monitor would be present during construction. The department had already seen to that.

Hartmann had sent his draft report of the cultural resources survey to the state transportation department on December 10, 2002, and his final copy on January 6, 2003. The department forwarded copies to the Lower Elwha Klallam Tribe, as well as to other neighboring tribes, on January 13, along with a form letter requesting comments. The next day Frances Charles, then a member of the tribal council, wrote to the city in response to its request, separate from the department's, to provide the tribe's views on the project. In her letter, Charles sounded a warning on behalf of the Lower Elwha people: "The tribe is concerned with protection of water quality and marine habitat in the harbor, as well as protection of cultural resources that might be unearthed as a result of this project." Then, in the last of eight items of concern listed, she wrote: "The Klallam people were present throughout the Harbor and a known village site was located in close proximity to the proposed excavation site. In excavation work, human and cultural remains and artifacts were unearthed. We are extremely concerned about any excavation work and strongly recommend that an archaeologist be present on site throughout this project."

But that warning wasn't clear to Johns, who said his confidence in the site was actually boosted by the tribe's letter. "There were eight comments; they were more concerned about fish, where the soil was going to go. It was eighth of eight. If it was first, if it was definitive—'This is where Tse-whit-zen was, we are confident.' But it was like, 'Oh, there might be something in the neighborhood.' I thought maybe they are back by the bluff; they wouldn't be on the beach." He toured the site with staff from the state Department of Transportation, to see it for himself. "I was trying to get a feel for the site, so I could describe it. I was kind of curious. It struck me as a kind of trashy old waste industrial site. I was thinking, 'How is this going to work, how do you make the sea gate open and shut?'—the engineering and scientific aspects of it—that is my training. It's that all-American stuff: If we have enough money, we can build anything. I had it in my mind that it was all fill. It was inconceivable to me that there could be a burial site."

After all, Johns had seen the picture, an aerial shot taken during World War II of Olympic Shipbuilders, Inc., an industrial shipyard built at the site. And that was *after* the Big Mill—another enormous industrial development—had been built, operated for decades, and demolished on the same ground. Johns was so impressed by the enormity of the shipyard that he attached a copy of the photo to the permit file. "I looked at that picture of the shipyard and thought, 'They would have found a burial ground if they did that.'" The total transformation of the site to industrial use by the newcomers, for whom its history *was* the mill, the shipyard, and piles of logs, heaped and pawed over by front-end loaders, hid the truth.

Yet the same development that convinced Johns and other reviewers that the site was all disturbed and nothing could still be there had actually sealed and protected what remained of Tse-whit-zen largely intact. Most of the early mill buildings were constructed waterward, on pilings. Early construction techniques didn't disturb the ground with heavy equipment. Utility lines were dug by hand. And the thick layers of sawdust for stacking lumber and the fill dirt covering the site protected the village site and burials like a blanket. There were other reasons, too, that Johns and others missed the site: They couldn't see past their own frame of reference. The possibility

Map of False Dungeness Harbor, 1853. Note the three Indian villages mapped on the harbor shoreline, including the westernmost, which may be Tse-whit-zen. U.S. Coast Survey, A. D. Bache, Superintendent Reconnaissance of False Dungeness Harbor, Washington, by the Hydrographic Party under the command of Lieut. James Alden, U.S.N. Assist. Courtesy Clallam County Historical Society.

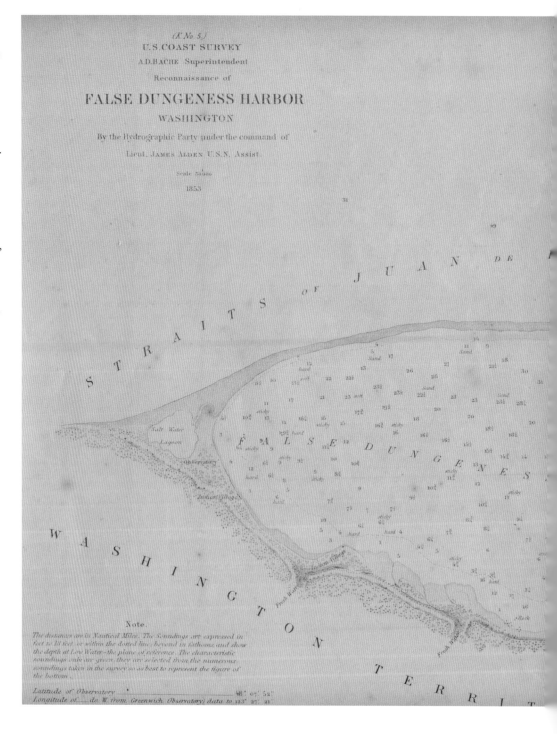

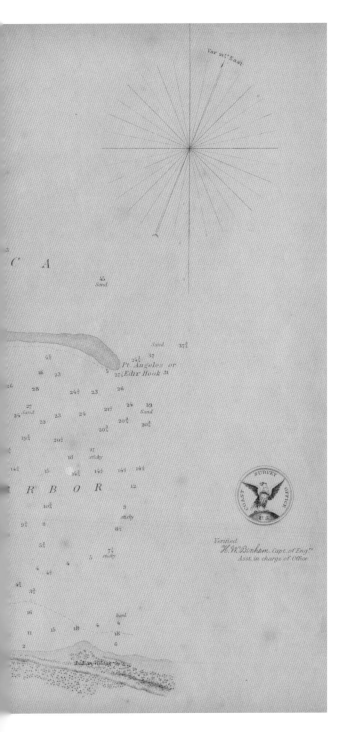

that Indian graves—many graves—*had* been discovered at the site in earlier construction and simply been shoved aside, didn't register. "It didn't occur to me, 'Yeah, they did find it, and they used it as backfill,'" Johns said. "I could kick myself, it is so obvious. When I think about it, it brings tears to my eyes. It has kind of haunted me. All those past uses there. I used that as justification. I thought, 'Somebody must have discovered this.' But somebody did. They found them and kept their mouths shut." Johns wrote a staff report recommending approval.

Next, on January, 16, 2003, Lower Elwha Klallam tribal employees Matt Bierne, then in the tribe's environmental office, Mike McHenry in the tribe's fisheries department, Rachel Hageman in the tribe's planning department, and Robert Elofson, head of the Elwha River restoration effort for the tribe, sat down with Jerry Moore, from the state transportation department, and two officials from the port to talk about the project.

Bierne used to work in the tribe's environmental office, reviewing developments planned within areas where the tribe has treaty rights to hunt and fish, both on and off the reservation. "We go through this all the time," he said in a weary voice, reciting the machinations of bureaucracy that govern development of the shoreline in Washington. "Anything within 200 feet of the shoreline, they have to have a review team, on which the tribe sits. All the jurisdictions knew our concerns." The tribal staffers brought the 1853 map of the Port Angeles Harbor, drawn when Washington was still a territory. The same map that bothered Hartmann. The map is a popular decorator item in Port Angeles, one of those bits of nostalgia people like to look at briefly and then move on. It's on the wall at the McDonald's on the main drag into town. Another copy hangs on the wall of a county commissioner's office, right behind his desk. "False Dungeness Harbor" was what they called it when the surveyors mapped the bay sheltered by the Ediz Hook. The character of the bottom—hard, sand, sticky—is written in neat script alongside precise soundings in fathoms throughout the bay. The long, sheltering arm of the hook is carefully drawn, and so is the lagoon that still pools at the head of the bay. There are the stippled banks, representing the trees that used to grace the shoreline. And in tight script, right on the beach, just east of the curve of the hook, is noted "Indian Village." There's a second village marked, where the surveyor also logged a stream of fresh water rattling down the hillside to the east, on the beach. A third village is mapped farther east.

"We brought out the map of the village sites. They didn't seem to take it very seriously," Bierne said. "There were no notes taken, no one asked to make a photocopy. We told them we have knowledge that there was tribal activity all throughout the harbor." Bierne suggested the archaeological firm the tribe would choose to monitor the site during construction. It was the same firm that had written the 1991 report warning of the likelihood of an archaeological find in any ground disturbance at the site. But he was told the department already had its own process for selecting an archaeologist. The meeting ended. And so, for all practical purposes, did the discussion about the project back at the tribe. "We had been cautioned by the tribal council, 'Don't bother the elders; they have been interviewed to death. We have hundreds of tapes,'" Bierne said. "We get these documents all the time, and we have no cultural resources department. There's been assumptions about the fill at that site. And it was on a fast-track process." Less than a week later, the city planning commission held a public hearing on the project. No one objected, and the city council granted its approval the same day, less than a month after the department submitted its permit application. The project was good to go. The city imposed the same default fail-safe condition everyone else had, requiring an archaeologist to be present during any construction, just in case.

Dennis Sullivan, tribal chairman at the time, replied to the department about Hartmann's archaeological survey of the site in a letter written February 5, 2003. He warned the department about the tribe's historic presence in the area. He relayed extreme concern about any disturbance of cultural materials. He, too, asked that a monitor be present during construction. And he essentially agreed with the report. "Our staff has reviewed this document and basically agrees with its findings," Sullivan wrote on behalf of the tribal council. "The proposed site within Port Angeles has clearly been significantly altered, however its proximity to known Klallam Village sites and traditional use areas argues strongly for caution. We also understand the inherent limitations in characterizing a site of this magnitude with small diameter subsurface borings. . . . We realize that this project is progressing on a fast-track schedule. . . . We look forward to continuing to work with you in the development and implementation of this plan."

But meanwhile, down a dirt road, a stone's throw from the tribal center that would be visited many times later by transportation department managers, Beatrice Charles and Adeline Smith say they could have told anyone who asked them about the cemetery and village at this site. But no one asked them about the proposed project, not even members of their own tribal council. Both women are adamant that they could have stopped the project before it started—if anyone had listened.

"The knowledge, the information was there before they started," Smith said. "We have said that a lot of times, but the younger generation, they didn't want to listen. We always knew there was a cemetery there. There is a lot of differences between the generations. What Bea and I know was handed down. It wasn't written. It was a duty for elders to tell the next generation. We didn't have knowledge like writing it down. You just had to have that memory and pass it on to whoever would stop and listen.

"They should have asked around. Instead they didn't tell anyone. To be truthful I didn't even know what they were doing until they were into it," Smith said of the council. "But people here are a lot younger. We know what we were told by our elders, passed on verbally, from generation to generation. I don't know whether people would have listened to us. We have to deal with our own people, too. We haven't been a reservation very long. And a lot of the history was lost. That's that younger generation, that is the way they are. I hope it will be a lesson to the younger people like the council. They should ask."

Even their own council didn't know about the cemetery, Charles said. "Maybe they have too much work to do, I don't know. But they didn't. They are so busy running the tribe, they forgot to learn the history. You have to learn your history to build your future. They just never bothered; they are just in this present world. They never bothered to find out what happened before. Maybe they don't want to know what happened before. Because it isn't very pleasant. Maybe it is our fault. Maybe we should have stepped forward. But who would listen? They just don't care about us."

Sullivan, chairman at the time the project was proposed, said he regretted not reaching out to the elders the way he should have. "We had to reach out and go talk to the elders. I didn't reach out to as many as I wanted to. This bothers me. Bea and

Adeline, I used to go down and talk with them. They used to summon me. I didn't reach out on this one. . . . Nobody knew exactly where the cemetery was. They probably could have given us some direction about where, I'll have to agree about that. It's been a very expensive learning process for all the parties." Later, as tribal chairwoman, Frances Charles apologized to Beatrice Charles and Adeline Smith for the council not coming to them sooner. The council made some attempts to reach out to tribal elders after the first discoveries at the site, Frances Charles said. "It's not that we didn't make an outreach to them. It was asking the right questions. They were asked but they weren't asked the right questions, and we didn't interpret it the right way."

In the early stages of the project, elders were also reluctant to talk, Frances Charles said. "We did try to talk to them, but they were not willing to talk at that time. It was the uncertainty. I think everybody doubted the survival of the cemetery itself. Because of the uncertainty, a lot of the elders didn't open up. But they knew the stories they were told. There was a silence all those months. Not only were the elders ashamed, but they were afraid. It was really hard for them to open up because we were going into painful territory. Generations were told their culture was evil. There still are some that have never opened up, and you have to back up. You are digging into those wounds that are so deep. From losing loved ones, or witnessing something they want to forget, or their guilt at something that happened that they couldn't do anything about, and a lot of the remembered hate and prejudice. You had to be real quiet. In order to stand up for your culture you've been beaten so badly, not physically, but mentally, that you are not to be teaching your culture. And it was not something that we wrote down."

In the past, the tribe had recorded oral histories from its elders about the location of cemeteries and village sites. But the council didn't consult those histories, Frances Charles said. "Why didn't we remember the documentation? Why didn't the staff know?" she asked in frustration. Some elders were irritated at being questioned again about painful history. "It was, 'I've already talked about this. Where are those tapes, those interviews, those manuscripts?' That was the difficulty we were having, that was the lack of ability of knowing the importance of preserving the tapes, those manuscripts, and here we are, putting the burden back on them." Charles remembered the first time she stepped into her council office. "I went up to my office and said, 'My God, we have a gold mine here. Why isn't this in the archives?' When you have changeovers in the council or the staffing, it might not mean anything to them, and

An Indian woman uses a sewing machine on the beach at the city waterfront east of the dry dock site after the Klallam people were displaced from their village at Hollywood Beach, ca. 1902. The tent, on sticks to her left, is made of cedar-bark blankets. The city waterfront was home to at least three Indian villages, of which Tse-whit-zen was the largest. Bert Kellogg Collection, North Olympic Library System, INDN ACTV-012.

it's tossed." But a trove of information also was available, right in town, in public files, about the tribe's historic presence on the waterfront. "It was all right there, we didn't have to go and talk to anyone," Frances Charles said. "All we had to do was research. It is on the map, in the museum, in the library, in the archives, and in our own archives. It's in the stories. I don't think anybody thought about it. Things were rolling so fast, we didn't have time to think about it. We were reactive, not proactive. We didn't have time. I don't blame WashDot. I blame the local governments. They knew it was there. All the signs were there. All the public information was there. But everyone forgot to go out and research."

Later, even when the first human remains were found, Charles said that the tribe still could not provide what the state wanted. "We are hearing there is a grave site. But what the state agencies want us to do is say, 'It's right there.' We can't do that. Don't ask me to put a dime on it. Draw a circle around it. We knew it was down here somewhere, but to say it's right here on this dime, that's what we couldn't do. It's like all of this testing that was done. Twenty holes in one grid and not once did we hit it. It's, 'Look at this map and give us an exact location.' We were being challenged: 'If

Dennis Sullivan, then chairman of the Lower Elwha Klallam tribal council, at the dry dock site, November 2004. He says he regrets not talking to elders to learn the history of the site when the Washington State Department of Transportation was considering it for the dry dock. "It's been a very expensive lesson for us all," Sullivan said. Steve Ringman, courtesy *Seattle Times*.

you don't know and we don't know, then there's nothing there.'"

It wasn't until the project was already well under way that the ground finally started speaking for itself, as artifacts, burials, and remains of the village were gradually revealed. "The ground itself told us," Charles said. "The more things started opening up to us, the ground opened our eyes even wider. The more the ground was disturbed, the more the expression of our spiritual and cultural traditions surfaced. To me, it was the ancestors stepping forward and saying, 'This is your heritage, and it still is.' It was very powerful to have the ground and the ancestors say it themselves. After the evidence of the ground opened up, it finally made it comfortable that the elders could open up. As soon as the ground itself started opening up, they started opening up. It was, 'OK, we can talk about this.' Once the ground opened up, that's when everyone started feeling comfortable with what the knowledge was." But by then, the state was well into its project.

Like Hain of the transportation department, Charles has her regrets. Since the dry dock project, a cultural resource checklist has been negotiated with the state and the city for the next time a developer wants to build on the waterfront. But also like Hain, Charles doubts that it will cover every situation. After all, the city had ordi-

The late Walt Bennett (*left*), a Lower Elwha Klallam elder, is pictured looking at a harpoon point dug from the site, shown to him by tribal member Arlene Wheeler during a tour elders took of the dry dock site in 2003 after the inadvertent discovery of Tse-whit-zen. As children, Bennett, Bea Charles, and Adeline Smith had to walk around, rather than through, the site on the way to school, to respect the sacred ground of a large cemetery located there. Courtesy Lower Elwha Klallam Tribe.

nances on the books long before the dry dock project requiring it to work with the tribe to inventory cultural sites—and avoid them. "Everyone would go back and say, 'What would we do differently?' It's good to have a checklist. But what is the next crisis going to be?" Charles asked.

"We have a city shoreline management plan that hasn't worked yet. It's not about policy. It's about communication and trusting each other. Where do you let down your barriers? I think everyone is trying to take that first step right now. I don't blame the DoT. I don't blame the federal highways. I blame the City of Port Angeles. They knew what was here 150 years ago. They knew the heritage, of what was here. They can't sit there and say they were unaware. They ignored it because of their greed. It's in the archives. In the library. But to them, we don't exist. We are the outsiders that are looking in. We are not of importance to them. We are just another John Doe Citizen with no impact on the City of Port Angeles, and they are the government overseers."

Tribal government has also changed and can fill only so much of the cultural gap. Tribal members used to advise a handful of elders, who executed the community's wishes. But today, the council is younger and acts for a community that doesn't turn out for monthly meetings unless it has an issue directly at stake. "They know when the community council is scheduled, for the first Monday of every month. They will attend a meeting to address a personal issue," Sullivan said. "The ones that do things are the same ones, over and over. A lot of them come to complain, not to share. The community used to make the decisions for the council. Today, the general community relies on the council to make decisions for them. What bothers me is I feel the community relies too much on the council business committee to make these decisions, which affect future generations."

Their tribal government has, in other words, become in some ways like local governments everywhere. And life on the reservation, like everywhere else, has also become more fragmented and impersonal. "When I was growing up, there was no TV set. Everything was by radio," Sullivan said. "The activity in my day was you would go to the river. Fish were plentiful, the creeks were alive with salmon. People walked everywhere in groups; there was a unity. You don't see that anymore. It was a community effort. The elders were on the council; you didn't have any young council members until later."

The professional government staff at the tribal center can't necessarily provide crucial cultural knowledge. About half the staff is non-Indian. And the cultural gap ripped into this tribe by more than 150 years of violence and forced assimilation has not healed. "I use myself as an example," said Frances Charles, then forty-seven. "There was that whole generational gap, there was that silence. From about age ten or twelve until about thirty, you were not to talk about your religion or your culture. There was a little bit here, a little bit there, and you were not to talk about it. Even within our own council, some of us choose life on the reservation and some didn't want to live on the reservation or be considered an Indian, even today."

Beatrice Charles agreed. "Our culture is just being revived. We were taught not to speak our languages. We forgot our tradition. We forgot our culture for a long time. Maybe that's what's happened. Within our families, we had that. But a lot of families didn't have the older teachings. That breakdown was . . . it was more modern. And you had rivalries between families. It's not communicating with them. It's politics." And many people in this tribe, which was without a recognized tribal government until 1968, are just trying to survive. "We were not recognized for so long. During that era everyone had to be for themselves," Adeline Smith said. "The Indians always took the worst jobs, or the dirty end of the jobs, or no job at all. In Port Angeles, it was rough. Her and I had to go to Seattle to look for work," she said of her niece

Beatrice Charles. "That's where we lost a lot of our culture," Smith said. "People were separated from their culture. The government erased the Klallam off the map. We were diminished from the smallpox. That's why the government put the military reservation here. They said all the Indians are all gone. We was supposed to have died."

The Lower Elwha Klallam people became strangers in their own homeland, plagued by conflict between the tribe and this town for more than 150 years. Even after the reservation was created, many tribal members lived in isolation there, just six miles from downtown Port Angeles. "I wasn't allowed to go into town," Adeline said. "There was an incident where a[n Indian] child was killed. He was clubbed to death with a two-by-four; he lived for three days until he died. You never heard anything about it. Indians didn't dare ask anything. They just got away with it. I never seen Port Angeles, just once or twice a year, when my grandmother took me." Ask at the Lower Elwha Klallam reservation if anyone has ever sought a position on the city council, school board, county commission, or port commission, and the answer will be a bewildered "No." Even the chamber of commerce, the planning commission, and the economic development council were all no-go zones for decades.

Jamie Valadez, a tribal language instructor, raised her kids, one of them a national wrestling champion, in town. "They get watched when they go into a store, or when they drive, they get pulled over more often," Valadez said. "My daughter is a hairdresser, and it's 'No, I don't want you. Can someone else do it?'" She has struggled to feel at home in Port Angeles herself, despite her work teaching the Klallam language at the public high school. "I've lived in town since I was sixteen. I like living in town, but you don't feel like you are a member of that community. You feel like you are a pet, under a microscope. They want to ask you questions, like you are some kind of expert, and you aren't. I fight this a lot; you try to fit in. I see myself distancing myself. Putting this thick wall around. When you fail so many times at trying, you get hurt so many times. I'm staying in that comfort zone, and that's where they all are staying, and we have to get out of that place. Or they are trying to meet their quota: 'We did our outreach to the Native population.' I feel like a quota number."

City officials made an effort to reach out to the tribe in 1990, building a longhouse at a city park with public funds. But the building was kept locked, and tribal members needed city permission to use it. What the tribe regarded as a sacred, traditional place was used for K-Mart employee get-togethers and storage for park department lawnmowers, baseball equipment, and soccer goals. When the city concreted over the traditional earthen floor, the tribe protested. The city took out the concrete, perplexed at the peculiar people in their midst. Then officials gave the tribe a key to the city, which perplexed the tribe, here long before the settlers first showed up to form a white utopia. "It was like having a key to the house when you are kicked out," Beatrice Charles said. "Then it changes every four years, when they elect someone else who has no history. They never did like us. We have been living through that ever since I was a child. Even today, we tell our kids never to go to town by themselves. It's not safe."

By June 16, 2003, the tribe had taken a closer look at the dry dock site and issued a report comparing its location with the villages on the 1853 map. That report pegged the location of the ancient Klallam village of Tse-whit-zen well south and east of the boundaries of the proposed dry dock.

On August 6, 2003, former transportation secretary MacDonald finally got his first look at the site. He and other department officials had traveled to Port Angeles from the state capital for an event relished by all government officials: a groundbreaking ceremony for a big, coveted project that would bring much-wanted jobs to a local community. He remembered his first impressions of the site vividly. "You didn't see a beach. You didn't see the land. You couldn't even, in fact, from where we stood, see the water. And if anybody had said, 'Do you understand that you are going to spend the next year and a half of your life dealing with the implications and the contents of the site related to Native Americans?' you would say, 'You've come to the wrong party. That must be something else. That is not here. I don't see any Native Americans here. Are there Native Americans in Port Angeles? Isn't that interesting.' There would have been no understanding that there was another overlay in time and in space with which we would soon be very involved. The past was invisible, and the Native American context of the site was invisible. There was a complete disconnect, a complete absence of understanding of where we stood in history and in space as we soon, to our astonishment, learned. The collective consciousness of the Port Angeles community is not contributed to by the tribe. It is part of the invisibility of the tribes. We do not connect between those cultural groups, and that is one of the reasons the Port of Port Angeles and our own engineers would never have given this a second's thought. This happened because the two communities that live in Port Angeles have never worked this out. They don't understand each other's history."

That, the city vividly demonstrated. Town residents and state and local elected officials turned out to celebrate the groundbreaking for the project. There was a band and yellow-and-white striped party tents for locals and dignitaries gathered

Port Angeles city officials and business boosters join transportation secretary Douglas MacDonald (*facing camera, foot on shovel*) at the groundbreaking for the dry dock site, August 2003. Within days, the first human remains would be found not far from where they are digging. Courtesy Washington State Department of Transportation.

to cheer the jobs that would soon be coming to town. Andrew May, 2005 president of the local chamber of commerce, had never seen such a big crowd—not even when the town gathered to watch the demolition of the stack on one of the last big, shuttered mills. "They had a plane flying around, taking photos," May said. "It was the multimillion-dollar thing. We're doing the big sandwich, celebration thing." There were drawings of the project to look at and a video running on a monitor to show how the sea gate of the dry dock would work. "People were singing, dancing, eating, celebrating, walking around, slapping each other on the back. It was who's who, everybody, Peter and Pam Public, everything was wonderful," May said. But as a town resident and a mover and shaker who made it his business to have his finger on lots of pulses, May's sense of Port Angeles was different from the one transportation department officials at the site had that day. Amid all the festivity, to him, something just didn't feel right.

"I'm talking to several people. There were definitely rumors that they didn't want to listen to what was really out here. Let them get started. I distinctly remember it," May said. "I was asking around. I'm getting this feel that there is an unheard, small minority saying, 'Well, wait until they see,' and later it was, 'Why didn't they say so at the time?' But listen, they were trying to tell folks that," he said of the tribe. "They did say, 'You are going to find a village, and we tried to tell you how big it was. But why piss into the wind? If I'm telling you it's here, and you are going forward with your tests and moving ahead, who am I to say no?' Nobody needs economic development more than Lower Elwha. And here's this [archaeological] firm that specializes in this saying it isn't there. Are you saying you know more than them? There was such momentum at that point. I view it as a Greek tragedy. You heard these things before it happened, you saw it hit the fan, then both sides entrenching." Thinking back over the moment local dignitaries pushed their shovels into the dirt, breaking ground, he shook his head. "That day was for me a very bizarre day. The word I got was, 'We are sitting on a powder keg.'"

7

This Ground Speaks

IT WAS A BIG HUNK OF CEMENT, AN OLD FOOTING, AND ROOTED STUBBORNLY. Heaving and hefting, the backhoe finally broke its grip on this ground, and on the past. David Garlington leaned over to peer into the hole for a closer look. A distinct, banded layer of bits of white shell gleamed in the walls of the hole. "It was clearly something cultural," said Garlington, the transportation department's site manager for the dry dock project. Made up of cooking and food debris, a midden is the remainder of a prehistoric refuse heap. It typically, but not always, contains bits of shell, fish oil from cooking, animal bones, and even human remains, of slaves, war captives, and others not high born who were buried in the trash heap. Sometimes a midden is just a very dark layer in the soil, with no shells at all. It is usually the first sign of ancient human habitation. And it was a red flag to any knowledgeable, ethical construction contractor digging up the ground in the year 2003. This was not the first time someone had dug here. The site had been churned up, filled, and built on for nearly a century. But for the first time since contact, when this ground spoke, it was heard.

Garlington moved the backhoe operator away from the area. Then, even though

First discovery of the Tse-whit-zen site, August 2003. The first clue that this was no ordinary construction site were the bands of midden layered in the ground. The dark, oily soil and bits of broken shell are often the first signs of human habitation at an archaeological site. Courtesy Western Shores Heritage Services.

it was a Saturday, he contacted federal and state archaeology officials and the tribe, as required under the monitoring plan for the site. Construction had been under way less than a week. The tribe didn't even know work had started. Hartmann didn't get the message Garlington left at his office until Monday. "I didn't go out there right away," Hartmann said. "There was a good chance it wasn't archaeology. David is not trained in archaeology. It could have been dredge spoil. It seemed to me the most prudent thing was to get someone there."

He sent an employee, Garth Baldwin, who arrived at the site Tuesday morning. He called Hartman to tell him Garlington was right. While they had thought they were digging only in industrial fill, the department had in fact unearthed archaeology. Once at the site, Baldwin asked tribal members to help him search the area. "Garth was put in a tough spot," said LaTrisha Suggs, a tribal employee and one of the first from the Lower Elwha Klallam reservation to get to the site. "He didn't have the authority to stop work down there. He was very upset that work was still going on. He was very sympathetic to the tribe, very patient with us. You could clearly see he was frustrated with the construction workers and the work that was continuing. He was trying to control the situation the best he could. No one knew what the boundar-

The discovery of artifacts such as this stone wedge (wíč), used for splitting planks, was a shock even to some tribal members, who had always heard that their people had a village on the waterfront but never knew where it was. Steve Ringman, courtesy *Seattle Times*.

ies were, and he wanted to analyze what was there and monitor what was happening, and he couldn't do both at the same time. It was really confusion and chaos.

"There was excitement, too, because of everything that was being found. For years the city's attitude was, prove that you lived here, come up with something. Here we have something, we finally have proof that this was our village, this was our homeland, all the things that were being found, this new information. It was history that was being opened up." Suggs asked more tribal employees to come down and help her assist Baldwin. "We helped provide eyes for Garth. We assisted in looking along the ground for artifacts. We had to be careful where we were stepping."

Mostly, tribal cultural liaison Arlene Wheeler, who joined Suggs at the site, remembers a sense of chaos and that something just didn't feel right, as trucks kept loading material and roaring away to a town landfill. "He started telling us, 'What you want to do is a top survey. These are the kinds of things you want to look for,'" Wheeler said. Minutes later, they found a human jawbone. "You can tell, those aren't animal teeth. You just know they are not," Wheeler said. "We were first trying to make sure this is what we are really looking at, and just from the look on the archae-ologist's face, we knew that it was. He was just really frustrated at that point because of what he was trying to accomplish, to get that one-hundred-foot buffer in, to right away come across a human bone. You could see the look in his face." Meanwhile, outside the buffer zone, backhoes kept digging up the ground and dumping the dirt into dump trucks that hauled it away. "It was a feeling that is very hard to describe," Wheeler said. "There were double dump trucks leaving every three minutes . . . it felt like these machines were ripping through your heart when they were tearing up the ground and hauling this soil away. After seeing the shell midden, the cultural material, and human remains, the thought came to our minds and to our souls of what was really happening here, and it literally felt like someone was jabbing our hearts."

Baldwin called the coroner and the police about the jawbone. He also called Hartmann. "He said we really need someone else out there," Hartmann recalled. So did Dennis Sullivan, the tribal chairman. "He expressed concern about why we didn't have more people there," Hartmann said. "I know Garth wasn't always comfortable. He told me he didn't think the construction people always listened. I know there was a certain level of unease on his part and mine. Was the monitoring as controlled as it should be?" Tribal members found a spear tip and herring combs. Mammal teeth and whale vertebrae. "And I had never dealt with archaeology, cultural resources, cultural material—it all was totally new to me," Wheeler said. "I never had been out in the field doing any fieldwork. We just kept going every day after that, and it was really chaotic because the site was so huge and there was so much going on. It was a very rough area to be walking around in. It was so torn up from the heavy equipment and the bucket scraping the ground, and you had to be careful because everywhere you looked there was something. You didn't have to look very hard."

Tribal members called an archaeological firm they had used in the past, Larson Anthropological Archaeological Services of Gig Harbor, the same firm that had written the report about the site next door, warning of likely discovery for anyone digging here. Lynn Larson and Dennis Lewarch, then principal investigators for the firm, came out to Port Angeles. They arrived to find a contractor chunking through the site with a backhoe, at Baldwin's direction. Hartmann arrived next and was chagrined to find archaeologists from a competing firm already there. Lewarch and Hartmann immediately got into a shouting match, as Lewarch accused Hartmann of allowing the destruction of intact archaeology. "He is running around with a track hoe, trying to find the boundaries of the site and at the same time taking big chunks out of it," Lewarch said. "I saw shell and fish bones and big pieces of deer bone."

In a report filed later with the tribe, Lewarch and Larson described a churned landscape of fill dirt and intact archaeological deposits: "The ground surface was rutted from tracked vehicles and tires from dump trucks, and had small, linear ridges of historic period fill and over burden mixed with archaeological deposits and human remains between ruts. Some areas had low mounds of mixed fill and archaeological material that had been removed by track hoes, but had not been placed in dump trucks. Intact archaeological deposits were visible at the base of the ridges as small, horizontal midden exposures."[1]

Tribal members felt their confidence slip. "My general impression was kind of overall disappointment that all of a sudden the tribe was thrust into a situation that could have been prevented," Suggs said. Tribal members demanded to know where the material dug from the site was going. And then they made a trip to the landfill. Slowly, carefully, they checked the surface of the piles that had been hauled away. "We found a lot of stone knives that were flaked and intact chunks of shell midden. A lot of it was probably buried or destroyed," Wheeler said. "The midden that was intact was in chunks, like the size of a bowling ball, and the other stuff you could tell had been destroyed. They flattened it out on the top with machinery and then drove over it, which was not good," Wheeler said. "There is this pile of midden that is not intact, and you could see the bones coming out of there—the elk bone, you could see everything. It was so rich, it was just really dark, black, oily, the cultural deposits, the oily black soils. Shell, sea urchin, all that stuff."

Mary Anne Thomas, a spiritual advisor to the tribe and a relative of Arlene Wheeler's and Frances Charles's, was visiting from the Esquimalt Nation in Canada. She led a prayer circle. "When Auntie got through praying, she is the one, because she had that power, she is the one that said that she feels there is a presence there," Wheeler said. "That they are letting her know that there are some bones there. We didn't really look to find human remains, but we are pretty sure that there are some up there because of the feelings that happened."

On August 26, 2003, one week after the initial discovery of human remains on the site, transportation secretary MacDonald shut the project down. All of it, everywhere on the site. A total shutdown beyond the area of initial discovery wasn't legally necessary. But MacDonald wanted to make a point. "We shut it down to make a statement to the tribe that we weren't going to just blow through this thing," MacDonald said. "We had to go talk to those people, and we couldn't talk and work at the same time. Good faith required us to show that we were going to listen. It was not a unilateral decision on my part. I think it was the fact that we didn't know where we were, and we had to get our feet under us and our bearings. I think when we found the first thing, it was a happenstance, a fragment. But there was a sense that this trickle could grow. It was the accretion. Partly it had to do with the relationship with the tribe. But it was also a pragmatic sense of a need to find out where we were."

Archaeologist Lynn Larson went out to the site again in September at the request of the tribe. Her assessment of the site, relayed in a report she filed for the tribe on October 10, 2003, sharply differed from the assessment Hartmann had made when he looked at the site of the initial discovery. In her report, she documented intact archaeological deposits at the site, including remnants of material removed to the landfill during the early days of construction, including possible human remains. Larson alerted tribal members that, while they had been told the site was all disturbed and there was nothing there, her opinion was far different. Larson and Hartmann disagreed on the most fundamental points. He said she located the ancient beach line in the wrong place. She said he missed intact deposits—and told the tribe the site wasn't being treated as the site it was. "I told them everything I saw was intact," Larson said. "That was such a confusing time for everyone. They really trusted me."

It took longer to convince the state. In conversation after conversation with Allyson Brooks, the state historic preservation officer, Larson insisted on the site's value. "I couldn't get anyone's attention until I yelled and screamed that this site is not being treated as the site it is. It is not all disturbed, it is intact, it is enormous, it is not disturbed. I said, 'This is an intact site, a deeply stratified, intact site. I saw a site that is intact.'" Brooks well remembered Larson's early warning. "She communicated to me she felt there was a site out there, and she communicated the fact to DoT. She was criticizing Glenn's work at that point," Brooks said.

Larson contended from the outset that Hartmann misinterpreted the site in the initial assessment. She said she saw lenses of a midden where he didn't in the photographs of the initial site survey—and he missed them again when the first excavation uncovered the village.[2] "She was pretty adamant that there was something out there," Brooks said. "There was a lot of animosity between the parties and mistrust. The relationships weren't very good. It was, 'She is being a bitch, just dismiss it.' Strong women are bitches, and strong men are intelligent. They went on what Glenn found. And she was seeing things that Glenn wasn't seeing. You get into a 'he said, she said.' Glenn had just cleared the site; he doesn't want to admit he's wrong. And here's this crazy woman screaming at him, and no one wanted to believe Lynn was right. It wasn't just the tribe versus white folks, it was girls versus boys. And agencies with different

The discovery of human remains in the backfill of old utility trenches was a crushing emotional blow to the Lower Elwha Klallam Tribe. While they had always heard about their ancestors' bones being carelessly tossed aside during industrialization of the waterfront, they had not confronted proof before. The bone fragments were wrapped in white blankets and stored in cedar boxes, awaiting reburial. Here Dennis Sullivan, chairman of the tribal council, bows his head as tribal spiritual advisor Mary Anne Thomas (to his right) leads a prayer. Courtesy Lower Elwha Klallam Tribe.

agendas—you have a review agency versus a construction agency. It was so poisonous. And Lynn was being sidelined. The push to do the project was enormous. Not just at DoT. But there was congressional pressure, pressure from the legislature, and pressure from the tribe, saying they didn't want the project to stop because they want the jobs. But I think Lynn was very clear about the importance of that site. She expected human remains and an important village from the word go. When she called me, I was holding the phone out. I always laugh, because it was like when my mother's calling me and I have to hold the phone out. She's yelling, 'It's an intact village, it's a large village, there's going to be human remains.' She was screaming."

Early in September, Brooks's office was formally brought in on the project. Brooks started asking the transportation department for more information. Most important to Brooks was an analysis of the deep history of the site: the shape and location of the ancient beach line, long buried under fill dirt, where the Klallam people typically would have lived and interred their dead. "We made a big stink that we needed this paleo-landform analysis so we could understand where there was potential for archaeology," Brooks said. "It took them three or four months to do it; they were reluctant. Normally you do that before you do your archaeology. When you know what your historic landscape is, then you can direct your testing program. There was a cart and a horse, and they never were connected. That was kind of off. I'm harping away that we need some geology here, and they hear the wife at the dinner table. They did it, but it's a little late."

But even after clearing the report and a monitoring plan for going forward with construction at the site, some things weren't adding up for her. "Our office still wasn't comfortable. You have that gut feeling," Brooks said. "We kept asking for more testing. There were villages all the way through there. All of us had that feeling in the pit of our stomachs, saying, 'Oh boy, this doesn't seem like a place where nothing would be.' And you put that together with the tribe and what they were saying, how can you put all that together and say, 'This is fine'? I think everyone in the pit of their stomachs knew there was more to come. I don't think anyone knew how much. But when you have been told the site is here, and you have already paid for the land, and because of the salmon there is nowhere else to go, how do you turn back? And all the while the bridge is falling and the pressure is enormous. You stand there, and you are hoping for a break."

The tribe took the bone fragments of their ancestors to a funeral home. The bones would not have filled a cigar box. But their discovery threw a hard emotional punch that hit the tribe's unhealed wounds from historic and repeated desecration of their ancestors' graves, on this very same ground, through a century of industrialization.

The problem facing the department was quickly apparent to Colleen Jollie, tribal liaison for the Department of Transportation. Hers was not an easy job. While not enrolled in a tribe, Jollie, descended from members of the Turtle Mountain Chippewa Tribe, often found hers to be a lonely voice as the department's first tribal liaison. Jollie had camped at Alcatraz Island when Indian activists sought to take it over in the 1960s. She participated in the demonstrations for Indian fishing rights in Washington State in the 1960s and 1970s. When MacDonald offered her the job, she went to pray at what she calls her power place: a big fir tree by her former cabin in Olympia, where fish-in activists used to plot strategy. MacDonald had asked Jollie to be a cultural translator, and a reminder, for the agency. The year was 2001—not an easy time for an Indian activist to consider a job at the department. Indians had just filed a lawsuit against the agency alleging destruction of salmon habitat all over the state. Failed road culverts were blocking salmon from their spawning grounds in streambeds, the suit alleged.

"I thought, the Department of Transportation? What the hell, I'm going to work for the devil," Jollie said. "And it was this huge, big-ass agency, all engineers and accountants." But the agency was also under a new director—MacDonald—and the job would bring a significant raise in pay and more stability than her current position in the governor's Office of Indian Affairs. Jollie's office would be down the hall from the secretary, with other agency brass. It was a high-ranking position. Jollie made an offering to her power place. She buried a quill work pendant gifted to her by Buffy Sainte-Marie, the Indian folksinger, and prayed for guidance. She decided to commit to the job. But she was wary.

It turned out to be worry well placed in an agency where she was sometimes avoided. "It was like, 'Oh God, here is Colleen,'" Jollie said. "'Let's see if we can get as much of this done as we can before Colleen comes in, because she just cares about the tribes. She is going to sell us down the river.' I keep reminding people that we are on the same side, we are not adversaries. We are one Washington State. But it's 'Go behind some closed door, and don't call the tribal liaison.'" As the agency worked to find its footing after the initial archaeological discovery at Port Angeles, Jollie felt out of the loop. "I was pissed at being left out of the room or off the e-mail list. I'm a mom. And I'm incredibly intuitive. I thought, 'It's too quiet in here.' It's 'Let's leave her out and hope she doesn't catch up.' I wasn't going to be treated the way some wives are treated, nice to have on their arm but not expected to think. Or, 'You helped us get in the door, now get out of the way.' I wasn't going to be a scout. Respect and inclusion are like a good healthy marriage. It's not a marriage of convenience or image. Look at the work we have done to have a place at the table. And it is not to be there to step and fetch it." MacDonald backed her. "He genuinely supported this work and ordered them to get along with me," Jollie said of her colleagues.

When the agency sent some of its top project directors to meet with the tribe on August 25, 2003, after the initial finds, Jollie went along. In the car on the way over, she picked up Hartmann's site survey for the first time. "And I'm reading this report, and it is full of red flags and bombs. And I'm thinking, 'Oh my God, am I the only one who sees an emergency here?'" It was Jollie who would help the agency take one of its first steps in handling this project that was like no other. On the advice of the tribe, she told MacDonald the agency would have to spiritually make amends on behalf of the ancestors for the desecration of the remains. It would require a burning ceremony.

The ceremony, which had not been performed at Lower Elwha for many years, was a sacred rite intended to initiate reconciliation with the spirits disturbed in their

Mary Anne Thomas (*center*) led a sacred burning ceremony at Lower Elwha to help heal the disturbance of the ancestors in their resting place. Colleen Jollie (*right*), tribal liaison for the department, attended the ceremony along with other state transportation officials. Jollie is examining an artifact shown to her by tribal member Arlene Wheeler (*left*), August 2003. Courtesy Lower Elwha Klallam Tribe.

graves. Being asked to participate in such a private, solemn, tribal ceremony was a first for a Washington State agency. And agency members wouldn't just attend as guests. They would help do the work. The agency was also expected to help pay for the expenses of the ceremony. As the date drew near, Jollie sent out a letter to agency staff relaying the importance of the spiritual work the department was required to do on behalf of the ancestors:

> The disturbance of the cultural material has set into motion a process that the tribe feels is absolutely necessary. This is a special and ancient ceremony that is usually done in complete privacy, as it is personal and spiritual. It is a lot of work. The Tribal Council and Elders, who have come down from Canada to conduct the ceremony, have decided that it is time we found out just how much work we create for them when this kind of disturbance occurs. It's not enough to hand them a check and apologize for the expenses and inconvenience. They want to see action and a learning experience so that we will be more careful next time.
>
> This is a generous invitation. Considering the honor and opportunity to participate in this kind of private ceremony, it cannot possibly be construed as penance. It is also a time to make amends. I do appreciate how inconvenient

it is to have this kind of "cultural" spiritual activity suddenly interjected into a major construction project. I would ask you to consider, however, the great lengths we go to for ribbon cuttings, groundbreakings, annual banquets, and various celebrations of our work. This ceremony is held in such a sacred manner that I hesitated to compare them, but there you go—celebration . . . ceremony.

The ceremony is called a *burning*. We will send traditional foods, and other necessities, to the spirits of the ancestors by burning them on a cedar pyre. This is NOT going to happen at the job site, too public. It is happening at a beach site on the Lower Elwha Reservation. We will have guidance and a lot of actual help, but remember this is our responsibility, we will be expected to work. I need your help and I need you to keep a positive attitude in the process. No whining and no diminishing the importance of the work. Done properly this will speed the success of our work in many ways.

Jollie's job was enormous. Mary Anne Thomas, the tribe's spiritual advisor, handed Jollie a shopping list of groceries for two meals, one to be burned for the ancestors and another to feed to everyone else afterward. And there had to be gifts, lots of gifts for the ancestors, to be burned along with the food, sent along on the smoke to the spirit world. Jollie's first task was to take the right attitude. She would be working in a new place, with different boundaries and different rules: the spirit world. "From the start, Mary Anne said, 'You have to ask for our help in a special way. You have to start like this: "On behalf of the ancestors, will you help me do this work?"' And I repeated after her until I got it right."

Jollie asked each member of the tribal council for help with the ceremony, just that way. It was difficult. "Asking for help, acknowledging my need for help, is one of my greatest challenges," she said. "So this was a very difficult exercise for me personally. Which is probably why I got the exercise." Jollie went back to the agency to recruit colleagues to help prepare the dinner. MacDonald supported her, and he encouraged—but did not require—his top project staff to go. Jollie went up to the reservation the day before the ceremony, to get the food and gifts and to help prepare the meals.

"I had a sinking feeling that there would not be enough help, enough cooks, enough firewood, enough fire builders, enough clean-up crew. I didn't know who was going to show up, how many, what to expect from the tribal community—was there going to be 50 or 150?" A friend from the Jamestown S'Klallam Tribe, Elaine Grinnell, whose mother had been born on the Ediz Hook, came along to help. She brought a drum. "A hand drum was on the list of things that needed to be burned, so I bought one from Elaine. She makes the best—it had a deep booming voice, hand-painted, just beautiful," Jollie said. "I'm sure it was well received."

Wheeler took on the task of buying the clothes, complete outfits for every age and gender. She bought baskets to be loaded with food and burned. She bought blankets to be burned and for wrapping witnesses to the event, in a gesture of gratitude. Jerry Charles, the tribe's grave digger and Frances Charles's father, brought cords of cedar for building the table where the food would be burned. Department staff helped split and stack the cedar near the beach, arranging the wood in crossed layers over a bed of crumpled newspaper. The split logs took the shape of a table three feet high, about twelve feet long, and four feet wide. A second fire pit off to the side was created to send the clothes and blankets to the spirit world.

Meanwhile, Jollie and tribal members hit the Port Angeles Costco. It took two carts to load all the food: bags of potatoes; flour; black tea; paper tablecloths, plates, and cups; dinner rolls; rice; salad fixings; chips; pop and juices; a box of apples; oil for cooking. Then there was the seafood—oysters, clams, halibut, and salmon—some $1,100 worth, purchased by the department from the tribe.

Jollie took it all to the kitchen in the reservation's tribal center. "Every refrigerator and freezer was packed to capacity." And she needed more: cash to pay the cooks, Thomas and her extended family, and witnesses.

"So I went to the bank and got $1,500 in cash and put money in envelopes with names on them. I was sure it wasn't enough, but it was all I could get. When Doug called to tell me he was in town and was there anything he could do, I said, 'Yes, bring money!' He got $200 from his cash machine." Jollie rose at four the next day to start cooking.

When she arrived, most of the crew was already at work. Frances Charles was filleting fish. Her father, Jerry, was mixing dough. Other cooks were peeling potatoes, washing rice. By six a.m., they had already hit their stride. "It was a happy and peaceful time of cooks. I washed and cooked and opened twenty dozen oysters," Jollie said. "We had to be done by noon and completely clean the kitchen so the next crew could come in and fix dinner." Their attitude was critical, Jollie said. It had to be one of real generosity. "We could not be wanting the food we were cooking for ourselves. We had to give it freely. No covetousness. We could not be hungry. And, miraculously,

I wasn't. I didn't feel any hunger until I went back to the hotel. Mary Anne said the ancestors wouldn't take the food if they thought we wanted it."

They packed the food on paper plates, put more food in baskets, and hauled it all to the beach. Jollie headed to the Red Lion Hotel and met up with MacDonald. He never questioned that he should go to the ceremony. But he did not go alone. MacDonald liked to bring his mother, Elinor, then eighty-four but lithe and mentally undiminished, to interesting department events. He called them "Elinor's Excellent Adventures." Employees across the agency, from rock-slide repair crews on mountaintop highways to ticket takers on ferry boats, had long been accustomed to seeing their peripatetic boss with his snowy-haired mother beside him. The type of department secretary to climb the tower of a bridge under construction or get on a paving machine to learn how it works, MacDonald would show up in person for the smallest neighborhood meeting on an agency project. "When Colleen said, 'There is going to be a burning ceremony. Are you going to come?' there wasn't a moment's hesitation that the answer was yes, because it was part of doing the job," MacDonald said. "It was out of a sense of duty and obligation that is the way I do the job. You have to be there where the people are. You have a duty to go." MacDonald bundled his mother into his car and headed out to the reservation. But the burning ceremony held August 31, 2003, would be no typical department meeting.

It started with the site: a wind-raked beach on the reservation, reached by a rutted, dirt road. It fronted the blue salt water of the Strait of Juan de Fuca and was on no beachcomber's path. It was a private place, and a tribal place, on the reservation, away from tourist traffic or almost anyone who had not been invited to be there. The beach, with its gray stone cobbles big enough to turn ankles, didn't invite strolling. It was a beach for carefully placing each step. MacDonald was surprised at how much the cold wind off the strait had already chilled what had been a warm sunny day back in Seattle. A fog bank parked just off the coast, and the wind pressed in close. He settled his mother into a nylon-web lawn chair and went back to the car to root around for blankets to keep her warm. Once she was swaddled and comfortable, he walked around the beach a little. He felt awkward. "I had no idea at all about what the drill was going to be for all this, and what participation would be asked of us, if any," MacDonald said. Log by log, tribal members slowly built stacks of cedar, forming the table. "I sort of felt I didn't want to carry logs around, and I wanted to stick with my mom. So I just kind of hung."

Construction workers from the job site had turned out for the ceremony. So had some of the project's directors as well as other agency staff and their families. They mingled with tribal council members and others from the tribe. It was the first time they had met one another. "The fundamental quality of respect for what was going on was high," MacDonald said. "I think this was something Colleen orchestrated and gets the credit for. It was understood by people that the invitation to be there was important to the tribe. There was a feeling of being in someone else's church."

Tribal members began arriving with baskets of food and paper plates loaded with complete dinners: clams, halibut, salmon, oysters, potatoes, fish heads, elk, dinner rolls, soup, bread. Glass jars of black tea for drinking (Jollie would return the next morning to pick up all the shattered pieces from the jars, which had exploded in the heat). Peanut butter and jelly for the children. The plated dinners were covered with foil and labeled with the name of an ancestor to be fed. The plates were carefully placed on the table, which had been covered with white plastic held down with rocks. There were also two beautiful drums on the table. Baskets of utensils. And thousands of cigarettes. People spread blankets on the sand and piled up clothes for adults and children, carefully folded and arranged into complete outfits. There were jackets, shirts, pants, and tennis shoes for children. Even canoe paddles.

"The burning ceremony burned a lot of stuff," MacDonald said. Most of it, he noted, paid for with agency credit cards. "I remember thinking this is a little bizarre, although not nearly as bizarre as the gifting," he said, referring to the cash handed out later, in thanks, to the cooks, witnesses, and leaders of the ceremony. "You don't ordinarily, even in quarters, just hand out public money. I was sufficiently nervous that when Colleen needed $200, it was my $200. I never did expense that. It was just a contribution to the cause, and I never even thought about it. It was fine." He wasn't sure how much the agency spent in all. "I haven't a clue, and in a funny sort of way I don't want to know," MacDonald said. "And in another way I made a decision right there that this was an expense of this project. There wasn't a doubt in my mind that I wasn't going to go to any ethical jail over this because this was a project cost. But it sure was a weird way of spending money. But not in the context of what had to be done."

The fire was ready to light. Thomas first gave a lot of instructions. For starters, no one could leave until the ceremony was over. For communication with the spirits to happen, everyone had to be there. Another teaching was the importance of the smoke. It would carry the offerings to the spirits. And the spirits would come to the table on the downwind side, to receive it. The offering, Thomas said, was a gift of reconciliation, for the disruption and the trauma caused to the ancestors by the disturbance of their resting place. But while that gift of reconciliation was welcome, even long overdue, the smoke was dangerous to the living. Thomas warned participants in the ceremony not to mingle with the spirits or even touch them. It was critical to stay upwind from the smoke. To stay on the correct side of the table. To not even smoke a cigarette so as not to attract the spirits too closely.

The fire was lit. A vast flock of seagulls flew overhead, as if acknowledging the start of the rite. And then, one by one, the names on the meals, unwrapped and placed on the table, were called out. Thomas, her face painted with red ochre and her hair wrapped in a red bandanna, asked everyone to pray with her. She stood, facing the table.

The fire flared. It didn't burn fast. It climbed slowly, first licking up the wood, then reaching up and across the white cloth. The meals started to burn. Polyester jackets melted. And quietly, almost imperceptibly, with a dirgelike cadence, Thomas's prayer and song rose with the smoke, mingling with gray streamers of fog, the cold wind off the strait, and the sound of the waves, breaking on the gray stones of the beach. An agnostic, MacDonald was surprised to find himself powerfully affected. "I remember thinking, if there is a spirit between here and Mount Olympus, this spirit is coming," MacDonald said. "I don't believe there is any damn spirits. But if there is a spirit, they are hearing this, because it was permeating everything. Everyone is quiet, and the fire is starting to crackle. And the power of the fire is just incredible. And you are sitting there looking at the fire, and you are seeing the smoke and you are hearing the chanting. And the more time passes, your knees are locking and you are getting cold and you are starting to shiver. And you are worried about your mother and you are taking off your jacket. But emotionally, you are in it. Psychologically, you have been totally the captive of this thing long enough to purge your brain of distractions other than what is here. And I just think, once that purging is done and into that void comes—who knows what. And I think one of the reasons this affects me so powerfully, I don't know what I was thinking, but I know that I was thinking deep and sad. Restless, edgeless thoughts. It took a long time. And you were alone with whatever thoughts you had and whatever you were feeling or whatever was in your heart for an hour and a half."

The table burned down to glowing coals. Slowly, people started to leave. But first, everyone—the construction workers, agency project directors, MacDonald—washed their faces and hands, dipping them in metal bowls filled with a tincture of snowberries. They splashed on the water, cool and silvery, ritually cleansing their skin in case they had been accidentally spirit-touched. Stiff, cold, exhausted, they drove back to the tribal center for dinner. After all the food, after the gifts of money and acknowledgments to the celebrants of the ceremony, the speeches began. With faces tired and sombered by the ceremony, tribal council members thanked the agency for taking part in the burning. Thomas spoke first. She said that hundreds of people—the spirits of the tribe's ancestors—had come to the table and were glad for the opportunity to recognize and repair injuries going back several centuries. As such, the ceremony marked the very first step in negotiations between the state and the tribe to continue the project.

Thomas reported a clear message back from the ancestors in response to the agency's effort to reconcile the injury caused by its disturbance of their resting place. "They understand it wasn't meant to be," Thomas said. "And that you didn't do it on purpose. But they are asking respect. The elders were just so overwhelmed about getting this message through to each of us today. The work that went on today is going to clear your way. It's really up to you. But don't try to do it yourselves. Work as a team." Jerry Charles Sr., the tribe's grave digger, rose and spoke, tears grabbing at his voice. "It chokes me big time," he said of the ceremony. "I've been burying my people since the early 1960s. Down at the beach I had a good feeling. I could picture all the people I buried, grabbing their dish and sitting down. I really hope through this project we can work together. It's going to be hard. But I am hoping as we work together we can both come out winners in this. One of the biggest medicines in all this is we can work together." His daughter Frances, then on the tribal council and soon to be chairman, rose next. Through tears, she uttered the phrase that would be the watchword for this project: To succeed, the agency and the tribe would have to walk together.

"This is an opening for us all," Frances Charles said. "We are going to work together. I know we are. It's been a struggle over who has the harder heads right now. But we are all starting to walk together to what's best for all of us." Tribal chairman Dennis Sullivan spoke last. He said he was startled by the agency's willingness to come out to the reservation and honor the tribe's culture. "We thought we were all alone," Sullivan said. "We were lost. We didn't know what we were going to do. We were talking with the DoT by phone, and then they arrived and asked to come to the tribal center and meet with the tribe. In my mind it's a very historical ceremony. It's not often that you have officials join in and witness a ceremony that we had. Agencies and archaeologists didn't have to walk the site with us, but they did. We stood in a circle. We held hands. We formed a bond. We prayed together. It means so much.

They thanked us for being allowed to participate in the blessing, and we are honored you were there standing with us. When something bad happens, usually a lot of very good things come out of it. This is going to be what happens here. A lot of good things are going to happen. With our relationship. With the bond we have formed. I just thank everyone from the very bottom of my heart. My heart has just opened up with this warmth."

Together, the agency and tribe had managed to cement the beginning, however fragile, of a relationship. With its gesture of reconciliation, the agency had taken the first step in negotiations with the tribe to restart the dry dock project. But MacDonald still had no doubt, even then, that the project was in deep trouble.

He drove his mother back to Seattle and continued on to his apartment outside Olympia, another hour away. He fell into bed before dawn, spent. He got up at noon the next day, still engulfed in a bottomless sadness opened by the ceremony. "I cried for hours," MacDonald said. "It was partly the emotion of it. It was partly the exhaustion of it. And it was partly that I had not a doubt of how badly this would end. I knew then. I knew it would be awful. I didn't have any doubt about where we were going. I told my mother, this is going to be the ruination of my career. I said, this will bring me down. It is fated to be the worst thing that will ever happen to me. I knew this was going to be trouble, trouble, trouble. I had no idea what we were going to do. So my sense was of the kind of personal frustration and the institutional catastrophe of the whole thing. I didn't know everything of it, but boy, it sure got totally and completely foreshadowed by this event, and I never had the slightest illusion about that. And that weighed on me very hard."

The agency's dry dock project was on ice. Begun as a routine construction job, the project was now also an archaeological site and, ominously, a resting place for an unknown number of human remains. For starters, a new, much more comprehensive archaeological assessment was going to be needed at the site, to figure out what was there. It would all take time. It would all be expensive. Just idling the contractor cost $30,000 in taxpayers' money every day. And at the moment, MacDonald had no restart date, no game plan. "I knew it wasn't going to be easy to put together anything about what to do," MacDonald said. "And I knew there wasn't going to be any playbook for it and that it was going to be culturally complicated. And I don't undervalue what the complexities are of cross-cultural settings. I've had plenty of them and I know how hard they are. And I live in this sort of fear, or recognition, or anxiety and angst about the shallowness of the process in which you operate, and the tendency of any single thing you do to default to the worst common denominator, and the shrillness of the scapegoating, and the bullshit. I just expect that as part of the environment in which I work professionally, and when you see it coming, you say, 'Oh brother, I don't want to do this. I know where this is going.'" MacDonald headed back to work. He needed to figure out what walking together might mean.

Enough is Enough

8

Walking Together

IT WAS MID-MORNING ON SEPTEMBER 21, 2003, WHEN EXCAVATORS DOING A second archaeological survey dug up the human skull, its eye sockets staring up from the backfill of an old utility trench. For tribal members assisting in this second, much more extensive archaeological exploration, the sight was a punch to the stomach. Then they found more bones: the remains of six of the tribe's ancestors, including an infant, backfilled like so much trash in old utility trenches.

To Arlene Wheeler, who accompanied the archaeologists and other specialists digging the test trenches, the ancestors were speaking again. "Our ancestors have been disturbed enough down there," Wheeler said. "They are going to wake up not only our own people but Port Angeles that have been desecrating my people for a hundred years." Frances Charles, also helping with the new survey, wondered how to explain to the watching tribal members the bones shattered and tossed back into the ditch during the first round of construction, in 1911. And how to explain the bone fragments amid coaxial cable, adjacent to a concrete pipeline with rubber gaskets, and a 1977 Pepsi-Cola can directly beneath the conduit.[1]

After the initial discovery, transportation secretary MacDonald shut the entire job site down and ordered a three-week archaeological survey. Despite digging more than one hundred test trenches with the help of tribal members and two professional archaeological firms, the true history of this ground was still not detected. Courtesy Western Shores Heritage Services.

"The hardest thing I still carry is looking at the young ones, who were looking at the burials in the pipes, and looking at their expression: How can someone do that to another human being? And having to explain to them that Indians weren't considered human, and it was not so long ago," Charles said.

"That was their question: How could another human being treat another human being like that? They are not animals, not dogs, yet they were treated that way. That was the hardest thing. It was tearing everyone up inside." Charles kept a stoic expression down at the site. "You knew if you fell apart, everyone would fall apart. You had to be real strong with them face-to-face and then go off and do your crying. They were so young, and a lot of those burials, especially the infants and the babies, you could see the anger, you would sense the confusion, the disappointment, and the frustration, and then they would look at someone [on the department's construction crew] and want to pounce on them: 'How could you do this to our people?' Knowing it wasn't their fault. But it really did bother them and get them angry." As the survey work went on, more fragments were found. It fell to Wheeler to care for them, on behalf of the tribe.

After work at the site shut down for the day, Wheeler would go to a Department of Transportation garage in Port Angeles to fill out so-called inadvertent discovery forms with an archaeologist, coloring in the correct bone on a drawing of a human skeleton. "I was not sure if I could do this or not," Wheeler said. "I prayed about it. I actually hauled them up in my own car," she said of the bones. "I knew that this work I was doing was for my ancestors, so whatever it takes, I'll do." Wheeler cradled the pieces of bone in her palm as archaeologists filled out forms. "I would hold it, and they would look at it, what part of the cranium it was, what part of the bone, the shoulder, the arm, the toe, and we would put it in a blanket. And we actually ended up taking these individuals to the funeral home. I didn't know what I was doing. I was just being sure they were being respectful to the ancestors. I had never, ever, ever held a human part in my life. The other guys had gloves on, but I didn't. I wasn't going to put gloves on; I just held it with my bare hands."

The survey continued for more than two weeks, as archaeologists, tribal members, and other experts walked the site and dug for clues. But elders weren't brought to the site. Oral history recorded in the tribe's archives, and known by community members, wasn't consulted. A deep landform analysis still wasn't available to guide the work, to steer it along the ancient beach line, where burials, houses, hearths, and other evidence of settlement were most likely to be found. Even after digging more than eighty new exploratory trenches, and with the combined efforts of the tribe, two archaeological firms, and other state and federal experts, the reality of the important village site and cemetery just below their feet remained hidden.

But the bones in the backfill outed the guilty secret of this ground. Keeping the project going would require dealing with the history now coming into plain view. Its ugliness, ripped open by backhoes, spread like poison gas. History would now sit, invited or not, at the head of every table, at every discussion between the city, the state, and the tribe about how to proceed. For now, everyone knew there were more bones in the ground. The earliest agreements between the state and the tribe about how work might proceed acknowledged the possibility of more human remains— possibly many more—being found at the site. "We continuously told them, 'We don't know if we are in the beginning, the middle, or the end of a cemetery,'" said Dennis Sullivan, tribal council chairman at the time. Sullivan early on warned MacDonald that the department might need to consider a new location for its project.

"If many additional remains and artifacts are disturbed, the Department of Transportation must be prepared to re-evaluate their current decision to categorically exclude options to relocate or redesign the project," Sullivan wrote to MacDonald three days after he shut down the job in August 2003. But no law required the tribe's consent before work could proceed on the site, which was on state, not federal or tribal, land.

The National Historic Preservation Act allowed the parts of the village in the path of the project to be destroyed as long as archaeologists also recovered artifacts and data from a percentage of the construction site, enabling analysis and preservation of some of the site's history. But before construction could begin, the Federal Highway Administration and state historic preservation officer had to sign off on a memorandum of agreement spelling out in great detail, in an attached site treatment plan, exactly how the site would be dug. The tribe did not have to accede to the agreement or sign it. Construction could start with them or without them.

For MacDonald, though, that wasn't good enough. He told the tribe early and often that he would restart the project only with the tribe's agreement. That wasn't new for MacDonald. A former general counsel in the mid-1970s for Boston-Logan International Airport in Massachusetts, MacDonald had been at the forefront of the movement to negotiate agreements with communities and even compensate them with public dollars for the nuisance of public facilities in their midst. "This was the first time when you took public money and you didn't pay it for something you did; you did it because you owed the community for your presence," MacDonald said. A Harvard graduate with degrees in history and law, MacDonald ran the defense in a case brought by twenty-three airlines protesting the use of landing fees for mitigation agreements. The payments, and the principle they stood on, stuck. MacDonald kept at it, working in church basements and people's living rooms and at kitchen tables to find out what else could make the airport a better neighbor, from night closure rules to noise abatement agreements. He did the same thing as executive director for a water authority building new systems for sewage treatment and drinking water delivery in communities in greater Boston, with mitigation agreements for everything from the Boston Harbor cleanup to a sludge-burning plant.

"It was a powerful teaching experience that says, if you do this right, it works," MacDonald said. "A lot of community work is going out and sitting and talking to people, and the power of commitment and transparency and willingness to communicate was huge. So I go up to the Elwha Klallam dinner, and it's just work. It's just the next place I'm going to be coming for a while. I'm listening, and learning, and it's what I've done my entire life. It's not an exercise in cultural anthropology; I'm just doing what you do. What I do believe in is the ability to talk with and deal with people. I know it works, because I have done it. You can't do projects in America today that trample communities. We are not going into communities, saying we are coming in, and you better move by next month. We have come to a better place, and a good thing, too."

A veteran of two years with the Peace Corps in Africa, MacDonald also felt comfortable working in other cultural settings. "You sit in a place that is not your place and eat food that is not your food with a fork that is not your fork. You come back having learned you can be in a place that is not your place and function there," Mac-Donald said. So when his contractors unearthed the first bone in Port Angeles, Mac-Donald, while deeply alarmed, figured he at least knew what he had to try to do. He had, figuratively speaking, dealt with lots of tribes, whether they were people in Malawi, Africa, or neighbors of airports or sewage treatment plants. And, MacDonald said, "This wasn't going to be the first tribe that didn't matter." He set about gaining the tribe's consent to keep going. Besides just getting the project built, MacDonald also saw broader value in securing the tribe's agreement. "We are teaching people there is a different way of doing it," MacDonald said. "You are working against an awful lot of accumulated wisdom about how you roll people. The fundamental notion that you pat them on the head and they will go away has deeper roots than Port Angeles."

MacDonald also brought personal history to the project. A distant grandfather on his mother's side fought in the infantry, and a distant uncle was scalped in King Philip's War, the bloody Indian war in seventeenth-century colonial New England, more than 100 years before Manuel Quimper even sailed into the Strait of Juan de Fuca. "You get a little sense that even we have an oral history, and other people can, too," MacDonald said. "And the notion that there are land conflicts that involve people I know is not remote. Those stories aren't happening to someone else. They are stories I know. Those people, my people, their gravestones are in a field today in Wakefield, Massachusetts, and I know where they are. And nobody is digging up their burials."

The talks got under way in September. Pressure on the tribe to restart the project was intense from the beginning. Local business leaders hammered the tribe on the importance of the jobs the project would bring to town and the urgency of fixing the Hood Canal Bridge. The Port Angeles city council, representatives in the state legislature, and even the local congressman also urged the tribe to go along. By the first week of October, the department was already asking the tribe to allow at least some work at the site, to install a drainage system before the winter rains. The pressure continued to build. All of a sudden, the tribe, so long on the periphery of public life in Port Angeles, was the center of attention. The local state senator came calling with the gift of an elk skin. Local politicians signed a letter apologizing for past desecration of the site, evidenced by the bone fragments in the backfill of the pipe trenches. Included in the letter of apology was a promise to support the tribe—assuming work at the site continued—for the sake of the much-needed repairs of the Hood Canal

Bridge. "Everyone was just loving the tribe up," said Sullivan, the tribal chairman and suddenly a sought-after speaker at business and community events. "I was the hottest ticket in Port Angeles. We felt they were real pushy, right from the beginning. The majority of the time while we were talking, they were pushing their construction work," Sullivan said of the department. "That's when the threats started coming: If the tribe doesn't do this, we will just go on and do this with you or without you, and this goes all the way back to Washington, D.C." And still no one involved in the discussions knew for sure what lay under the ground. Larson's firm threw out an estimate of twenty-five burials, but only as a basis for estimating her fee for taking over from Hartmann as the site archaeologist, a gesture of conciliation from the department to the tribe. But twenty-five was a number, and everyone seized on it.

Yet the possibility of finding many more human remains at the site was no secret. Brooks, the state historic preservation officer, wrote in an e-mail in February, "We have the potential for a large number of human remains throughout the site." She requested direction from the state attorney general's office as to the state's legal obligation to remove all burials in the ground, not just those directly in the path of construction. A critical question. It went unanswered.

The tribe's discussion at that point was about how to build the project and respectfully remove their ancestors' remains from the state's construction site. But among tribal members, beneath the meetings and conference calls, memos, e-mails, and words about policy, procedure, and law, there also flowed another river. It was just as real as the Elwha and just as much a part of their life and culture. It was a river of memory, of dreams. Of spiritual and family connections, flowing in blood ties, to this ground. For while the tribe had lost control of the property years ago, as with the Elwha River, the site was not just any piece of land. This was the tribe's homeland, with the remains of their ancestors' belongings, bones, and blood. No decision about what to do was ever divisible from that fact, deep in every tribal member's genes.

"I was really searching for answers," Sullivan said. "I used to lay awake late at night and wake up early in the morning. Sometimes I would go out to the end of the Ediz Hook and say a silent prayer. I would ask the ancestors for guidance. I don't know that I got any." He and other council members felt both hope for what the tribe would gain if it said yes to continuing the project and dread of what would befall them if they did not. That dread was based on bitter experience.

Council members carried painful memories of what had happened in Port Angeles the last time Indian people stood up for themselves. They remembered the backlash in 1974 when the court decision was rendered in *United States v. Washington*, dividing off-reservation fishing catches equally between Indian and non-Indian fishermen. Resentment over that recognition of tribal treaty rights still simmers today in many parts of Washington State, not only in Port Angeles. Tribal council members didn't want to stoke that resentment by stopping a project the town wanted for the jobs. Mostly, they worried that it would come back at their children in the public schools. "It was, if we don't go along with this, the kids are going to pay," said Verna Henderson, a member of the tribal council. "We have to think about them. But if we don't preserve this, we are not doing the right thing by our children either."

But tribal leaders also saw an opportunity to get things they wanted: a museum and curatorial facility, like some other tribes had, and a cultural resources department. They also hoped to make right the treatment of ancestral remains disturbed at the site by prior construction. By doing the project, the tribe wanted to recover those remains from the site and finally give them a proper reburial. "We were led to believe good things might happen. There was a lot of cooperative talk about a curatorial building, a museum, help for us to find property to rebury," Sullivan said.

Negotiations over two items began at the same time: a site treatment plan, to address how the site would be dug, and a mitigation payment from the department, which the tribe hoped to use to build a curatorial facility and buy land for reburial.

The tribe was zealously represented by its lawyer, Russell Busch, of Seattle. Busch, a warrior for the Lower Elwha's causes since 1976, had been named an honorary member of the tribe for his previous work, a rare honor intended to convey the highest levels of affection and trust. Mary Anne Thomas, from the Esquimalt Nation, provided spiritual support and guidance. Thomas packed a monumental force. Hers was a moral authority inherited from a family line of shamans and chiefs, and she wielded it with practiced ease, power, and precision. Her charisma could silence a room.

History also played an important role. It sat in on every discussion, as a goad to the agency and the tribe to do better this time. But it also imposed a burden of resentment on both sides. The 1855 Treaty of Point No Point, signed just five generations back, might as well have been signed yesterday for tribal council members who were once again dealing with non-Indians in their homeland, wanting something. "I know what they felt like now when they had to sign that treaty," Henderson said. "And then they wanted to start talking about money. I always say, 'Remember Manhattan.'" Agency staff in turn resented being held captive by a history they didn't create. "It was awful," said Steve Reinmuth, then a lawyer in the transportation division of the state attorney general's office. "It was, 'You guys, you people.' We walked in as the big government, threatening the little tribe." It seemed impossible, at times, to establish what he wanted: the sense of a fresh start between people of good faith, working together for a common goal. Without that, Reinmuth couldn't see how the negotiations could go anywhere. "Maybe it was naïveté on my part," said Reinmuth. "I said, 'I can't believe that you would sit here and say "We don't care," and you have to knock it off.' We weren't going to get anywhere if it was just 'We don't care, we don't care, we don't care.'"

Jollie, the department's tribal liaison, understood the tribe's skepticism. "They saw us as those white government workers, 'We know your type. You're going to just plow us over.'" It didn't help, Jollie said, that when bones had been first discovered at the site, the department's site manager, Jerry Moore, got into an argument with Frances Charles that instantly became legend on the reservation. "I said, 'How would you like it if we dug up your mother's grave?'" Charles said. "'It's no big deal'—that was his attitude about it. It was like, 'So what? Just move it.' It was like a stone face, with no heart. To him, it's his job. His responsibility. And 'I'll be damned if Indians will tell me what to do.' He told us, there will be no delay in the project. His attitude was, this project is not going to stop." That attitude got no support at the top of the department, where Jollie and others were working hard to earn the tribe's trust. But the argument fed the tribe's worst expectations about dealing with the department. "Talk about an uncanny ability to lead with the wrong foot," Jollie said. "We paid for that. They would not believe that we were there with good intentions to make things right. They were expecting the old school. The 'This is the way it's always done, and we don't care about you. We don't even care about our own grandmothers.' And they saw that face, so who could blame them? How could I be any different? Or Doug [MacDonald]?"

But in truth, many at the department, and outside of it, didn't support negotiating an agreement with the tribe. "All the lawyers in my office were like, 'What the hell are you doing? That's not the way it's done,'" Reinmuth said. "There was discussion

Tough-minded and outspoken, spiritual leader Mary Anne Thomas (*right*), who married into the Esquimalt Nation in British Columbia, provided crucial and influential guidance to tribal members. Courtesy Lower Elwha Klallam Tribe.

early on about an option the department had to just notify the tribe and move on. There were a lot of people internally saying, 'We pave things over all the time. It's OK.' Well, it might have been OK for the state in the past, but not this time. We made a fundamental decision to get together with the tribe and work this out. Throw it out the window. The playbook's gone."

While the department was taking heat from local politicians and business leaders in Port Angeles, Reinmuth was also picking up little sympathy for the tribe. "There was a sense among the state representatives and local folks that we have dealt with the tribe before; we can do this," Reinmuth said. "It was a kind of, 'Go pat them on the head and it will be OK.'" But it wasn't OK at the Department of Transportation. "Our clear direction was 'Make this right,'" Reinmuth said. "You reach for the law, but ultimately you are talking about matters of the spirit and of the heart." And that required new ways of doing things. Way beyond Post-Its, faxes, e-mails, and conference calls. Department staff scheduled meetings at the reservation instead of at their government offices. They held hands in prayer circles at the site. They shared meals, cooked by tribal elders, at the tribal center. As they walked the site, some agency staff wore red ochre, stroked on their faces by the fingers of tribal members seeking to protect them from the spirits of the ancestors. "That crossed some lines," Reinmuth said. "It bothered me initially. It ultimately didn't bother me. It felt like it was a dominance thing. Was it really about protecting you or about telling you what to do?" And while some tribal council members said they felt threatened, so did some agency staff. "Mary Anne [Thomas] would effectively summon the spirits and say that terrible things would happen to people who didn't understand what the tribe wanted," Reinmuth said.

Randy Hain, administrator of the department's Olympic region, also took a lead role in the negotiations. He often felt uncomfortable. It started with the total shutdown of the project by MacDonald, beyond the area of the initial find. The shutdown disrupted every contractual agreement that had been carefully put in place to build the project on time and on budget. For Hain, it was a departure from the ways of doing business he had learned in more than thirty years at the department. He was used to having clear lines of authority within the agency and sticking to contractual agreements with anyone outside of it. For Hain, the terms of interaction and negotiation with the department were set only by agency policy and state regulation.

The shutdown would be only his first surprise. The second was when MacDonald showed up during Hain's briefing on his first day at the site, arm and arm with Thomas.

Then, as Hain spoke, the two walked off together for a private discussion of their own. Hain, still talking, watched with amazement out of the corner of his eye. Suddenly, not only had the usual line of authority on the project jumped, with one gesture, to the highest level of the department, but MacDonald's inclusion of the tribe's spiritual leader was a literal embrace of values MacDonald had signaled would be as much a part of this project as anyone's rule book.

"I thought two things," Hain said. "Number one, wrong basis. And number two, I knew at that moment, on the first day, that I had lost all authority to speak on behalf of this project." That arm-in-arm walk was an invitation and a welcome from the department's most senior executive, a kind of talking and listening that opened new channels, fed from different headwaters. And they would eventually flow, in a way not seen or felt in this town since the Elwha was dammed to power the mills built over Tse-whit-zen. With that walk together, MacDonald signaled an invitation to a larger walking together: building the project by accommodating each other's values and needs, to mutual benefit.

Hain picked his way carefully, working to build a relationship with the tribe from scratch while remaining true to himself—and the agency's imperatives of schedule and budget. He had his limits. He politely refused when Thomas urged him to wear red ochre at the site. And he turned Jollie down flat when she invited him to the burning ceremony. "I am not going to go up there and act like I'm down on my hands and knees," Hain said. He also told Jollie he was appalled by the burning of clothes and food bought with public money.

The open-ended nature of much of the negotiations with the tribe also drove both Hain and Reinmuth nuts. A meeting agenda for talks held on the tribe's territory was considered rude. "That drove the lawyer in me crazy," Reinmuth said. "What was amazing to me was all the subplots," Hain said. "I have never in my career at the Department of Transportation of thirty-plus years faced a situation where it has been quite this emotionally draining. It was an emotional roller-coaster." Hain and Reinmuth struggled to keep the process on track. "As a consultation model, it broke every rule you learn," Reinmuth said. "It was just, keep talking until you agree. You thought you had an agreement and then you would find that you didn't." Weeks turned into months, as the job site sat idle at a cost to the public of about $30,000 a day.

Meanwhile, Reinmuth's kids learned how to make fry bread. Somewhere, he turned an internal corner. He saw the situation differently from the way staff at agencies and congressional offices in the other Washington saw it, wondering what was

U.S. congressman Norm Dicks (*front, left*) and his staff with the tribal council as Frances Charles, then a council member, helps lead the discussion. This meeting, in the winter of 2003, held in council chambers at the reservation's tribal center, was one of many, as the transportation department, local community, and political power structure turned up the pressure on the tribe to restart the project. Courtesy Lower Elwha Klallam Tribe.

taking so long. "It was interesting to watch staff from D.C. come out in their Prada shoes for their quick tour of the site," said Reinmuth, himself long past quick tours, or anything quick at all, for that matter.

Two months turned into three. Then four, then five. Then six. Communication proved a struggle for both sides. "We are like ships passing in the night, and it's not dark," wrote tribal staff member Ralph Kopansky in an e-mail sent December 23, four months into the negotiations. "We have given WSDOT stipulations on mitigation, which includes the property and curatorial facility. They say yes, then they seem to disappear." And then there was Hain's trip out to the reservation, a drive of more than two hours each way, to get a signature from the tribal council on an agreement to allow drainage work at the site. A simple errand, he thought. "All I'm going to do is walk in and have them sign this and it's, 'Can you excuse us?'" Hain said. He waited on a couch outside the council chambers—room 13 at the tribal center, as it happens. "An hour and a half later, I'm called back in, and it's, 'We're really disappointed you have come up here to get this signed. We are really disappointed it's not Doug [MacDonald], and it really should be the governor for this to truly be government to government. So we are not signing this today.'" But since Hain had driven all the way up, council members invited him to join them at the tribal center's dining hall for lunch, saying they would be down in a minute. "What I really felt like doing was getting in the car and driving away," Hain said. He went down to the dining hall. "I'm here with all these tribal people, and a biologist finally said, 'Can I help you?'" Hain sat down to wait for the council. "They never came back," Hain said. "I got a few things on a plate and stuffed it in my face. I thought, that's a great way to treat people."

But finally, on March 16, 2004, seven months after shutting the job down, the state, tribe, and federal agencies reached agreement on restarting the project. The site treatment plan executed as part of the memorandum of agreement committed to extensive archaeological exploration and analysis of portions of the site destroyed by the project. Artifacts, field records, and photographs from the archaeological dig were to be repatriated to the tribe and curated at state expense until the tribe could provide a permanent facility. The department and federal agencies were to work with the tribe to find sufficient land for reburying human remains discovered during the archaeological dig. The department was to pay the tribe for employing tribal members at the site. The tribe and the department were also to cooperate in the creation of a public education program that would include an interpreter, a video, a community meeting in Port Angeles, and an educational curriculum for elementary and secondary school students.

Under the site treatment plan, the state committed to paying an estimated $4.6 million for a predicted fourteen weeks of fieldwork, digging about 6 percent of the intact archaeological deposits in four areas of the site. That payment would include up to $800,000 paid to the tribe to hire as many as 100 tribal construction monitors, who would shadow construction workers, and professional archaeologists to watch for human remains and artifacts wherever the site was being dug. The monitors would actually pace the work by checking the ground, centimeter by centimeter, for their ancestors' bones and belongings before excavators could disturb the site for construction. The $4.6 million would also pay for about twenty-four months of analysis of data from the site and a report documenting what the site revealed about the early Klallam people and their village.

In a side agreement, the department also paid $3.4 million to the Lower Elwha Klallam Tribe in return for the tribe's agreement to allow the project to restart by April 1, 2004. In this agreement, the tribe also gave up its right to sue the state for any claim arising from the project.

The side agreement helped clinch the deal. Wrapped up in it were some of the tribe's most closely held hopes, to finally have the money to create a cultural resources program and have a museum, like many other tribes. It also wanted to buy land for the reburial of human remains disturbed in previous development of the site and long awaiting proper reburial. The payment was both novel and controversial among some regulators and archaeologists. "The mitigation payment was unprecedented and a matter of concern," said Ken Ames, professor and chair of anthropology at Portland State University and president, in 2006, of the Society of American Archaeologists. "It establishes a precedent nationally, in which people are being paid in a sense to do things that are required by law. It is probably a bad idea. The state agency could have gone ahead and done the project, and in terms of precedence that is probably what they should have done. And I think it is very strange, very odd. It establishes a precedent which people can follow and require state agencies or federal agencies to make a payment for doing something they had a legal right to do. The payment is troubling. From the outside, it looked like, what's the "b" word—it looked like a bribe. I would rather they had not done it."

But to the signatories, the agreements represented hard-earned high hopes for the work that they were about to begin together. Sullivan, then chairman of the council, and Hain signed the agreement not at the tribal center or at the state capitol but in an agency conference room in a town midway between the two. "It was this cheesy little conference room," Reinmuth said. "There was a microwave with a Cup o' Noodles on it. But someone spoke of how the spirits were there that day. It was warmer and sunny, and whatever religious belief you brought, whatever your worldview, everyone had a sense it was right. Everyone breathed this huge sigh of satisfaction, that we had done a good job and it was the right thing to do."

Work at the site began at once. Construction, archaeological data recovery, and burial removals went on at different locations at the same time. Archaeologists dug one-meter-square grids at selected locations, so that they could record artifacts, structures, hearths, and other archaeological features in their precise location. Human remains encountered in the grids or in the path of construction were removed under the supervision of archaeologists paired with tribal members. The tribal workers slowly, tenderly took their ancestors' bones out of burial boxes, cedar mats, and final resting places, one brush stroke and prayer at a time. Meanwhile, tribal members also worked at screening platforms, picking their ancestors' bones and belongings out of dirt dug from the site. Tribal construction monitors also hand-troweled through piles of dirt, gingerly lifted ten centimeters at a time by excavators. Their task was to clear the ground for construction by checking the area first for archaeological material and human remains. As weeks went by, heavy-equipment operators were building roads,

After six months of painful negotiations, the tribe signed an agreement allowing the project to go forward. The department hired more than one hundred tribal members to work at the site alongside archaeologists from all over the country. Here tribal construction monitors carefully comb the ground for their ancestors' bones and belongings, as an equipment operator waits to proceed with his backhoe. Steve Ringman, courtesy *Seattle Times*.

Tribal spiritual advisor Mary Anne Thomas starts the workday at the construction site with instructions for the department of transportation crew. The tribe sought to teach the department that this was no ordinary construction site; it was sacred ground. Courtesy Lower Elwha Klallam Tribe.

digging trenches, vibrating massive metal sheet piles into the ground, and doing other heavy construction work to build the dry dock. But this was no ordinary construction job. From the very beginning, contractors found themselves stopping and working around archaeology or burials as the ground was opened like a panoramic window into the past.

The tribal members on the job were paid about twelve dollars an hour, the best money some of them had ever earned. The job also drew archaeologists, self-described shovel bums, from all over the country. They camped out in their trucks, slept in travel trailers, and packed the local motels. They filed weekly summary forms describing their finds, like court reporters recording the testimony of a witness revealing all that had happened in the long history of this site. They found pieces of milled lumber and corrugated roofing. Scattered fragments of human remains, sawdust, copper power line, Styrofoam, and plastic water lines. They noted gravel and brick and metal fragments. Woody debris. A cedar plank box. A woven mat.

"Disturbed and damaged human remains continue to be recovered," an archaeologist noted in April 2004. "A six foot concrete pipe cuts diagonally through this area. Bones are in the pipe fill zone. Human remains are disarticulated, scattered and often crushed." They found kneecaps and thigh bones and pieces of bone too small to identify. They found industrial-sized belt rollers and human vertebrae. "Began screening half a track hoe bucket of material that came out from under a very compact layer," an archaeologist wrote on April 6, 2004. "No inventory yet. But basically have both legs and most of the skull from a robust individual." They found old wooden pilings from the mill, driven right through burials. "Collection of human remains continues," an archaeologist wrote on April 1, 2004. "A pit feature is evident, with at least four individuals recovered so far. Cedar, possibly woven, fish bone are occasionally coming up. There is a wood piling driven through the center of this feature that has affected the conditions of the remains."

They found railroad ties, bricks, and cobble. They found asphalt on top of fill dirt, imported to the site, laid down like frosting over sand. And then the fragments of a skull and a human skeleton lying on its left side. They found human neck bones and teeth and the thick shaft of a thigh. Then another human skeleton placed in a fetal position: a pelvis, leg bones, bits of spinal column, arm bones, skull fragments. The rest had been crushed during earlier industrial development. They also found human remains probably inadvertently crushed by department contractors.

"Bones were found in a low spot that was previously brought down to grade by a bulldozer," an archaeologist wrote. "Cranial bones are fragmented and were all found along the A line, running east west, likely due to the act of bulldozing." They found cardboard and diesel fuel stains. Two-thirds of a thigh bone found on March 16 seemed to match up with the rest of the leg found the day before. They found ground so mixed up and disturbed that the top two meters were a blend of wood from construction of the Big Mill along with asphalt, concrete, bricks, pipes, buried tree branches, human jawbones, and teeth, all suffused with "a strong unnatural odor." The material had been dug and transported several times, the archaeologists noted.

There were chunks of lumber. Pebbles. Cobbles. There were intact beach sand deposits from the ancient beach line. They found bone points for hunting. A fire hydrant. Gravel. Bricks. Shards of metal. Then, less than two weeks after signing the agreement allowing construction to proceed, archaeologists found the first intact Indian burial.

The skeleton was wrapped in a cedar mat, in a flexed position, knees to chest. The skull faced toward the rising sun. When told the news, MacDonald said, it took his breath away. In continuing work at the site, one of the things he and the tribe had hoped for was healing. The idea was that bones found during construction, shattered in earlier work at the site, could be removed and given the proper burial needed to reconcile the history of this ground. But suddenly, his department was creating new disturbance, new grief, new anguish. His agency was uprooting intact ancestral Indian burials.

9

Walking Away

THEIR PICKUPS AND CAMPERS FILLED THE DRIVEWAY OF A SIMPLE BLUE HOUSE
hard by the highway leading into Port Angeles, a makeshift lab for sorting through
the artifacts dug from this village site. The word "lab" conjures images of gleaming
surfaces and white-coated experts with pipettes of glistening liquid held up for squint-
eyed inspection. This, the archaeologists' lab was decidedly not. The first impression
on coming in the front door was of claustrophobic clutter: people, bags, boxes, trays,
stacks and piles everywhere. Plastic sheeting on the floors tracked with mud and dirt.
A large bottle of ibuprofen on the kitchen counter, its label papered over with a
handwritten one: Prozac.

The house was a hive of people, hard at work. And like the site, the house brought
together people from two different worlds: professional archaeologists doing the scientific work of data recovery and tribal members surrounded by the bones, belongings,
and spirits of their family members. As the archaeologists picked through trays of
matrix, taking out bits of bone and shell for analysis, tribal member Amy Carter
worked at a card table set up in the living room, a candle burning on the mantelpiece

just overhead in honor of her ancestors. Carefully, patiently, she recorded in a ledger the labels on bag after bag of material dug from the site. "I was just a house mom; I didn't have a permanent job before all this started," said Carter, formerly a night manager at a fast-food restaurant. "I wanted to know. It was just curiosity. This is part of my history, and I see myself as a caretaker kind of person. This is my way of wanting to know how they were being taken care of, actually identifying bones, looking at the etched stones, the projectile points."

Just holding the bone harpoon points cut with stone tools, sanded smooth, each a different size depending on the animal it was used to kill—seal, salmon, otter—amazed Carter. "It makes me wonder, the time and the patience [it took] to make these," she said. Archaeologists seated around her picked through trays of material with tweezers or the side of a credit card to find the ear bone of a fish, the leg bone

Back at a makeshift lab in a house in Port Angeles, archaeologists and tribal members worked to sort and log every artifact (čəćən) for later analysis. Courtesy Washington State Department of Transportation.

Archaeologists came from around the country to work at the Tse-whit-zen site, which some called the opportunity of a lifetime. Here tribal members and archaeologists sort artifacts and bits of bones and shell from soil. The bags piled up at the right have yet to be sorted. Courtesy Washington State Department of Transportation.

of a bird, a bit of mussel shell amid the gravel. The popular image of the swashbuckling archaeologist as Indiana Jones had no place here. These archaeologists spent far more hours in the lab than at the site, drying, sorting, and cataloguing samples. As word of the importance of the site spread, the staff assembled a box of artifacts, a kind of collection of greatest archaeological hits. They kept it handy for the few visitors allowed in here, who, under supervision and with the tribe's permission, could actually hold the artifacts in their hands.

There were hairpins crafted from pieces of bone, no longer than the lifeline of an adult's palm. Smooth and creamy colored, they were carved in the shapes of animals—perhaps the head of a fawn or a fish. There was a stone adze, cool and heavy in the hand, made from dense, black nephrite rock shaped and polished glassy smooth. It would have been hafted to a handle and used to chip out canoes from cedar logs

This hairpin shows the fine work done by craftsmen at Tse-whit-zen, where an abundance of food left the winters free for song, ceremony, protocol, and art. Courtesy Lower Elwha Klallam Tribe.

and hew cedar house planks. A bone comb, as long as a woman's hand, was carefully carved front and back into the shape of two musing cormorants. Their delicate beaks just touched, forming an arch over a crouching human figure. Nearly every long, slender tooth of the comb was still intact. A gleaming, obsidian projectile point, chipped into shape with stone, was still sharp enough along its edge to cut skin. And everywhere there was more: on trays arrayed in baker's racks, in boxes in the closets, in the basement, along the walls, in the bedrooms. The volume of material was staggering, with 10,000 Ziploc quart bags catalogued by late summer of 2004, and much more still to go. The archaeologists heaped laundry baskets full with cobble spalls. Boxes, stacked to the ceiling, sometimes cascaded to the floor in what the staff called "boxalanches." On sunny days, the front lawn was covered with trays of gravelly matrix dug from the site, drying.

Meanwhile, over at Tse-whit-zen, more material was being dug every day. Heavy construction work was under way, with contractors digging trenches, building roads, grading and excavating, pouring concrete, and using a machine to vibrate steel sheet piles deep into the ground, to enclose the pit that would form the dry dock.

At the same time, archaeologists were laying out and excavating their meticulous grids and recording the location of each item found in the layers of the earth. That

For some Lower Elwha tribal members, working at the site was their first encounter with their culture. Steve Ringman, *Seattle Times*.

way, everything they found would have a reference point in place and time, to give it context and inform its meaning. Meanwhile, tribal construction monitors kept an eye on the backhoe buckets, looking for artifacts and human remains. They picked through piles of dirt, sometimes on their hands and knees. For them, the work wasn't science. They weren't doing data recovery from a site. They were combing their homeland by hand for their ancestors' bones and belongings. The clash between their personal, cultural bond to the site and the science the archaeologists were committed to had consequences. The tribe decided it wanted no analysis of the human remains found at the site or of the earth clinging to them. This meant that no scientific understanding of the age of the bones or documentation of a link to an epidemic could be gained from the burials.

And there were arguments. Thomas, the spiritual advisor, demanded that a dog found at the site be reburied without documentation or analysis. It was, she decided, probably a family pet and should rest in peace. That prompted a stern e-mail from

As they worked side by side at the site, the job became personal and friendships developed, all the way up to the highest levels of the Lower Elwha Klallam Tribe and the department of transportation. Here Elinor MacDonald (*seated*), the transportation secretary's mother, examines an artifact with tribal spiritual advisor Mary Anne Thomas during MacDonald's tour of the site. Courtesy Lower Elwha Klallam Tribe.

Allyson Brooks, the state historic preservation officer, to the Department of Transportation, demanding that Thomas get in line. "Mary Anne's behavior on the site is extremely troublesome," Brooks wrote in July. "We agreed to consider removing her from the site if she continues to give direction to the archaeologists. She has no authority under state or federal law to be providing direction on methodology. . . . This problem needs to be corrected. Her role was to say a prayer over the human remains after they were appropriately excavated by archaeological teams. Anything other than this violates state law." But tribal members felt that they and Thomas, not the archaeologists, were the experts on how their own ancestors and the belongings of those ancestors should be treated. Resentment also went deep over the dictum that tribal members could not exhume their ancestors' bones unless they were under the direction of a professional archaeologist. But to Brooks, spiritual values were muddying her job of following the March agreements governing work at the site.

"We have a separation of church and state. Well, they didn't sign up for that," Brooks said of the tribe. "It throws into chaos what we as government officials have to do. We have no way to respond to religious values. I would try to talk to Mary Anne about what we need to do at the site and she wants to talk about spirits, and

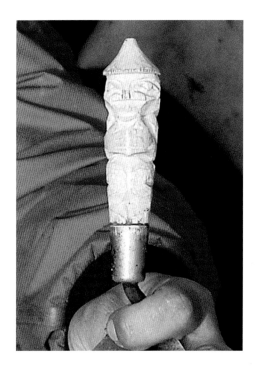

Some tribal members carved the handles of trowels and other common hardware-store items for use at the Tse-whit-zen site and shaped small scrapers from cedar for the most delicate tasks, such as digging graves. The tools helped provide comfort and strength for difficult work. Courtesy Lower Elwha Klallam Tribe.

you can't interrupt, or you are rude. You can't dialogue. You have a spiritual advisor whose role is to tell you about the voodoo that is done so well, and I'm sorry, I'm just here to implement the law."

Brooks hadn't attended the burning ceremony or approved of the department helping to pay for it. "I don't see people coming to the Department of Natural Resources on Yom Kippur and saying, 'I had a bad year—give me a goat,'" Brooks said. "There are starving kids out there without clothes. I am just a big redneck about this." She dismissed the tours of the burial tents and boxes in the bunker, which tribal members conducted for selected visitors, as "the trail of tears."

But people also developed friendships and mutual respect across barriers of race, class, and education while they worked at the site. Partly, it was the excitement. Together, working in the dirt, tribal members, archaeologists, and construction workers employed by the state's contractor found museum-quality artifacts every day. The site grew to some 1,200 features—living areas, cooking areas, ceremonial areas, and more, spread across three acres of beach berm and landforms. Slowly, on parts of the site, a picture emerged of more than 2,700 years of continuous use. There were houses and refuse pits dating back 500 years. Post molds, house posts, vertical planks, and stone hearths dating back as far as 1,800 years. Hearths for reducing red clay to ochre powder for ceremonial use were even older, dating to 2,700 years ago.

The presence of houses and other structures along with cooking areas, tools, and other artifacts offered a rare trove of clues to the past, said archaeologist Lynn Larson, principal investigator for the site. "Usually, we get a piece of a site. Here we get the whole thing, where the houses were, the cooking areas, the ceremonial areas, the drying racks," Larson said. "Here we have all of it. For us, it's a once-in-a-lifetime opportunity." The assemblage of stone and bone tools was also spectacular, Larson said. "It's the biggest assemblage we have ever seen, and it is over such a long period of time. There are barbed harpoon points in ten styles."

The large number of tools can shed light on the technology used by early peoples, and the variation of styles can teach about the interconnections among the peoples of the Strait of Georgia, the Strait of Juan de Fuca, and Puget Sound. Tools are also a clue to diet. Leonard Forsman, chairman of the Suquamish Tribe, a neighboring

One of the best things about the discovery of the site, tribal leaders say, was that it gave tribal youth the chance to discover their culture with their own hearts and hands. One worker at the site, Lower Elwha Klallam tribal member Phillip J. Charles, even decided to teach himself how to make replicas of his ancestors' tools. "To actually get out there and find things your great-great-grandpa may have used, was pretty exciting. I would try to imagine who these people were, what they looked like, how their lives were," Charles said. Steve Ringman, *Seattle Times*.

Lower Elwha Klallam tribal member Mark Charles remembers finding this spindle whorl (sisúy̓ətəŋ) and the thrill of learning that it was carved from a single whale vertebra. Charles said he was guided to the find by intuition. "Something just told me, keep digging," he said. Courtesy Lower Elwha Klallam Tribe.

tribe, said the uncovering of the tools and belongings of the Lower Elwha people's ancestors rekindled the tribe's sense of itself. "The artifacts are important for the tribe because they provide them with some inspiration for future artistic endeavors," Forsman said. "It also gives validation to their identity, which is always important for Indian people, because we have so many threats to our culture and our way of life from the disconnect that occurred during assimilation. It helps us get stronger in a cultural way."

The variety and number of structures also was a valuable find, Larson said. "We were delirious to have more than one house. That was a huge surprise, and the zonation of the houses, on the berm, with the cooking areas behind them, that was very surprising to me. The ochre-processing pit is even farther south; we have never seen that before. Usually houses and camps and cooking areas are next to each other, not stacked from north to south. One of the houses at the site may even be a dancehouse or potlatch house."

Dennis Lewarch also found the 2,700-year span of use in parts of the site unusual. Other sites, such as the Makah village site of Ozette, out on the coast of the Olympic Peninsula, don't go back as far in time. And the West Point site in Seattle shows only a partial view into the past. A wastewater treatment plant was built over parts of the site, leaving only the oldest and newest areas for excavation.

For some tribal youth, working at the site was the first exposure to their culture. Courtesy Lower Elwha Klallam Tribe.

"A lot of sites don't go as long in time as this one, and you don't have continuous occupation," Lewarch said. "We had that at West Point, but we couldn't sample it because of the location of the treatment plant. The period from about 2,500 to 1,500 years ago we are missing. We had early and late, but not the middle part. The question is, when did the ethnographic pattern start? Was it 1,000 years ago, or 1,500, or 2,000? What we can see at Tse-whit-zen is it was at least 2,700 years ago, and it helps cement that understanding."

The site also rendered thousands of animal bones that can help tell the story of ancient wildlife biology at the site and teach about the seasonality, species diversity, and even the size of salmon long ago in the Elwha River.

Tse-whit-zen also offers a look at a different ecology, because of its position on the outer Strait of Juan de Fuca. And its preservation was remarkable, said Ken Ames, the archaeologist at Portland State University. Ames visited the site when it was first uncovered. "The thing I remember was the extraordinary quality of the preservation," he said. "I was amazed. This was an extraordinarily well-preserved site. And unlike Ozette, which is not that old, it also had the potential for looking at a slice across more than one piece of time. It's of unparalleled importance in the way this gives us

Tribal member Michael Q. Langland was thrilled to find a stone maul amid the construction debris at the site. Courtesy Lower Elwha Klallam Tribe.

access to that in an area that is not that well known archaeologically. What is emerging is a set of data for the North Olympic Peninsula. It is ecologically distinct, in that it's on the open strait, and that is different from a lot of what we know now. In terms of a vantage point from which to look at things to go on, regionally, it might be quite an interesting vantage point. And then there is the sheer scale of the project, and the sheer number of things."

The site also may be the only one in the Northwest that provides an archaeological record of the epidemics that struck down the Native peoples of the Northwest Coast. "We have been looking for something from that time period, but we never found any evidence of that contact period," Lewarch said. "The thing that is really important here is there has been all kinds of speculation. There is the historic documentation, but what actually happened to the people? And here is some concrete evidence about what happened and the cultural response to the crisis. That is just invaluable. We see what did happen to the people. We kind of know some of those things that are in the written documents, but here is a really large burial population and lots of information on that."

The etched stones found at the site are also unique, in their sheer number and their range of styles and forms. The first time an etched stone was found north of the ochre pit, nobody knew what it was. Wheeler remembers showing it to Thomas, the spiritual advisor. "That was a moment I will never forget," Wheeler said. "She had that smile on her face. She said, 'I know what this is.'" The lines and shapes etched in the gray stone were not doodles, Thomas said, but inscriptions with meaning. One stone was marked four times: for the brain, for good memory; for the eyes, to protect self-esteem; for the nose, to breathe in and out; and for the mouth, to always have a voice. More than 800 etched stones were found at the site altogether, more than at any other single site in the Northwest. No two were alike, and some were more than 1,000 years old. There were weaving patterns. Instructions for blessing a pool of water before drinking. A stone to hold to the cheek, to catch the tear of a bereaved spouse. Some stones were for healing rituals, and the large number found at the site may indicate efforts to stem or treat epidemics in the village, such as smallpox.[1]

Some stones depicted entire ceremonies, such as the proper way to reintroduce tribal members to eating certain foods after losing a family member in death, Thomas said. Those ceremonies are still practiced in Klallam culture today—but no one had seen the stones that hold the knowledge. At Tse-whit-zen, that circle was reconnected. Tribal members also found a large round rock in the big house, just where the late spiritual leader subiyay (Bruce Miller) of Skokomish said it would be. With a great-grandmother who had been married at Tse-whit-zen, he knew of the big house and knew of this village. After visiting the site, subiyay's family gifted back a song to the Lower Elwha from Tse-whit-zen that had been held in his family through the marriage tie. "You start thinking about all the different things that have been coming to us and that have been brought in front of us," Wheeler said. "It was overwhelming. Each day every one of us, when we come through those gates to the site, we ask the ancestors for permission to be here and pray to the Creator to ask them to open your eyes and ears and give you what you are supposed to see and hear and find."

It was the first time any tribal member had worked at an archaeological site—and going into it, most didn't like the idea of archaeology. "I couldn't tell a rock from a bone. I didn't know anything," said Michael Q. Langland, a tribal member whose prior jobs included working in the tribe's river restoration program and at its fish hatchery; selling beads; and working as a welfare caseload manager, a truck driver, and a forklift operator. "I had never used a trowel; I had never done that kind of work. Basically, my impression of [archaeologists] was they just robbed graves. I had no idea what they did. They had us measure off an area into a block and we would dig. There I am, a fifty-year-old man on my hands and knees."

But Langland figured out a way to work that blended their science and his culture. "I would go to a certain spot and say a prayer every morning to my ancestors for allowing me to be on their land, our land, and that whatever it was I was doing, it wasn't

Uncovering the posts of a longhouse at Tse-whit-zen thrilled members of the Lower Elwha Klallam Tribe. Courtesy Washington State Department of Transportation.

out of disrespect and to protect me from anything evil," Langland said. "I never, ever took it for granted. It was an honor to be there. I know it changed my life, the way I look at everything, the way I perceive myself."

The first thing he found was a stone maul, used by his ancestors to soften leather. In another part of the site, he realized he was in a cooking area, one of his ancestors' kitchens. He found all kinds of shells, tools, hooks, mauls, an adze, hammers, bone points, urchin shells, antlers, fish-cutting spalls, and bones carved into harpoon points. He sometimes felt guided by his ancestors to what he found. "I had dreams that I could not interpret at first, but they were very powerful. It was the ancestors' way of thanking me for what I was doing," Langland said. "We had been digging in the same spot for a while and got to an area where we thought everything had been depleted, and we were going to do one last pass. I was standing off to the side and looked into this big mound, where the excavator was putting the soil, and something just caught my eye. It was almost like someone guided me there; it wasn't that there was any reason to look there. I started troweling around. I didn't know how fragile it would be, and the color of the soil was an indicator, too. It was very black. I exposed it a little more. Then I pulled it out with my hand; it was just caked. With a lot of work, I tapped it clean with a cedar tool. It was an eight-point barbed harpoon point, ten inches long. I held it up and did a little dance. When you would find something really cool, you would go around and show it to everyone."

As they discovered more burials at the site, tribal members' feelings shifted from excitement to grief. Here they work alongside archaeologists in a burial tent to take the bones of their loved ones out of the path of construction, November 2004. Steve Ringman, courtesy *Seattle Times*.

Langland found more than his ancestors' tools and belongings at the site. "I saw my grandfather down there. I saw other ancestors; I heard voices, heard songs. It was a once-in-a-lifetime experience. It was very spiritual. When you have things like that happen to you, it is going to change your life. I took this very seriously. I think I am more patient, loving, caring, considerate. I feel better about myself. It changed me for the good. It made me a kinder person. Being down there, it was just something the moment I set foot there, the first time I could feel the presence, how powerful the site was. I am more in touch with my culture now. It humbled the hell out of me. It was a very spiritual experience, very healing. Peace. That is what I found."

As the ground slowly revealed its secrets, elders, who had been silenced for years about their own cultural knowledge, also began to share what they knew. For the first time, elder Johnson Charles Jr. got out a family photograph of his father, born in the last smokehouse along the Elwha River. Johnson hung the photo of his father, wearing the paint of a blackface dancer, on his living room wall. "I was really surprised when he brought that out," said tribal chairman Frances Charles. "I didn't ever remember it being on the wall. Generations had been told it was evil. They were told there was a generation that turned bad. That the medicine men were paid to harm people. We were told we were wrong. We didn't do the ceremonies and the dances. We didn't wear the paint. The elders were told not to talk about it anymore. Some were burned on their hands or whipped. As time itself has showed it on the site, some of the elders started slowly sharing with us what their grandparents did and the things they were told not to talk about. And they would just sit there and cry. Even within ourselves, you had some that didn't have the teachings. They didn't believe. They were apples, is what we call them. Red on the outside, white on the inside. They were not to think of themselves as native, because in order to be thinking Indian, you need to be living Indian. A lot of them won't eat fish or elk or deer. They would rather eat a burger and fries. You see the gaps in the generations. There was that big time lapse, when there was no culture and no teachings. The ancestors stood up for us. They are the ones who showed us—we did have these practices, we used these medicines. Our elders, what they were beat for, what they weren't allowed to talk about, that's the big gap I see in the generations. The ancestors themselves rose up and spoke. And then you see the richness, the heritage now."

So much material was being screened at the site that normal hand-sorting methods were too slow. The department rented a power screener called the Turbo Chieftain. Nearly forty tribal members divided themselves into two lines, one on each side of the conveyor belt that rumbled material from stockpiles through the screen, looking for artifacts and human remains so they would not be discarded. Screeners picked through the matrix with trowels, heads intently bent to the work, looking for clues, hints, and bits of the intimate life of people they had known all their lives—and not known at all. As they worked, they slowly uncovered a trove of artifacts: bone and stone points, etched stones by the hundreds.

Meanwhile, heavy-equipment operators lifted the ground ten centimeters at a time under the watchful eyes of tribal monitors. But it was heavy equipment. "It crushed anything it touched," said Mark Charles, known as Hammer on the reservation. "It made a certain sound. It would crack craniums open, as soft as they were trying to be. The soil was so dark, just black. You try to train the eyes to see that and to listen. If there was bone, you could tell the difference between rock breaking and bone breaking."

Some tribal members sorted carefully through the dirt using trowels with handles carved into eagles and ravens and hand tools cut from cedar. Just being in their ancestral village was very powerful. "It changed us," said Carmen Watson-Charles, a Lower Elwha tribal member who worked at everything at the site, from digging burials to photographing artifacts. "It felt like home down there, like the same family feeling between a mother and a child, a warm feeling. It was a sense of home, it was a sense of stillness—this is where we belong. Dignity. I didn't feel naked anymore. It was a spiritual connection."

But for many tribal members, the excitement of working at the site began to change to grief. Discovering their ancestors' tools and belongings, their houses, cooking areas, and tool-making sites was one thing. Finding their bones was another.

Digging their ancestors out of their graves was yet something else again. And they found their ancestors everywhere on the site. In middens, in structures, in pits excavated in beach sands. In rock cairns. In wooden burial boxes and in cedar mats. In wood-lined pits. In sand pits. Surrounded with a thin covering of pea gravel. With cobble headstones. In flexed positions, knees tucked to chin; on their backs; lying facedown; and on their sides. The very youngest children were buried seated.

They found their ancestors buried facing east, west, north, and south. Their hands held to their faces. Or raised, as if in praise. There were intact burials and skeletons shattered, cut in half, crushed, disarticulated and skewered by pilings, by heavy equipment, and by pipelines. They found burials saturated with diesel fuel, burials in a trench partially filled with asphalt, and burials burned by fire.

They found bones of adults, teenagers, children, and infants. They found skeletons buried alone and amid jumbles of other skeletons. A pair of skeletons was placed in an embrace, one lying atop the other, with the head of one person resting on the chest of the other, their arms and legs entwined. One foot was found all by itself. Some burials were so decomposed that they appeared only as faint traces on the ground, suggesting the shadows of ancestors, like ghosts. They found bones dusted with mica. Bones glowing salmon pink with red ochre. Skeletons with flattened skulls. Burials interred with fishing gear, shaman's telling sticks, Chinese coins, glass beads, a notched tooth pendant, and a ground slate knife. Burials with sea urchin spines, shells, and fish bones. A burial with a whalebone club.[2]

For tribal members, these were not just bones in the ground. They were family members in a living community of spirits. And those souls were not crowded in some distant heaven, to be reckoned with only in an afterlife. They were living close around them, here and now, in direct and not necessarily benign communication. Disturbance of their rest was not acceptable—it was even dangerous, inviting death, illness, and accident. Each bone tribal members touched was connected to the spirit world and to an individual life in communication with their own, across a boundary negotiated with red ochre, snowberry tincture, cedar boughs, and prayer. The work of digging the burials penetrated them, took them over.

"I can still see his hands," Watson-Charles said of one of the first burials she carefully took out of the ground, piece by piece, starting with the feet. "And there was another one, where I was literally looking into the eyes of my ancestor. I can feel him still. It's one of the ones that touched me." Stroke by stroke, with a brush, she drew back the ground covering his bones until she revealed teeth. They were flat, from being used to make tools and fray cedar. Tribal members were careful to include the dirt that touched the bones as they placed the remains on white blankets inside the cedar boxes. They only minimally cleaned the bones, for to them, the dirt was sacred. "It has their skin and blood," Watson-Charles said.

For tribal members, the burials, which mostly dated from two periods, 1420 to 1800 and 380 to 620,[3] also told stories about their ancestors' lives and culture. A skeleton in one grave carried a harpoon point embedded in the side of his pelvis. The harpoon toggle was buried along with him, at his feet, along with all his fishing tools and a round ball of red ochre. He was one of the few intact skeletons found with his head facing the sea. Another grave contained fifteen severed skulls, mostly of young men, probably taken as war trophies and mounted on stakes on the beach to warn the Klallams' enemies. When the flesh on the skulls deteriorated, women usually collected the skulls in burden baskets. To some tribal members, that find proved what they had long heard, that their people had been formidable in war. "That's a trophy case," said tribal member Lonnie Charles of the pile of skulls.

Another skeleton was found decapitated and laid flat on his back. A leather pouch containing eleven copper Chinese coins was found crooked in his arm. His entire skeleton shimmered with silver mica, and he was buried with a copper pendant and a shaman's telling sticks, made from bone. To tribal members, the gifts and elaborate dusting of mica were a clue to his high status and role as a medicine man in the village. The coins bore the reign date of the Qianlong (Ch'ien-lung) emperor (1736–1796) on the obverse side, and the mint mark of Yunnan province on the reverse side.[4] Other trade era goods, from 1736 to 1800,[5] found with the burials showed tribal members that their village had been a crossroads of trade and culture. Tribal members found a burial with a bayonet, a metal spoon probably from 1760–1800,[6] and a tin can. The bayonet, possibly an heirloom, was a typical English spike bayonet, probably manufactured before 1700 and obtained from early English explorers or traders.[7] Other gifts for the journey to the spirit world included blue glass beads, probably obtained in trade with Europeans in the mid-to-late 1700s,[8] a copper ring, net weights, a bone needle, and harpoon points.

For some tribal members, working at the site was their first encounter with their own culture. "When I first started, I was really excited. I didn't know anything about it," said Teresa Sanders. "I didn't know anything about my culture at all. My mom

Tulalip tribal member Michael Watson-Charles exhumes a grave at the Tse-whit-zen village site. At the request of the Lower Elwha Klallam Tribe, this photo was altered to delete the piece of human skull that Watson-Charles is brushing clean. Courtesy Lower Elwha Klallam Tribe.

was white and my dad's Indian, so when we were kids my mom wouldn't let us live on the reservation. She kept us more or less separated from anything tribal." Sanders, with bright blond hair and blue eyes, took a lot of guff. "I looked like a little white baby. People would say I was the milkman's baby. I hated it," Sanders said. "And when I'd go to the tribal functions, I wouldn't expect people to accept me. When I started working at the graving yard, I was so honored they would trust me with that." She found herself getting angry as she began to learn about her tribe and the history of her homeland. "I learned more and more about my people, what they did to them. They took their land, their language, and all the things that were not given to me, and a lot of children, because their parents didn't talk about their culture either, because it was painful. It changed who I am. My whole life is in a different direction now. It started out as a job, but all these artifacts, that's all I think about anymore. We are looking back on the past to find out the answers they already had. From that first week I was down there, I knew my whole life was going to change. This is our link; this is how we find out who we were before. I want it to keep going. We can take back what was taken from us." Sanders worked over on the western end of the site, where archaeologists encountered the grave with more than one hundred burials in an area the size of a single-car garage. It was the way people were buried—in sand, on top of and right next to one another—that made tribal members think it was a smallpox grave. That the living had to work quickly to bury so many dead, to protect themselves and their families.

"So many of those burials, you looked at them and saw so much sorrow. It came off of them. That was what affected me the most, all the sadness," Sanders said. "It takes so long, you are on your side, brushing on the bones, and you are thinking about that person. When I saw all those people, especially the infants. You are taking in so much hurt. It was so sad because the cedar boxes for them were so small."

The growing number of burials unearthed as the construction job continued shocked everyone. First ten, then twenty. Then one hundred, then two hundred, three hundred. More. Tribal members felt their feelings shift. "At first we were saving them from being disturbed, getting them out of the path of that bulldozer," said Wendy Sampson, a language instructor for the tribe who dug burials at the site. "I was really excited to work down there. It was a brand-new experience. It was a big wave, and I wanted to get into it. It was proof—there it is, look at this, it's not just a story anymore. There's 10,000 artifacts and more than three hundred burials that show we were there. We have been talking about this and telling people for a long time, and no one listened. There has not been a lot of recognition; we were overlooked. Now the entire world has proof. Listen next time."

But as she kept digging graves, she grew uneasy. "It wasn't until I was talking with my elders and I realized how they felt about it, how disgusted they were, and there I am, I'm digging graves, too," Sampson said. "We are down there voluntarily, getting paid. I'm sitting there picking the flesh off somebody's bones, and with the elders being so mad about it. Then it was, that's what we are doing. One more disturbance. It makes me cry to think I'm the one down there, picking the flesh off these bones, breaking bones one at a time and putting them in a box. Why do we have to be doing that? And there I am with my little wooden pick. I'm down there, getting paid. Digging graves. I don't know who said it, but it was really true: It was a funeral every day. I cried, digging up people. And our elders would say, 'We would rather you be down there doing it, because you are going to do it with care and tenderness.' Better than with a machine, going fifteen feet before it stops. A lot of tribal members felt that way. A lot of people felt they needed to be there. A lot of it was the ancestors, helping us along, so that we were the ones there to do it."

Wendy Sampson kept a journal of her work at the site, writing the Klallam words for what she was finding: rock (sŋánt'), shell (kʷáʔŋənor), hearth (sčqʷaʔcáyə), wedge (wíč), bone (scúm̓), skull (scaʔméʔqʷ), rib (yəkʷx), ancestor (sčiyúʔis). "But they

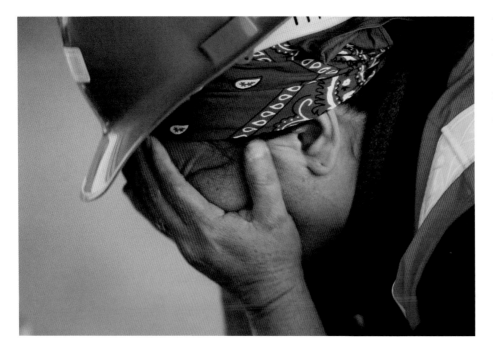

Working at the site also meant grief for tribal members who were taking their ancestors out of the ground with their own hands. Here Frances Charles is washing (ċaʔkʷúsəŋ) with snowberry water for spiritual protection before leaving the site for the day. Tribal members observed the traditional protocol in order to avoid bringing accidents and illness upon their families from contacting the disturbed spirits of their ancestors at the site. Steve Ringman, courtesy *Seattle Times*.

didn't have a word for 'digging up people,'" Sampson said. "That just didn't happen."

Sadness washed over Carmen Watson-Charles as she walked this ground, dotted with burial tents as more graves were discovered. "A lot of times I would go out there and let the wind blow on my face and just listen. It would be a feeling of pure peace and stillness, and then you would have a rush of sadness because of what was taking place around you. It was like losing your first love. You can't eat, you can't sleep, you feel lost, helpless. I felt like there was nothing we could do for our ancestors. It was overwhelming."

Bones sometimes broke as they were lifted from their graves. Or tribal members could not fit them back together the way they had been so carefully placed. "We uncovered a couple that were holding each other, and their bones were perfect, they were beautiful," Watson-Charles said. "They were wrapped, holding each other, her head on his chest, and their legs entwined. I started at their feet, digging the sand out from underneath. I said, 'Please, I don't want to break your bones.' Out loud. I said, 'Please, break when you are ready,' and dug the ground out from underneath. And I held a dust pan to catch the pieces bit by bit. I got to where their chests were, and they didn't want to break. They are not ready. Finally, they let go. I had to place them both in a small box, not big enough to place them just the way they were placed

As news of discovery of the site spread, so did support for the Lower Elwha Klallam among neighboring tribes. In the summer of 2004, tribal members making the annual Canoe Journey in the waters of the outer coast and Puget Sound stopped at the Tse-whit-zen site. Tribal members working at the construction site came to hear the paddlers' songs and prayers, offered for the ancestors. Courtesy Washington State Department of Transportation.

when we found them. That was really hard. That is what hurt the most."

For Watson-Charles and many tribal members, the turning point came when they realized that every burial was not going to be removed from the site. Over budget, its schedule blown, the department resisted digging even more burials outside or underneath the area of the dry dock, areas not covered by its March agreements with the tribe. "I thought, 'Oh my God, we are not taking all ancestors out. We are leaving some of the ancestors behind,' Watson-Charles said. "I felt so lost. I said, 'I can't do it anymore.' First, I felt I was saving them. Now it doesn't feel right. After that, I could not dig up any more of my ancestors. I wasn't saving them. I was doing more harm. And it happened so fast, it was a feeling of a loss of control. You were hoping and praying it could stop." And still, the number of ancestral burials kept climbing. "The more they pushed us, the more they showed themselves," Watson-Charles said.

By May, tribal members were sending a steady barrage of letters to the department, urging a slowdown in work so that they would be able to get all of their ancestors out of the path of construction. Tribal leaders did not ask that the work stop for good. The question was how to build the state's project while still meeting the tribe's spiritual needs. The tribe repeatedly put the department on notice that the burials were part of a living community of spirits that could not be separated. To leave burials behind would condemn those spirits to an industrial under-world, spent in an eternal search for loved ones now missing because they had been dug from their graves.

The department poured the first portion of the concrete dry dock floor. The expanse of concrete put even more distance between the tribe and the department. With so many bones found all over the site, the tribe wanted the state to check for remains below the level of its excavation before pouring the floor, work the department contended it was not required to do. Relations were unraveling. "It was the lack of being able to come together in those two different worlds, to come together fully. We couldn't make the transition complete," said Colleen Jollie, the department's tribal liaison. "We are pushing that schedule, and [the department] went and paved that area, and they freaked," she said of the tribe. "You don't get to pull out in front like that; you don't get to do those power grabs. And we just couldn't help it, they did it," she said of the department. "They couldn't resist the urge to control."

Jollie kept a journal during the project that became a silent scream: "keep insisting on doing things the old way—muscle through—our might makes us right. They paved too early on the south half. If this ends up in court we may have to pull up a shit-load of concrete," she wrote late in November 2004. A prophetic insight, as it turned out. Meanwhile, time and money kept draining away. "How deep? How deep before we quit?" she wrote, as the department kept chasing burials. "I have to find out what is right by the tribe, what is REAL justice? Is it okay to cap? Is it the best option, as believed by some: do not disturb, leave it, cap it for eternity. . . . How DEEP? Frankly—we are out of our league—out of our element. This is a problem for God, or people who know about spiritual stuff. Not engineers and accountants."

For MacDonald, the project had become a nightmare. Spreading a map of the site over a tabletop, he pointed to thick clusters of triangles stacked one on top of the other—burials found in the course of the construction project. MacDonald was sure that there were more in the spaces between the clusters, not yet explored. Possibly many more. In the western end of the site lay the densest cluster of graves, the possible smallpox burials. Like the first intact skeleton, the discovery of the mass grave had hit MacDonald hard. "There is a profound sense that this is not some accidental thing here," MacDonald said. "We are still living the contact experience of living on this

Word about disturbance of the burials at Tse-whit-zen angered area tribes with relatives buried in the cemetery. Here Delbert Miller (*left*), spiritual leader of the neighboring Skokomish Tribal Nation, meets at the site with other Skokomish tribal members and Lower Elwha Klallam tribal member Arlene Wheeler, November 2004. Courtesy Lower Elwha Klallam Tribe.

land. We are connected to those burials. That's a piece that's relevant to this damn problem." The possibility that removing just a few more burials would finally clear the project for completion had, for MacDonald, become a chimera. "When you look at this, how do you talk about doing a little more?" he said, a finger on the triangles indicating the burials salting the map. "I'm looking at this, and I'm thinking 'Where are we a year from now?' It is like pulling a thread from a sweater. And every time we dig, we are uncovering archaeological material. We are not going to say, 'Throw away those fish hooks. We've already got 10,000.'"

He wanted a bounded solution. But Frances Charles, elected tribal chairwoman in June, was pushing back at the department. Elected to the council in 1992, Charles was the longest-sitting council member and one of its few women chairmen ever. She walked into a room with her arms and hands swinging loose, ready as a prizefighter. The tribe's small size, with just 760 members, seemed to make her stand all the taller. "We are the small tribe with the big bite," Charles would say. Before her election to the council, Charles worked in the Strait of Juan de Fuca, earning as much as $8,000 a month fishing for coho salmon, back when the fish runs were still strong. She earned a commercial truck driver's license, then worked a dozen years in the woods for the United States Forest Service, running forest fire crews choppered into remote areas all over the country. They burned slash, cut trails, snuffed flames. Charles coordinated the supply lines, ran the crews, drove fire trucks. Back home on the reservation, she was known as Gator for a throwing arm on the baseball field as powerful as the swat of an alligator's tail.

Charles was just as assertive off the field. "She knows when to be sensitive and tender, and when to give the snake bite," said her niece, Carmen Watson-Charles. "People love her for that." And by November, Charles was out of patience with the department. "The main part of it is we want to go back in there and take our loved ones out of the ground," Charles said. "The reason is we don't want to leave a mother and child separated; we don't want to leave a family out there in the spirit world searching for a soul mate. We want to unite them, to keep them together. It's a cultural belief. What we were told is if you separate loved ones that have already been buried, you are going to be separating their souls when they thought this was their final resting place for all eternity. And it all goes back to the beginning, of what we thought was here. It's not just a little corner with burials. It's the whole twenty-two acres."

But getting every bone out of the ground, MacDonald knew, would be impossible. "I am personally very conflicted about it. We are going to entomb people here,"

MacDonald said. "That is what is making this so difficult. Leaving burials undisturbed as much as possible, digging the archaeology and doing reburial, that was my touchstone. Since that has come apart, I am unmoored. The tribe doesn't want to lay its people below concrete. It's a new card." As the conflict deepened, alarming things also were happening. Tribal members working at the site dissolved in tears they could not explain. They felt unseen touches on their backs or their shoulders. They heard drums. Wolf pups crying. The traffic death toll on Route 101, the main road in and out of Port Angeles, climbed. Tribal members felt they knew why. To them, it was the disturbed spirits of ancestors, their bones stacked by then in more than three hundred cedar boxes up at the bunker.

The tribe also began fielding questions from media outside of Port Angeles. Frances Charles walked the site during a tour for reporters in November. In jeans and boots, hard hat, and safety glasses, she picked her way among burial tents, her long braid looped up so it would not brush the ground and be spirit-touched. Red ochre was painted in stripes under her eyes. "Everything has changed now," Charles said. The whole basis of the project needed to be reconsidered, she explained, in light of all the burials that had been uprooted. "Our assumption was there would only be twenty-five individuals. You are wiping out our existence; you are wiping out that we were ever at the village site. How do you ever pay the tribe for the anguish of what has happened and wiping out one of the most valuable archaeological sites? And yet it continues on."

Meanwhile, MacDonald was starting to take heat from legislators and city officials, who were putting on the pressure to keep the project going. He wasn't the only one with political problems. By November, Charles was getting beat up on all sides. She and the rest of the tribal council continued to reassure the department, both in private conversations and in statements to the press, that the council didn't want the project stopped—it only wanted the ancestors relocated. But the council's position was eroding under a rising tide of opposition, on and off the reservation. The daily spiritual violence at the site—uprooting their ancestors, grave by grave—even though it was being done by agreement with the department, was becoming too much to bear. As the body count ticked higher, no words on any paper, no signed memorandum of agreement, no legal right, however enforceable, could stand up to the political reality of what was increasingly feeling, and looking to the public, like a moral wrong. "Visualize the caskets, and if it was your family member there on the ground, for everyone to see," Charles said. "How would you feel about them being exposed in that public setting, and where would you want them to go back to? How would you feel if it was your mother, your father?" The side agreement the tribe had negotiated with the department had become an albatross.

"That $3,400,000 is hush money," Charles snapped as she toured reporters around the site in November. "It's always thrown back to us, the Hood Canal Bridge. The issue to us is the heritage, the cultural resources that is being demolished. In the earlier times it was agreed to be real quiet and discreet. But once people see what's actually happening, they have a change of heart. Then it's, 'You guys agreed to it, you signed it, and if you shut this down, it comes back on the tribe.' The city, the port, the county, everyone would be angry with us. They would penalize the tribe and bring no economic development." It got uglier. Tribal members still talk about hunters who stood on the bluff overlooking the project site, pointing rifles with high-powered scopes.

And increasingly, Charles and other members of the council were being criticized by their own people. Some elders who had never blessed the project in the first place now wanted it gone. "I'd stop it," Beatrice Charles said. "Why can't they find another place? I just feel sorry that my ancestors are being disturbed again. It is not our fault that this is happening. There is nothing that we can do about it, it seems that way." And then she said the words that became the rallying cry for the opponents of this project: "We have been defeated for so long. But we are going to come back strong. And say enough is enough."

By November, Mary Anne Thomas was also telling the tribal council the project should be shut down. "My heart is crushed for the ancestors and what they are going through," Thomas said. Thomas had no tolerance for the archaeologists and their dig. She had little interest in the department's bridge project either. "No one put them in the hole where they are. They did it to themselves," Thomas said. "And now the tables have turned. It is a burial site. We need to tell them enough is enough. Who in the world would dig out their ancestors to put them on a shelf? And every day there is some accident happening. It is because of the spirits traveling. The ones in the cedar boxes, there is no burial that stays out of the ground, and some of these have been out a year. The ancestors here are so powerful. These old souls live." To her, the need to stop the project was plain.

"They should leave," Thomas said. "They have to put themselves in our place. How would they feel if we digged up their ancestors and put them on a shelf because of letting money come before life and death? The Creator never put us on the land to suffer. We are the ones that create it, through our decisions. We have to be account-able, and that goes for the DoT. Whatever we put out, it's going to come back."

The department kept trying to make the project work, both for the bridge and for the tribe. It deployed ground-penetrating radar equipment to search for burials, offered to bring in cadaver dogs, and invited elders to search for burials using their intuition, dreams, and knowledge. MacDonald set engineers to calculating the pounds per square inch of pressure exerted by paving, to assure the tribe that paving would not crush artifacts or bones left undisturbed in the ground under the dry dock floor. But he couldn't respond to the tribe's insistence that their ancestors just plain didn't want to live underneath a concrete slab. Searching for a bottom, any boundary, some limit to the state's obligations, MacDonald finally sought and got a ruling from the federal government. It stated that the department was not obligated to remove every bone. "You thought you were going to lawyer this issue. Then you thought you could engineer this issue," MacDonald said. "If you start building things in stupid little pieces, you get more stupid little pieces." By December 2004, work crews were still unearthing more burials, many never before disturbed. By then, a petition was circling online and in Port Angeles to stop work at the site. It quickly gained about 1,000 signatures.

The annual meeting of tribal leaders from across Washington with the governor and his cabinet became a heated referendum on the dry dock project. Here Lummi elder James Hillaire (*standing*) tells Governor Gary Locke (*third from left*) that disturbance of tribal ancestral remains is unacceptable. Steve Ringman, courtesy *Seattle Times*.

The department was also taking criticism over the project after a major story in a Seattle newspaper.

U.S. Senator Maria Cantwell decided to drive out to the dry dock site for herself to see what was going on. She came alone, the Sunday after Thanksgiving, dressed in jeans and a sweater. She walked the beach line where tribal members were finding so many of their ancestors.

"It was incredible from my perspective," said Cantwell, who, uninvolved in the project until that point, brought a fresh eye to the situation. Then a first-term Democrat who had featured her bond with her mother in her first campaign, Cantwell was hit hard by the sight of the burials. "Who among us would go and dig up their relatives?" Cantwell asked. "I thought all the options had to be put on the table and explored. There is more there at that site than anyone imagined, and we have to explore all the options to deal with that. And this is just going to continue to be a more expensive proposition."

Once back at her office, Cantwell knew what she wanted. "I am trying to get everyone involved in this to say, 'We really can't go forward, and this is actually a great opportunity.' Mistakes have been made, but it's not about embarrassing people. If people can be willing to say that we can just move on, and I think they are there, it's about who wants to pull the plug. I think what is there is of great historic significance. It is something the whole state can appreciate. I think we should look at all the options, including moving the project somewhere else. That has to be an option."

As she talked with tribal members, an idea took root. The tribe could ask the state to stop the project—for good. "She got the whole push on," said Carmen Watson-Charles, who helped escort the senator around the site. "She asked very good questions and seemed very sincere and open-minded. She said things that put it all in perspective for us. We felt powerless. I know I did. She gave us back that power we needed. Almost like a parent giving consent." Frances Charles also felt a sense of relief. "It gave us all an uplifting. You lost a few pounds of that heaviness."

In early December, MacDonald traveled to Port Angeles with Hain and other top project staff to meet with the tribe. As they gathered in a circle at the site, MacDonald asked Frances Charles to go for a walk with him. He wanted to talk with her alone. He told her the department could not continue the work at the site without the tribe publicly endorsing it. As he spoke, the tribe's lawyer, Russ Busch, walked over and interrupted them, demanding to be part of the conversation. MacDonald felt something snap.

"I just reached a breaking point of frustration," MacDonald said. "And I turned away and I just left. And I came very close to not going back. I just walked all the way as far as you can go on the property by myself, just on the beach, just trying to calm down and get control of myself, of what the hell was I going to do next. It was one of those moments: 'Doug, if you just keep walking, nobody is ever going to give a shit. Just walk back to Port Angeles and call on the cell phone and have somebody pick you up. You are not going back to this crazy, crazy situation. It's become utterly intractable; there is nothing here but bullshit. You can't do anything.'" But leaving would not be that easy.

Cantwell convened a meeting later that week in Seattle with MacDonald and Allyson Brooks, the historic preservation officer. The senator warned them that trends at the project didn't look good. MacDonald assured her he thought there was room for more discussion with the tribe. "A fish in the water doesn't see the water," Cantwell said. "I couldn't do this. I can't ask them to."

She told MacDonald she would support him politically if he stopped the project. So, quietly, did other members of the congressional delegation. The department was already figuring the cost of decommissioning the site as controversy about the project built in Indian Country. It burst out at the 2004 Centennial Accord meeting.

An annual gathering of the governor and entire cabinet of Washington State government, the Centennial Accord meeting is an opportunity for tribal and state leaders to assess their work of the past year and chart a course for the next. The agenda usually covers health care, transportation, police policies, all the things that governments do. But that winter, it soon became anything but. As the meeting began, John Loftus, the editor of *Muckleshoot Monthly*, a tribal newspaper, passed out reprints of a four-page, color special section he had written about desecration of the site and burials. He made sure everyone got a copy.

Jollie, who had heard about what was coming, got ahold of MacDonald. He was at his apartment, recovering from cataract surgery, and hadn't intended to go to the meeting. "I told him, 'You have got to be there,'" Jollie said. MacDonald took his seat at the head table, alongside the governor, Frances Charles, and the governor's chief of staff. Then one by one, the Indian elders spoke. And they did so in the style of the longhouse. Standing. With no microphone and in slow, carefully measured, penetrating words. Grief cries, about the disturbance of burials in Indian Country. The room went silent, so quiet that the lack of sound became a sound itself, expectant, a podium for whatever would come.

As tribal leaders continued their meeting with the governor and cabinet, Lower Elwha Tribal Chairwoman Frances Charles stepped outside with Transportation Secretary Douglas MacDonald. She told him that after eighteen months of trying to make the project work, the tribe would be sending the department a letter in a few days asking him to stop the project. Steve Ringman, courtesy *Seattle Times*.

Lummi elder James Hillaire stood first. "We as Native people live by a supreme law that is our culture," said Hillaire, his gray hair falling to his shoulders above a Pendleton vest. "Once our ancestors are laid to rest, they should never, ever be disturbed again. It is very disturbing to me and to our people that these things are allowed to happen. How many times does this have to happen before people realize it hurts us and it hurts us deeply? As I stand here before you, my heart is aching, and the hurt, the anger, is so deep I can hardly control my speech. I'm glad our governments are finally talking. For so many years it has been only a one-way conversation. Now we are finally being heard. We have been here for generations upon generations. We are going to remain here. I want to say to the Elwha people that your hurt is one hurt, and it's all across the nation."

Next, Mel Tonasket, an elder and former tribal chairman from the Confederated Tribes of the Colville Indian Reservation, across the Cascades in the Columbia River country, slowly, deliberately rose to his feet. And he spoke of the building of the great dam, Grand Coulee, one of the largest in this country, and how it had strangled the upper reaches of the Columbia, killing the salmon runs in a third of their homeland, the fish that had sustained his people for thousands of years. And the dam created an artificial river, ramped up and down by remote control, as hydropower engineers released water to turn turbines, spinning electrons onto the western grid to make toasters glow in Seattle and Portland and run air-conditioners in California. And then the engineers would back up the river's flow, storing it for release on demand in the engineered Columbia, in one big series of battery packs—reservoirs. As they held the water back, it flooded unnaturally high up the riverbanks, climbing the soft sands laid down by centuries of erosion. And then the water was released again, run through the turbines, yanking the water down the soft banks. And sometimes the washing and stripping away of the ground would lay bare the bones of the ancestors of the Colville and Spokane people.

"I can still see the faces of our people, preparing to rebury their people, the ground washed out," Tonasket said, holding the governor with a level gaze. He paused. Let the subject shift to the Tse-whit-zen site and burial ground on its own, like a salmon gliding to a deeper pool. "I look at things really simple. I try to make things not more complicated than they have to be," Tonasket said. "It just dumbfounds me that such a magnitude of things are being found, and work is still going on. I don't understand that." He shifted his gaze to Frances Charles, who nodded in agreement as he spoke. "In my opinion, this is something worth fighting like hell for. My tribe will stand with you on your land. So that it can't continue to go on. If we need all tribes in the state to show a presence, so it don't happen anymore. Find another location. It might not be as good financially. But what better reason than to stop digging up people? I just cannot comprehend it."

The room cleared. Everyone headed to the dining room for lunch. Governor Locke and MacDonald stayed where they were, side by side at the head table. They huddled together, conferring in the empty room. No one knew that in that moment, the governor, a lame-duck Democrat, asked MacDonald what he wanted. Locke had been to the site and had also been struck by the value of the history.

Locke was the country's first governor of Chinese descent, and his father had once worked as a houseboy not far from the governor's mansion. A two-term governor, Locke had a practical bent. He often said pruning and home repair were his favorite hobbies. As a legislator in the state House of Representatives before his election to the governor's mansion, Locke had a reputation as a budget wonk, delighting in micro-managing state spending. Yet he saw the value of the Tse-whit-zen site not in terms of the money the state had already spent there but in terms of its historical value.

"Had we known of the extent of this historic village and grave site, no one would have supported starting the project. This is such an incredibly significant site," Locke said. "If we had proceeded with this and paved this thing over, knowing there was such an incredibly significant archaeological site there that was thousands of years old, people in the future would say, 'What were they thinking?' I don't think future generations would forgive us for ignoring this and just paving it over. I just don't see how we can proceed with this project at this site, knowing there is a several-thousand-years-old village and grave site there. I believe that people years from now will say it is more important to preserve that, and educate future generations of what was there and document the findings and tell the story of Washington's first people. If we continue there and build this huge concrete pool, it would be akin to paving part of ancient Greece and ancient Rome, and that would be just absolutely unacceptable and unforgivable. The job of replacing the pontoons and replacing the bridge does not go away. We simply must find another place to build them."

Locke leaned over to MacDonald and told him he would stop the project then and there, at the Centennial Accord meeting, if MacDonald desired. "I told him it was not that easy," MacDonald said.

The meeting shifted back to its usual agenda, with sessions on policing and health care and environmental policy. But meanwhile, Frances Charles and MacDonald stepped outside. She promised him a letter would be coming soon. And in it, she said, the tribe would be asking the state to stop the project, to find another place. She sent it the next day. MacDonald, in consultation with state and federal officials, agreed to walk away from the site and some $90 million spent on the project. Two weeks before Christmas, he shut the job down for good.

At the site, cold rain and wind blew over the ground, silent except for the breathing of the paper plant next door, blowing its great wind socks of steam. The archaeologists' sampling pits, stripped of their evidence, were filling with water. The only thing left to do now was cover the ground to protect it. Contractors put black landscape fabric and fresh sand over the ground with its uneven jumble of broken bits, all mixed together.

It was a rumpled landscape, cold and abandoned in the weak winter light. Bits of shell, fire-modified rocks, and cobble spalls showed at the surface along with broken pieces of brick, oil stains, old mill pilings, fill, and dredge spoil. The archaeologists' work tents and portable toilets looked as misplaced as if they had been brought in for a circus. The blue steel sheet piles towered over puddles bouncing with rain. Monuments to a lost world.

10

We Were Here—We Are Still Here

HE SHUCKED OFF HIS JACKET, TUGGED OFF HIS TIE, AND OPENED HIS COLLAR. Behind him a hand-lettered banner yelled the sentiment in this packed union hall: SAVE OUR GRAVING DOCK. Transportation Secretary Douglas MacDonald had a long night ahead of him. In work clothes and big boots, in hickory shirts soft with years of work, and with their hands rough and ropey, knitted tight with worry in their laps, these construction workers fixed their eyes on the man who had snuffed their jobs two weeks before Christmas. Their wives were there, too. Some of them had moved to this town especially for the high-paying, union, government-rate jobs the project had promised. Most of the people in this crowd, though, were longtime locals. And they were stunned that anything could be stopped in this town because of anything Indian. MacDonald rose to his feet.

A veteran of a professional lifetime spent connecting with all kinds of people in meetings like this one, he opened a Pepsi and looked over the crowd as the room settled. He was alert and connected with the audience, like a doctor ready to give a bad prognosis to a patient. He started right in, skipping the pleasantries and icebreakers.

The decision to walk away from the dry dock project, laying off construction workers less than two weeks before Christmas, hit Port Angeles like a bomb. Here transportation secretary Douglas MacDonald (*standing*) explains the decision to workers and their families at a Port Angeles union hall. Steve Ringman, courtesy *Seattle Times*.

Used no microphone and no notes. "We decided our obligation is to fix the bridge, and the most important thing of all is to move to a place where we could get that done," MacDonald said. "We were going to face a tsunami of public opinion. The time had come to get honest with ourselves about where the project stood. We decided we were going to have to walk away. Can lightning strike? Is there a way that we can put this back together and people can go back to work there? I think that is very unlikely. That site has got to go quiet."

People shifted in their seats. Waited. MacDonald refused to make it easier for them, or himself, by blaming the tribe. "It's important this not be positioned as 'Why didn't the tribe get it?'" MacDonald continued. "If we were sitting in Alabama digging up a Civil War cemetery, people would be sitting there saying that is not the right thing to do. There's three hundred bodies. How many more are you going to dig up? What's your pain threshold?" The department probably couldn't keep going legally, even if it wanted to, he explained. It was vulnerable to lawsuits against the project, done with expedited permitting. Anyone could sue to demand the full-blown environmental impact statement that had never been done for the project, which would delay work another year or longer. "We might as well be building new pontoons," MacDonald said. He felt the crowd's resistance, every face in the room with the same

Nothing before had ever been stopped in this town for anything Indian, and the decision to walk away from about $90 million invested in the site did not go over well, as the faces in this union hall meeting show. Steve Ringman, courtesy *Seattle Times*.

"no sale" expression. But he offered no sugarcoating. "You don't in an ordinary day, on an ordinary project, run into three hundred dead souls," he said. After he finished, speaker after speaker rose to protest the shutdown. The tribe was "just living in the past." Surely, going forward with the project simply required fixing a price with the tribe. The tribe had to be held to its agreement.

MacDonald listened, but wouldn't placate them. "Nobody signed that agreement to cover digging people up by the score," he answered. And ultimately, he told this crowd, they were a part of what sank the project, too. "It has to be dawning on people there are folks in this community who aren't talking to each other well, maybe these past three weeks, past three months, the past one hundred years," MacDonald said. "We managed to misunderstand each other pretty well." That misunderstanding would continue.

At a meeting the same day with state and local leaders and tribal council members, MacDonald couldn't get the fact through to city officials that the project was dead. "Their whole deal was for the tribe to hear how important it was to get this started again," he said. "It was, 'Give 'em the word.' You could cut the tension with a knife. I said, 'Stop. You don't understand,' and I got on my hands and knees and unrolled a map of the burials on the floor. I said, 'Look at this. We are not going up this beach line. If you think we are just going to go up there and keep on digging, you don't get it. It's done.'"

No sale with them either. In a letter to their local state representatives, the entire membership of the local chamber of commerce called once again for a turnaround. The chamber asked for an order from the legislature that would require the department to stop looking for a new site and come up with a plan to keep the project going. "This impasse that the tribe and DoT have reached has to be broken, and in the Chamber's opinion, it is time for some very forceful action," the letter stated. "We do understand the tribe's request, but we feel that they need to be willing to compromise some of their ideals and make decisions that are in the best interest of the entire region. Contracts were in place." The letter was leaked to the local paper before it could be sent. The chamber killed the letter and apologized for it.

As 2004 came to an end, the state and the tribe began working on a plan to close the site and move on. Nothing was settled: Who would own the property, what development, if any, would be possible there, and what would be done about reburial of all the skeletons still up at the bunker. For tribal members, the only acceptable solution was to respectfully rebury the bones in cedar boxes on the site, as close as possible to the original graves. To them, anything else would be just like the last time, with their ancestors' bones used as backfill in an industrial site. But every push by the tribe for land for reburial at the site met a push back from local officials. They feared setting a precedent.

"It's not just this city," said City Councilman Larry Williams, who had first invited the department to consider the site. "This is the Three Mile Island of harborside community development. What TMI did for the nuclear power industry, this has the potential to do for any harborside renovation, development, and redevelopment. If the tribe's assertion is enough to make a state capitulate on this, then we need to very quickly figure out where the line is. This is definitely a precedent-setting event. If we don't get this resolved amicably, I think we might as well pack our bags, crawl back to England, kiss the queen's feet, and beg forgiveness. There is a concern that there is a larger agenda driven by this. If it starts there, where will it stop?"

Williams had an ally in former state representative Jim Buck, a Republican from Joyce, the next town over. Buck, a retired army captain who sported logger's work clothes on his days off, had gifted the tribe with an elk skin when he first heard that their ancestors' bones had been found in the backfill at the site. And he had brought a letter that day, with a pledge of support for the tribe and an apology for past desecrations. It was signed by every state and local official in the area. "It was a very big leap of faith, an extension of an olive branch to a community from a community that had not had a lot of sympathy in the past," Buck explained. But the support was for continuing the project at the site—not for stopping it. And once the tribe asked the state to leave, Buck went into high gear to try to save the dry dock. He offered to push through the legislature a gift of three hundred acres of state land if the tribe would reconsider. The tribe rebuffed him, calling the offer a "poor attempt at bribery." Buck tried again, this time with a request for an attorney general's ruling on whether the tribe had any authority over the land, which it had ceded in the treaty of 1855.

A deal, Buck insisted, was a deal. Not only on the dry dock, but in the treaty. To him, the two were intimately related. The tribe's assertion that it had any say-so over the land was a direct challenge to what had been the status quo in this town for more than 150 years. "What you have is a tribe that decided to be intransigent," Buck said. "They violated their agreement. There is a constant complaint of 'You have to understand how we do things.' But there has to be a quid pro quo of understanding how our process works, and how we do things. We are not going to take it. It is not OK or realistic to say 'OK, you can turn the clock back to 1855.'"

The negotiations now weren't about reburial; they were about control of the waterfront. And Buck believed what the tribe really wanted was payback. "I think there is a question here of what is actually a good-faith thing to do for the tribe, and where does that end up turning into 'Let's get even with the white guys,'" he said. The property remained in limbo, the boxes full of bones at the bunker. Archaeological material that state contractors had mistakenly trucked to the landfill was still there, overgrown by now with tall weeds. Months went by. In August 2005, the tribe finally decided to sue, claiming deliberate, knowing desecration of its burial ground. The state countersued, arguing that everything that happened at the site took place with the tribe's knowledge and consent, because the work was a collaboration, executed by written agreement and carried out on the ground every day, side by side with tribal workers. Walking together had deteriorated to winding up in court.

The impasse didn't surprise John Brewer, publisher of the local paper. He thought of the town's response to the Tribal Canoe Journey hosted by the Lower Elwha people in 2005, just before filing its lawsuit. The canoe journey was a major event for this small town. Tribal members from around the Northwest traveled to the Lower Elwha reservation for a weeklong celebration and revival of Coast Salish culture, with hun-

Despite the disturbance of intact burials and bone fragments, many in Port Angeles still wanted the dry dock project to continue for the sake of high-paying construction jobs at the site. Steve Ringman, courtesy *Seattle Times*.

dreds of participants arriving by canoe. The event drew about 10,000 people to town, packing motel rooms throughout the city. Many also camped on the reservation, where traditional songs and dances and ceremonial protocol were conducted under a vast, white tent late into the summer nights. Brewer, a recent arrival recruited from the *New York Times*, was enthralled. He assigned his reporters to do story after story, and he himself helped out as a volunteer, cooking in the kitchen at the tribal center. And then the complaints started coming in from readers.

"I get this voice-mail from this little old lady. She says, 'Mr. Brewer, Mr. Brewer, you can't keep putting the Indians on page one. My husband will cancel our subscription,'" Brewer said, imitating a squeaky, cranky voice. "Most of the people who called said, 'If you put those goddamn Indians on page one, I am canceling.' We lost thirty subscribers, complaining along the lines that this is way too much on the Indians, you are singling them out." When he went to canoe journey events at the reservation, he was surprised at how few white people from town bothered to attend—maybe a hundred. And it was the same group he was used to seeing at any event for a progressive cause in town.

"I remember the last dinner, sitting out on the lawn with a nurse friend of mine, and we were about the only white people at this great community dinner. Thousands of people showed up. It was very poignant; it bothered the hell out of me," Brewer said. "I felt terrible about it. I thought, 'These people don't understand what they are missing.' It just doesn't sink in on anybody what is going on around them. People

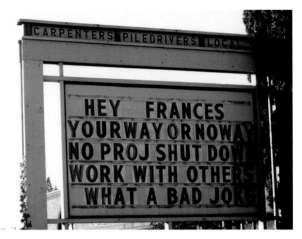

think it is a culture that is scary to them. You would want to bring your kids down, you would think. Nobody showed up for the reservation events. They didn't even know where it was. We could have run a map, but it didn't even occur to me that people wouldn't know where it is." Six miles outside of downtown, that's where.

Bigotry—and just plain lack of curiosity or interest in the tribe—were at the root of the dry dock project's downfall, Brewer said. "You have some enlightened people, but then you have the homeboys who grew up with the tribe and it's 'You are the Indian and I am the white guy, and guess who counts?' And then there was this cultural thing, a lot of people couldn't understand, 'Why can't you just move this goddamn cemetery? What is the problem?'"

He didn't buy the assertion that the loss of the project hurt the town economically. After the project shut down, housing sales and prices continued to climb. Businesses that wanted to add a second manufacturing shift couldn't do so because of the shortage of workers. "There are tons of jobs in this community," Brewer said. "But you have to know how to be a marine carpenter. You need skills. You need to know how to do marine fiberglass. You are talking about work ethic, too. 'Do I really want to do this, or hang out with my pals, or make meth?'"

With the loss of the project, the town's long-running dispute with the tribe returned to its usual sullen simmer. "It's like a bad dream or a divorce. They didn't have any profile anyway," Brewer said of the tribe. "They were never players before, and they aren't players now. It's not like we are shunning them now, because we were shunning them before. I'm not sure there is much you can do. You are talking about putting a romance back together that was never there in the first place. There was

Transportation secretary Douglas MacDonald and Lower Elwha tribal chairwoman Frances Charles bore the brunt of the town's anger when the dry dock project was shut down, as successive displays on this reader board at the union hall in Port Angeles show, winter 2005. Courtesy Lower Elwha Kllalam Tribe.

probably an opportunity for them when it all started, but this is a small town and these are small-town people. I have people who come in and yell at us because we didn't run their club notice. 'Why didn't you come over and cover our coin club?'"

The tribe also did a lousy job of making its own case to the public, Brewer said. "They are cooperative when you ask them, but they are not good at initiating. You had to go down there and dig it out. And if you didn't, you never heard about it, and they didn't care. They are very, very friendly when you talk with them, and very, very helpful. But it doesn't even occur to them that you would be interested. The reason they didn't ask for help is it didn't even occur to them that anyone would want to help them or be interested. No one else has ever cared, why would you?"

Andrew May, elected president of the local chamber of commerce, said the project was forcing the town and the tribe to take a look at themselves. No one should have been shocked at what was ultimately found at the site, May said. "The skeletons were in the ground, not the closet," he said. "They were in the drain fields, in the pipes. Everyone knew what was going on. It was the dark secret." He acknowledged that the tribe gave warning about what was at the site but not very well. "Yes, they told you. But why did they sign off then? Because you sold out economically just like we did, and just like the port did. Because you didn't want to look bad, you signed off on twenty-five of your ancestors. Everyone shares the blame. They are as complicit as the survey company that missed the site. Everybody had an eye on this prize. At that time we were leading the state in unemployment. And suddenly, here comes a chance for jobs. It was too much of a shiny object. You got a state's interest, you got a county's interest, and a city's, and a tribe's."

May, a landscape designer by trade—he calls himself "the toothless gardener" because he lost a front tooth long ago in a soccer match—was amazed that local business and political leaders didn't grasp the political demise of the project, as outrage built regionally over digging up more graves. "That's what I could not believe, the stupidity of local leaders in finding a solution," said May, who moved to Port Angeles from Michigan in 1995. "It was force it, pave it over, make them do it. Sue the state. In sailing, we all know that when the wind changes, you change tacks. But we just kept the course. Everyone is going to know Port Angeles as those crazy fuckers who just don't get it. If the toothless gardener can get it, why can't the mayor get it? Gardeners are supposed to be simple. We don't know things. If the gardener can get it, Jim Buck can get it. I lock horns with the old guard. If the people will lead, eventually the leaders will follow. The nice thing about the old

At a Port Angeles Chamber of Commerce meeting in December 2004, after the project was shut down, chamber members ponder a map of the site thickly dotted with pink and green symbols, each representing human remains disturbed during construction. Steve Ringman, courtesy *Seattle Times*.

guard is that first word: old. They are moving, they are dying, they are retiring."

But Port Angeles is also a town in transition, May said. Newcomers are more sympathetic to the tribe and want to heal the mistrust at its root: the history between the tribe and this town. "The precedent was, this was the first time for Port Angeles that something got stopped," May said. "Every other time it was, bring in the bulldozers and move these people out. It was the first time Port Angeles had to come into the civilized age. The atrocities are not even past history; they're in the elders' memories. I don't drive by every day and look at how people have polluted and trashed my home. I'm not reminded every day that this is where I used to be."

Instead of ignoring the tribe's historical tie to the site, May, as head of the chamber, supported giving it to the tribe for reburial and construction of a cultural center to showcase artifacts from the site. He saw not a loss for the waterfront but an addition that would help attract tourists and diversify the economy, part of his dream of creating a renaissance city in this old mill town. "Couldn't this be a catalyst?" May asked. "We don't have to live with the old model. We could give way to the new model of cooperation on this."

The department asked Tim Thompson, a former legislative aide to Congressman Norm Dicks and already working as a consultant on the project, to help resolve the dispute. Thompson was a veteran of complex, controversial negotiations, but this problem quickly became mission impossible. "Any reasonable person could go to Port Angeles and look at the history, and at how the tribe was treated, and see that it was egregious and deeply punitive and disrespectful of all aspects of the tribe's culture," Thompson said. "What the tribe wanted more than anything else was to have that felt and understood. They knew there was a lack of tribal attention to this matter as well, and there was culpability on the part of the tribe for letting the project get sited where it was. But that doesn't excuse the major responsibility of the community, of the Department of Transportation, of all the players to understand that the reason it couldn't get dealt with was because you were dealing with one hundred years of deep-seated feelings and abuse. You would think about the processes we would normally have set forth in government to manage these kinds of sensitivities, but the fact was that the tribe was never respected. And their oral histories and the map with the Indian villages, all that was dismissed because there was a lack of respect for the reality on the waterfront. It was a conscious act to ignore that. How did we get here?

"You have a piece of property that was sold to the department with high hopes that there would be great economic development. The reason I think all this happened was largely due to the fact that people were not respectful of the past, or the history of the past. There was a lack of attention and respect given to this site, and it was ten times worse because the tribe felt they had contributed to the problem. One of the reasons they were so angry is they felt they should have been paying closer attention; they didn't do their due diligence. And there is the spiritual element, which they also take very, very seriously. And here we were, digging up body after body after body, doing harm, and more harm, and more harm. And the inherent hurt of all that was compounded by the original problem. The stage was set for this. The stage got set decades ago. I think the relationship between the tribe and that city is still very, very damaged, and I think they have a long journey in front of them.

"It was impossible in my view to settle this if you don't acknowledge the pain and the hurt and the decades-old bad relationship. It was ugly, and it was racial. It is hard to negotiate with someone you don't consider worthy of negotiating with. If you can't figure out the motivation of the other side, and try to accommodate and respect it, you will never get anywhere. The communication was just terrible, and I have the marks on my back and my ass to prove it. It was ridiculous. You could never get to the negotiations, because the city could never let go of the fact that they couldn't use the site. Literally, they would just go apoplectic. You can say, OK, looking back, the tribe should have done more due diligence and the department should have, but in the end, who sold this land to the department and who in the local community and the port did not know this could be a potential problem? With all due respect to the hanging of Doug MacDonald or anyone who came in to fix the problem, why was there not enough fairness in the process to acknowledge that we were all guilty in this?"

The talks went nowhere. By Christmas 2005, Frances Charles, desperate to get the ancestors' bones back in the ground, went to Washington's new Democratic governor, Christine Gregoire, and asked her to assign an independent mediator, not one hired by the department, to reach a settlement. Gregoire agreed and assigned her chief of staff to steer the process. As the talks got under way in the spring of 2006, Charles pushed hard for reburial. One day she started the meetings by passing out a photocopy of a burial at the site: an intact skeleton, in fetal position, exposed in its opened grave, the bones glowing red with ochre. "This is why we are here," she said.

As the second round of talks ground on into August, Gregoire finally threw money at the problem. The Port of Port Angeles, which sold the property to the state in the first place, was handed a promise for $7.5 million from the state legislature for economic development projects. Not only would the port not have to pay taxpayers back for the site, which might as well have been radioactive as far as its unsuitability for the project, but it was rewarded for its actions. So was the city.

The city claims it didn't know precisely where the village was, but it never did the survey that required it, by ordinance, to inventory and map cultural sites on the shoreline. And the city kept rooting for the dry dock project even after construction inadvertently unearthed the site. That was despite the same ordinance, which stated "Due to the limited and irreplaceable nature of the resource, public or private uses and activities should be prevented from destroying or damaging any site having historic, cultural, scientific or educational value." Nonetheless, the governor's settlement agreement promised the city $7.5 million from the legislature for economic development projects as well as $480,000 in state tax dollars to hire an archaeologist to conduct the survey the city had committed to doing years earlier. Port Angeles also received up to $500,000 to attract and keep businesses in town.

The tribe was given eleven acres at the site for reburying its ancestors along with $2.5 million for reburial expenses, to preserve artifacts from the site, and to build a museum. Under the agreement, the tribe was forbidden to use any part of

the property for a casino. And it would have to share the cemetery with industrial uses right next door in perpetuity, because of land also gifted to the port as part of the waterfront deal.

As for the department, MacDonald's prediction proved accurate. The department was made out to be the goat. Under the agreement, it would be forced to obtain permits and contractors to dismantle its work at the site, including breaking up the concrete pad, just as Jollie had foreseen. The department would also have to remove the steel sheet pile, custom made and imported from Germany. The governor's office announced the agreement on a perfect August day in 2006 at a full-dress press conference at a community center in Port Angeles. Heavily scripted, it was intended to ring in a new day of reconciliation and cooperation in Port Angeles. But the reality in that concrete-floored room felt different. Port Angeles city council members, port commissioners, and economic development boosters filed in and took seats together on one side of the room. Tribal members, many in button blanket regalia and cedar hats, sat on the other. There were no happy handshakes or backslaps or hugs across the aisle, or visits back and forth to share delight or mutual relief. The two sides sat quietly apart, with the media set up on a platform between them in a kind of electronic demilitarized zone.

The governor strode to the podium in slacks and a yellow sweater. A native of the blue-collar town of Auburn, Washington, Gregoire had risen to the highest posts of state government, sweeping into the attorney general's office on a reform tide that saw a record number of women elected to statewide office in 1992. As attorney general, she became nationally known as the lawyer who brought Big Tobacco to its knees through her role in negotiating the $206 billion settlement between tobacco companies and forty-six states in 1998. She also gained a reputation at home as a friend to the tribes, working with tribal leaders to negotiate state compacts enabling economic development on Indian reservations through expanded video slot-machine gambling.

While her predecessor, Gary Locke, was the one who agreed to shut down the dry dock project, the controversy followed Gregoire to the governor's office. She would often say later that the canceled project was the first problem to hit her desk when she took office as governor. Within days, a delegation of angry city officials from Port Angeles told Gregoire they wanted her to restart construction at the site. That, Gregoire said, she would not do. And when she and Frances Charles greeted each other on August 14, 2006, to announce the settlement of the suit, it was with a hug and a kiss. Charles also gifted the governor with a hand-carved canoe paddle, in appreciation for her work on the agreement, and a sweat suit for relaxing in the governor's mansion. As she readied the gifts to take up to the podium, Charles briefly considered giving the mayor of Port Angeles, standing next to Gregoire, a handmade cedar basket. But at the last minute, she thought better of it. The basket stayed in a Tupperware container.

The prevailing feeling in the room was one of exhaustion after a long battle, and a wary tension. What was meant to be a happy, hopeful day felt more like a shotgun wedding. Without the money supplied as lubricant, it was hard to imagine that this town and this tribe would have hooked up at all; certainly no warmth flowed between them. Even in her official remarks to the crowd, Gregoire noted the strain. "I wish we could say this is a truly joyous occasion," she said, "but for many, I recognize it is more of a relief than a celebration. Hopefully, we will see at least one thing in common: this is the end of a long and painful experience."

Among the Lower Elwha, there were no claims of victory. There were tears and weariness. "We took what we could get," Frances Charles said. And the boxes full of bones were still in the bunker. "We cannot rest until the ancestors are back in the ground," she added. She knew reburial would be a long time coming, as permit applications to allow more disturbance of this ground wound their way through the bureaucracy. That deeply worried the tribe. The heart attacks and strokes that had already crippled two elders at Lower Elwha, including Charles's father, were no mystery to tribal members. On the reservation, the permits required to ensure a white version of safety were wreaking havoc in Indian lives connected, here and now, with the bones in the bunker. The spirits were still restless. Still dangerous.

Arlene Wheeler watched as the governor left the room with the mayor and city council members to go talk to the TV reporters. Her eyes were spilling tears. Her emotions were mixed. "We know we are doing the right thing in getting the land for reburial. It's been a long time coming," Wheeler said. "But we don't know where the relationship with the city really stands. Because of the history. It's going to take a lot of building relationships and trust. It's going to be a while. I don't think anything is going to happen overnight. Hopefully it's a new beginning for us all, for generations to come." She had no doubt that all of it, the finding of the village and the relentless way in which the ancestors' graves showed themselves—burial after burial after burial—was meant to happen. "They had been disturbed before. And they said, 'Enough is enough. We are going to do something about it this time,'" she said of her ancestors. "They set us all up to figure out what we are going to do to stop it, long term. And it's happening. I believe that. This is something they wanted to happen. They were tired of seeing this happen, and we've learned so much. They brought everything to our faces."

Across the room, Randy Hain stood alone. The man at the department of transportation with the most day-to-day responsibility for the dry dock project was not recognized, even briefly, from the podium. As the press conference wound down, he stood against the back wall, taking in the speeches and noting the divided room. Hain, who helped lead the settlement negotiations for the department, had been surprised by the $15.5 million offered to the city and the port. The department was not in the practice of offering money for lost profit when jobs are canceled. And he doubted that 120 family-wage jobs had been lost when the project shut down. "I thought, I wonder where that came from? There was no basis for it," Hain said. There weren't that many local hires for the jobs at the site, outside of the tribal construction monitors, because the contractor mostly brought its own specialized help. He wondered if the money alone had sealed the deal. Or if the department, intending to build one bridge in this town, had helped break ground on another, different kind of bridge. "I hope this is something that helps them on their way to being a community," he said. "I think the test of a good outcome will be getting through all these things that we have committed to. It's premature to say anything today. We'll see if the words we have said are what we accomplish. Maybe the simple fact that we brought something to light out there, that's a good thing."

The project brought profound change within a department long used to the idea of a road prism. It's an engineering term encompassing all the things that must be considered to build a road with structural integrity, the shoulders, the crown, the cut and fill. Never before had the department included history in that calculus. Tse-whit-zen changed that. "From a political standpoint, this project has been very important," said Leonard Forsman, chairman of the neighboring Suquamish Tribe. "It has made archaeology an issue. For years we had trouble convincing people of the importance of that, especially in local government. Tse-whit-zen was a way of waking them up, and waking up the legislature, and waking the state agencies up to the issue."

When the department undertook its next major project, construction of a new bridge over the Columbia River, it took a different approach. This time, the department started with a day-long history symposium, held in March 2007. Months in the planning, the symposium brought together tribes from around the region with academic experts and government officials from Washington and Oregon. Tribal members provided a Native perspective on the history and culture of the project area. Academics discussed explorers' expeditions, the fur trade, and the histories of the local cities of Vancouver and Portland. Tribal storytellers, basket weavers, and beadworkers provided a sense of the culture of the region. The department had never done anything like this before. It was the kind of beginning that might have prevented the ending in Port Angeles.

For the dry dock project, it was way too late for history seminars. That much was clear at the reception following the press conference to announce the lawsuit settlement, and a reconciliation not yet actually achieved. After the speeches, the TV interviews, and the presentations, the gathering fizzled; it had no cohesion beyond a scripted program to keep it going. A few people picked at food laid out for the occasion. The room quickly emptied out.

Restless, feeling incomplete and unfinished, Hain didn't trust himself with the long drive back to Olympia just yet. "I didn't feel like I had any closure. I needed to do something in my own mind to settle this," he said. He walked out to his car and knew what he had to do. He headed downhill to the waterfront and turned in at the site. It was deserted, anonymous. There was no sign, no piles of flowers or other memorials or mementos outside the gate, no outward indication of what had unfolded here. Steam from the paper plant unspooled over the site, just as before. Weeds grew up the chain link fences. Plastic sheeting covering mounds of stockpiled material flapped in the wind off the Strait of Juan de Fuca. Hain fished the master key for the gate from his pocket, slipped the padlock, and opened the gate.

Still in his street shoes and good clothes, he walked across the dusty ground and let his mind wander over all that had happened here. "All the milestones, everything came to me, the bad weather days, the good weather days, the looks on people's faces as they found things, all of this just washed through me," Hain said.

He found a wooden ladder and leaned it against a sheet pile wall. Climbed to the top and sat down on the ledge atop the wall, ten feet in the air. Hain looked out to the blue salt water, felt the wind on his face. Then he turned and looked at the site, with its jumble of archaeology and burials and construction, each a piece of the history finally made visible at this site. Ready to leave, he headed to the gate. The chain tangled. The lock fought him. "I thought, 'All this fumbling, just the way this thing has gone. Why should I expect I should just go, zap, with this lock?'" he said. The padlock clicked shut. "I thought, 'Well. Finally.'" And then he was gone.

Epilogue

OUT OF THE WATER, SINGING

IN THE DEEP WINTER DARK JUST BEFORE DAWN, THE TUGBOAT SIDLED UP TO the concrete pontoon, bigger than a barge. With a snort of black smoke, the tug eased the massive concrete structure through the sea gate of the dry dock and floated it out to the open waters of Puget Sound. It was the first real progress in the state transportation department's project to repair the Hood Canal Bridge. Delays and the eventual abandonment of the Port Angeles site had stalled the project for nearly two years. Some $90 million in state and federal money already sunk into the site was a big, bitter pill to swallow when the department agreed, at the tribe's request, to leave. That meant finding an alternative place to build pontoons and anchors for fixing the bridge. In the end, the department chose an existing dry dock in Puget Sound— one of the sites it didn't choose earlier because regulators frowned on it the first time around. It wasn't as big as the preferred site in Port Angeles. It wasn't as efficient for getting the work done, which added time and cost to completing the project. Department staff also had to rewrite their entire plan of work. But despite it all, as the full moon pulled the tide to its highest point that December night in 2006, dozens of workers and managers from the department turned out in the middle of the night to witness the float-out. There was hot coffee. And finally, with that first pontoon afloat, a sense of progress.

As the tide rose so, too, did prospects for better outcomes in disputes like the one that happened in Port Angeles. For both avoiding them in the first place and dealing with them when they inevitably arise in a rapidly growing nation. For regionally and nationally, plenty of learning came out of what happened at the Tse-whit-zen site and how the dispute was resolved. Much of what happened there was without precedent. Not the disruption of Indian burials—that happens all over the country. Many other hearts, in many other places, have been broken because of the violence done to ancestral burials and sacred sites. Projects all over the country have also been stopped, redesigned, or delayed at a cost of millions of dollars because of burials or significant archaeology encountered during construction work.

In west Los Angeles, the Gabrielino Tongva San Gabriel Band of Mission Indians had to stand by and watch as developers of the Playa Vista development complex, which was to include residences and retail and office space, dug up and relocated 411 Indian burials. As with Tse-whit-zen, the tribe and the developer signed an agreement allowing the project to go forward as long as the remains were excavated for reburial. And, as also happened in Port Angeles, the agreement was signed before anyone knew how many remains would be found. But when the tribe asked the developer to stop the project, the company refused. "When I said, 'Enough is enough,' we told the developer to leave them in place; they wouldn't do it," said Anthony Morales, tribal chairman and chief of the Gabrielino Tongva San Gabriel Band of Mission Indians. "That was the route they were taking, and they weren't going to divert. I want [the remains] right back where they originally were found. They should never have been disrupted, uncovered, or unearthed. People say it is just a skeleton, a bone. It's very disrespectful. It is not right. We would not do that to anybody else's ancestors or ethnic groups. Why do this to us? It tore me apart. It is a shame, a crime. Even a hate crime." Reburial of the ancestors was finally accomplished in December 2008, after fifteen years of controversy and litigation.

Outcomes like that make what happened in Port Angeles extraordinary, said Jack Trope, executive director of the Association on American Indian Affairs, a non-profit founded in 1923 specializing in cultural preservation and sacred lands. "The magnitude of the amount of money already invested, and the solution of turning some land back to the tribe, that is not unprecedented, but it is not the norm either," Trope said. "It

At a healing ceremony hosted by the tribe, tribal members from around the region joined with Port Angeles residents to circle the site one last time and pay their respects to the ancestors, January 2005. Sheet piles, driven into the ground for the dry dock project, rise in the background. Steve Ringman, courtesy *Seattle Times*.

is the exception rather than the rule. When you put all those things together, the extent of the investment, the scope of the project, the agreement to turn some of the land back, it is a pretty extraordinary example."

Trope ticks off other milestones notched at Port Angeles. The $3.4 million mitigation payment the transportation department made to the tribe was unprecedented at the time and not required by any law. Under Section 106 of the federal Historic Preservation Act, all the department had to do was consult with the tribe. Once the department had the agreement of state and federal historic preservation agencies on a mitigation plan, it was free to give the tribe notice and start the bulldozers. Instead, the department obtained the tribe's consent before continuing the work. And the Lower Elwha Klallam Tribe was fully engaged in crafting the site treatment plan governing work at the project. The tribe made the decisions about how the remains of its people would be treated and vetoed any scientific examination of the remains. The department's decision to hire tribal members to work alongside archaeologists at the site was highly unusual and put $1.3 million in wages into tribal members'

On a bitter winter day, wrapped in a blanket and painted for spiritual protection, Lower Elwha Tribal Chairwoman Frances Charles asks tribal members and town residents gathered for a healing ceremony to join with the tribe in forging a better future, January 2005. Steve Ringman, courtesy *Seattle Times*.

pockets. Some 111 tribal members were on the agency payroll at the height of the dig in the summer and fall of 2004. And when the Lower Elwha Klallam said that enough was enough, the region's political leaders honored their request.

"The outcome in the case of Port Angeles was something people felt really good about," Trope said. "It wasn't a given that it would play out that way; you hope it would, that you get people with genuine interest and concern. I thought it was pretty remarkable that the state was willing to do that, and I was glad to see it, when you are talking about a site that large and that many graves, given the profound importance. So often it is all about the money—'We know this is important to you, but we have so much money in this.' They got beyond that, and they were able to say, 'What does this site really mean?' And they were able to find a way to do what they needed to do. Too often you get agencies just digging their heels in, and that is enormously frustrating and infuriating to Native people who say there are other ways to do this. I'm glad to see the state was willing to say this is something that we need to get done, but we can do it another way, instead of getting caught up in 'We have already invested so much in this approach, and we have to do this. It's too late now.' They figured out how to do this without creating that kind of permanent psychological and social harm. I think it is great when they can do that, when you can turn traditional cultural properties back into tribal hands. That is a good thing."

What happened in Port Angeles could be an important example for finding solutions when remains are found. "It can have a positive effect, in terms of a precedent," Trope said. "In the sense that when you run across something where they say, 'We can't possibly do x,' now it's 'What do you mean you can't? They have done it in other places. Look at this example.'" But Trope said the outcome in other projects also shows that more legal protection is needed for Indian burials.

Section 106 of the federal Historic Preservation Act offers only a process but no mandated result when a site is encountered, and it comes into play only if federal funds are involved in the project. The law doesn't state what amount, or type, of consultation with affected tribes is sufficient. So the outcome of the law is only as good as what goes into it from the agencies and the good faith of the people participating, Trope said. "It's about whether they really want to figure out a way to work it out, or are they just going through the motions so they can get on with the project, and that is the problem with the laws. That is what it comes down to." The federal Native American Graves Protection and Repatriation Act, passed in 1990, applies only to federal lands. And it doesn't stop disruption of Native burials. "From a tribal perspective, the laws are not as strong as they need to be," Trope said. "They are tools that didn't exist in previous periods. At least there are some tools now. But the outcome can still be pretty bad from a tribal perspective despite all that."

It is yet to be seen whether Tse-whit-zen and other discoveries lead to changes in federal policy. But the Tse-whit-zen case quickly led to policy changes at the state level in Washington. The transportation department went to work with tribes all over Washington to craft a major revision of a written agreement spelling out just how federal requirements for consulting with tribes on development projects would be implemented. The agency also made internal changes. When the agency, one of the largest transportation departments in the country with a $5 billion biennial total budget in 2005–7, initiated the Hood Canal Bridge project, it had no professional archaeologist on staff. By 2006, it had five, as well as two more historians who joined the one already at the agency. The department also revamped its approach to pre-construction review of sites for other projects. The agency's understanding of where it needs to look to learn the true history of potential construction sites is far broader, beyond the mere physical footprint of the project. Tse-whit-zen taught the agency to reach out to elders and meet with tribal leaders face-to-face to learn the social, cultural, and historical context of lands it is considering for development. The Washington State Legislature also acted during the 2005 session to elevate the status of the state historic preservation office to department level and provide the budget for additional staff to handle project reviews.

But perhaps the most powerful legacy of what happened in Port Angeles is that this time, the story had a different ending, simply because people decided it must. To some longtime tribal advocates, that was the most encouraging and potentially influential lesson from Tse-whit-zen. "It sounds to me like they tried to do the right thing," said Walter Echo-Hawk, staff attorney at the Native American Rights Fund since 1973. "You just need a change of heart. That is something you can't legislate. It's a very significant and noteworthy milestone in our evolution as a nation. It's safe to say that had this taken place ten, fifteen, twenty years ago, they would have run roughshod over the site without giving it a second's thought. With the change in attitude toward Native American people and burials, we can see things like this. There is a whole new set of values that has kicked into place. There are laws and policies in place, of course, but there is also a change in perspective and values. That we need to try to do the right thing about it and not just run roughshod over it as if they were nonhuman remains. They did the right thing and walked away. It was very significant. You would hope to see more of these. Whenever money is involved, a walk-away is unusual. There is that mentality of construction and progress and civilization and everything must bend to that, almost as an attribute of Manifest Destiny, that God intended this, and we are not going to walk away from that almighty dollar."

David Nicandri, executive director of the Washington State Historical Society, sees the growing power of tribes to preserve their cultural heritage as a natural progression of their assertion of treaty rights. "What is different now is tribes are really the third leg of the government stool. You have federal, state, and tribal governments, and that structurally re-creates the intergovernmental dynamic that we have not seen in the Northwest since the 1840s and 1850s, when the tribes had military power sufficient to cause the federal and territorial and later state officials to calculate what they might want to say and do with the tribes. That was dissipated throughout the later half of the nineteenth century and into the twentieth century. By the 1950s and 1960s, they didn't give a damn. Tribes began to fight back, and they have had significant victories. The tribes have an infrastructure to assert their rights and priorities, and it plays out across the whole range of issues. They have to be taken seriously.

During the healing ceremony, spiritual leader Mary Anne Thomas (*front row, left*) joins in prayer with Lower Elwha tribal members Arlene Wheeler (*center*) and Carmen Watson-Charles (*right*). Port Angeles town residents shiver along with them, at rear. Steve Ringman, courtesy *Seattle Times*.

They don't have everything they want, but they have considerably more clout than a generation ago, because of the reassertion of tribal sovereignty."

Nicandri found that out the hard way when the historical society tried to work with the state transportation department to reroute a state highway for a new national park commemorating the explorations of Meriwether Lewis and William Clark. The park would be a badly needed boost for a southwestern Washington community fallen on hard times with the depletion of the fishing industry. Local officials badly wanted the park completed in time for the bicentennial of the Lewis and Clark expedition. But when contractors for the project began their pre-construction testing of the site in 2005, they uncovered longhouse planks and a trove of artifacts dating back to the fur trade years. The artifacts documented the world trade carried on by the Chinook people of southwestern Washington and the Columbia River country long before Lewis and Clark showed up. Undaunted, Nicandri entered into an agreement with the tribe, securing its permission to proceed with the project in return for paying $120,000, hiring a half-time employee for the tribe, and redesigning the park to encompass the tribe's history at the site more fully. Work got under way again, and then contractors hit human remains. The job shut down again. Then tribal members declared in a referendum that the agreement they had signed with the agency was null and void. A deal was no longer a deal. As he worked to save the project, Nicandri learned, as the transportation department had in Port Angeles, that Section 106 of the Historic Preservation Act gave no guidance on resolving the issues. "The statutory and procedural agreements in place only work if there is no problem. And if there is a problem, they don't work," Nicandri said. "The people in charge of managing cultural resources in a developing world need a new solution." That's because even though the law allows it, public agencies can no longer disregard the wishes of tribes. The political climate has simply changed. "When the tribes didn't have the leverage they have over federal and state and local government, there was no issue," Nicandri said. "But now they do. And it's a tremendous issue. The mechanism in place putatively to resolve this can't. Certainty is out the window."

Two years of delay later, and with some $400,000 sunk into the cost of the inadvertent discovery, on top of the $1.5 million already spent to develop the park, Nicandri was hoping that neither the agencies paying for the project nor the tribe would give up on it. One thing he knew for sure was that the challenge of working within a shared understanding, rather than just forcing the issue, is pressing the normal workings of government in the majority culture very hard.

"You are dealing with two different worlds," Nicandri said. "The majority culture gets upset with delay and views the time cost of money and wants to move on to the next big thing, the issue du jour. That is just not the way tribes look at things; they are looking at it from a multigenerational, 6,000- to 10,000-year perspective. It's bridging that divide that is the problem. But the reward is—arguably in the modern context, this is the only way you do succeed—in finishing projects and coming to common ground. It is not a practical alternative for government to act like it did in the old days of 'We consulted with you, and we are going ahead anyway.' But to say it is the cost of doing business never seems quite sufficient." Nonetheless, with Tse-whit-zen, he saw a paradigm shift. "It completely re-altered the frame of reference," Nicandri said. "My instinct tells me what happened on this [park] project was heavily informed by the success the tribe up north [in Port Angeles] was having with bringing the state of Washington into compliance with its view of things."

Port Angeles has, in spite of itself, become a precedent and ground zero for rethinking what constitutes true progress and wealth today. Settled and developed with the mind-set of conquering the last frontier, and anyone or anything in the way, this city is now an experiment in a new vision of wealth, based on restoration and renewal of its native ecosystem and culture. The Elwha dams, built in the heyday of unfettered industrialization, are slated to come out. It won't be with a bang, but with a whimper, with the dams taken down bit by bit. The dismantling was ordered not by a judicial decree but by a 1992 act of Congress, which mandates restoration of the Elwha River ecosystem. After years of bitter debate, the people of the Pacific Northwest determined there was more value in a restored, native ecosystem than in two dams without fish ladders that no modern regulatory agency could relicense.

When the Elwha River finally surges unleashed past the concrete, it will be chaos on the move. Tons of sediment, held back for decades by the dams, will rinse into the flow. The Elwha will be muddy, turbid, and messy. It will be a dangerous, liminal time for the fish that have hung on in this river. To protect them, scientists will trap and haul the salmon to safety. The people in this community don't have it nearly so easy. They have to live in the murk of change so that they may find their way together to a homeland that is shared with the Native people of this place. For breaking ground at Tse-whit-zen uncovered not only the past of this place but its present. It revealed a community's inability to anticipate the find or deal with it.

A spirit of collaboration can't usually be announced into being at a press conference. Nor will money buy it. Whether it will flow in this community or remain dammed by mistrust is yet to be seen. A cycle of history, begun more than 150 years ago, will come full circle for this tribe, this town, and this river. And while some see failure in the canceled dry dock project and the dismantling of the dams, others see hope.

Still to be determined is the fate of the archaeological analysis promised for the Tse-whit-zen site. The original, March 2004 site-treatment plan for the dig included a commitment to analyze the thousands of artifacts recovered and features mapped during archaeological excavation, in order to interpret and preserve the history of the portions of the site destroyed by construction. But that promise was abandoned in a new agreement approved in April 2007, after the dry dock project was shut down. That plan was silent on archaeological analysis for the site, which is without funding now that the project has stopped. As of this writing, the federal promise contained in the National Historic Preservation Act, to preserve the history of Tse-whit-zen, awaits fulfillment.

Also in a holding pattern are the artifacts themselves. Kept under lock and key in boxes at the Burke Museum in Seattle, their stories have not been told through archaeological analysis, nor has the public had a chance to appreciate their wonder. The tribe may petition for repatriation of its ancestors' belongings only after it has a suitable place to keep the artifacts, such as a museum, which the tribe is raising money to build.

Lower Elwha tribal member Vanna K. Francis, sixteen (*far left*), gives a speech in her native Klallam as tribal officials, Washington governor Christine Gregoire, and city officials sign an agreement returning a portion of the dry dock site to the tribe for reburial of its ancestors, August 2006. Many tribal members would later remark that for the first time they could remember at a city event, the flag of the Lower Elwha tribal government (*far right*) was placed on the podium alongside the United States, Washington State, and City of Port Angeles flags. The moment would prove bittersweet: In 2007, Francis was killed in a car crash. Courtesy Lower Elwha Klallam Tribe.

The tribe is enjoying a cultural renaissance. The Lower Elwha Klallam people, once beaten for speaking their language, today teach Klallam in the public high school. Artifacts, history, and culture unearthed at Tse-whit-zen and the tribe's historic use of the Elwha River are also part of the public school history curriculum, created in cooperation with the tribe and the public school system. There's a tribal liaison on the payroll at every public school in the Port Angeles area, to ensure a welcome and safe harbor for every Indian student. A Klallam greeting hangs over the door at the school district office, carved into a cedar plank. And in 2006, teachers, students, administrators, and Lower Elwha parents gathered for the tenth annual potlatch at the tribal center, to celebrate the children they share.

A van full of students travels each week to a neighboring reservation, to meet with other Klallam people who are learning their language. As they practice, the sound of the words, so uniquely theirs, is as steady and soft as the tide just outside the classroom door. Attendance at the weekly language classes at the Lower Elwha tribal reservation doubled after the discovery of the Tse-whit-zen site, and students included non-Indians curious to learn more about their neighbors.

Asked what more they hope for going forward, most people here on the reservation at Lower Elwha don't hesitate. They want the salmon back in the river. Their

ancestors at rest in their graves. Their language and culture alive in all the generations of their people to come. And they want an understanding in this community, and beyond, of the true history of the places we all share now. "Maybe they will believe it. Finally," Beatrice Charles said. "That we were here. And we are still here."

Postscript, September 2008

As day broke, the air was so still by the Strait of Juan de Fuca that the candles did not flicker. A tangerine sunrise glowed and grew brighter in the east as a full moon set to the west. A doe picked its way carefully across the Tse-whit-zen site, and a great flight of seagulls wheeled in the brightening sky. It was time to rebury the ancestors' remains, some now five years out of the ground. The steel sheet piles had been pulled out, the concrete slab broken up and hauled away. Eleven acres of this ground at Tse-whit-zen have been turned back to the tribe, who gathered at the site on September 15 and 16, 2008, for a reburial ceremony as small and private as it was long awaited.

Holding candles for the ancestors, a thumb smudge of red ochre on their cheeks for spiritual protection, Mary Anne Thomas and other spiritual leaders from across the water in Canada helped a small gathering of Lower Elwha tribal members carry the burden of the work. Johnson Charles Jr. came with his flute. Arlene Wheeler was there and Mark Charles, too, with a group of singers and drummers. Frances Charles and Phil Charles from the tribal council were there. And gravediggers traveled from Canada to help, so that the Lower Elwha Klallam people would not risk carrying grief home from the work. The gravediggers were ready with their shovels as the first pickup truck arrived from the bunker with a load of cedar boxes. It was finally time for the ancestors to come back home.

By hand, pallbearers, four to a side, walked the boxes from the truck and laid them next to each other in a mass grave. Care had been taken the night before to find the remains of family members who must be placed together, as they had been originally buried, as well as the couples, and identify the headstones to go with each grave. The work was slow, deliberate. As she walked to the site, elder Elaine Grinnell from the Jamestown S'Klallam tribe, here to witness the reburial with her grandson, suddenly noticed that her woven shawl was swinging loose. The hand-carved blanket pin that she used to secure it was missing. She searched for it for a time, then stopped. "I think they liked it," she said of the ancestors. She asked the gravediggers to tuck it in amid the rows of boxes, if they found it. The pin belonged here, she decided—like the ancestors.

As the row of boxes grew long, filling the grave from side to side, gravediggers shoveled the dirt of the ancestors' homeland over them, to the sound of softly spoken prayer and the ringing of a single bell. Fifty boxes. One hundred boxes. Two hundred boxes. Still so many more to go.

Nearly as soon as the ceremony began, the sounds of workaday Port Angeles intruded on the quiet of the reburial rite. Logging trucks rumbled past. In easy view just hundreds of yards away, front-end loaders snorted and stacked logs on the industrial properties that sandwich the burial ground on two sides. A truck lumbered along spraying water to keep down the clouds of dust raised by heavy equipment. The pulp plant steamed as always, right next door to the west. This site, returned to the tribe by the state of Washington, seemed small indeed, even virtually ignored by an indifferent world.

Yet there alongside tribal members was Clark Mundy, a non-Indian carpenter and lifelong Port Angeles resident, who helped build these burial boxes and who showed up to help carry them, one by one, to the grave site. A non-Indian backhoe operator, a trusted friend of the tribe for years, helped move piles of dirt for the gravediggers to shovel. Doug MacDonald and Colleen Jollie, both now retired from the state transportation department, rose before dawn to quietly bear witness. And when the tribe went to buy shovels and wheelbarrows for the reburial, local business owners sold the tools at reduced prices, according to the Port Angeles Daily News, which devoted two front-page stories to the reburial. This tribe was not invisible anymore.

Yet as the first day of reburial continued on to the next, and word spread through Port Angeles about what was happening down at the waterfront, there was no spontaneous groundswell in the larger community to in some way honor these dead, or any invitation issued from the tribe to join the observance. The relief participants felt in seeing what everyone wanted for the ancestors was paired with an awareness of how much work is still needed to keep history from repeating itself, not only in Port Angeles but beyond. That piece of healing has not come yet.

But for some people at the Lower Elwha Klallam reservation, a story comes to mind. It is a story of a man suddenly swept up into a powerful wave. He is tossed and thrown, pummeled and spun in the cold, green water. As he prays and prays, he suddenly finds his feet. And then he walks out of the water, singing. So it seems for the Lower Elwha Klallam people, battered by disease, dispossession, and industrialization, yet still walking forward as Indian people in the modern world, with a living culture.

The work of reconciliation, if it began at this grave site, certainly has not been fully achieved yet. But the bunker, so long full of boxes holding Native ancestors' displaced remains, is empty. The ancestors finally rest once more in their homeland. They face the rising sun.

A Klallam Glossary

ancestor sčiyúʔis

artifact čəcən

bead qʷəỷqʷi

bone scúmʼ

chinook salmon sčánəxʷ

comb tšéʔqʷən

dancehouse sqʷəyíyəšháwʼtxʷ

dancer's pole with deer hooves kʷčmín

Elwha River ʔéʔɬxʷə stúʔwiʔ

etched stone niɬ cə xəỷɬ

fish hook kʼʷúyəkʷ

head strap cəŋaʔtən

hearth sčqʷaʔcáyə

lightning ƛ̓əmƛ̓əmcínəŋ

otter bones scúmʼ ʔaʔ cə čaʔmús

point, or arrowhead yəčt

Port Angeles, or Tse-whit-zen čxʷícən

Pysht pəšct

rattle kʷčmín

red ochre təmʼəɬ

rib yəkʷx

rock sŋánt

sea otter scúmʼ ʔaʔ cə čaʔmús

shell kʷáʔŋənor

Skokomish təwánəxʷ

skull scaʔméʔqʷ

spindle whorl sisúyʼətəŋ

stone maul cə́stən

washing cʼaʔkʷúsəŋ

wedge wíč

white person xʷanítəm

winter dances syəẃən

Notes

2 Abundance

1 Sarah Sterling, Donald Tatum, and Dennis Lewarch, "Geomorphology of the Ediz Hook and Port Angeles Harbor," in *Final Data Recovery and Archaeological Monitoring at Tse-whit-zen Site*, ed. Lynn Larson, 3-1–3-55. Gig Harbor, WA: Larson Anthropological and Archaeological Services, 2006.

3 Calamity

1 Henry R. Wagner, *Spanish Explorations on the Strait of Juan de Fuca* (Santa Ana, Calif.: Fine Arts Press, 1933), 108.

2 Ibid., 110.

3 Ibid., 131.

4 Robert Boyd, *The Coming of the Spirit of Pestilence* (Seattle: University of Washington Press, 1999), 3.

5 Boyd, personal communication, October 2006.

6 Boyd, *Pestilence*, 58–59.

7 Mary Ann Lambert, "Smallpox Ship," in *Shadows of Our Ancestors*, ed. Jerry Gorsline (Port Townsend, Wash.: Empty Bowl Press, 1992), 204–7.

8 Matthew I. Gill and Glenn D. Hartmann, *Burial Recovery at Tse-whit-zen* (Bainbridge Island, Wash.: Western Shore Heritage Services, 2006), executive summary.

9 Hayley E. Kanipe, *Final Data Recovery Excavation and Archaeological Construction Monitoring at the Tse-whit-zen Site, Clallam County, Washington*, vol. 2, *Burials* (Gig Harbor, Wash.: Larson Anthropological Archaeological Services, June 2006), 113–14.

10 Charles M. Gates, "The Indian Treaty of Point No Point," *Pacific Northwest Quarterly* 46, no. 2 (April

1955): 53.

11 Ibid., 53.

12 Ibid., 55.

13 Ibid., 55.

14 Lambert, "Point No Point Treaty," in *Shadows of Our Ancestors*, 66–68.

15 M. T. Simmons, 1860 report, *Letters, Volume 1*, Culture and History Collection, Jamestown S'Klallam Tribal Library, Blyn, Washington. Quoted in Joseph H. Stauss, *The Jamestown S'Klallam Story: Rebuilding a Northwest Coast Indian Tribe* (Sequim, Wash.: Jamestown S'Klallam, 2002), 139.

16 Edwin Eells, 23 September 1873 report, *Letters, Volume 1*, Culture and History Collection, Jamestown S'Klallam Tribal Library, Blyn, Washington. Quoted in Stauss, *The Jamestown S'Klallam Story*, 143.

17 Beatrice Charles, interview by the author, digital audiodisc, Port Angeles, Washington, March 2005.

18 Paul J. Martin, *Port Angeles, Washington: A History*, vol. 1 (Port Angeles, Wash.: Pen Print, 1983), 1.

19 John McCallum and Lorraine Wilcox Ross, *Port Angeles USA* (Seattle: Wood and Reber, 1961), 55.

20 Gretchen A. Kaehler and Stephanie E. Trudel, "Trading Posts to Timber Mills: Historic Period Land Use at the Tse-whit-zen Site," in *Final Data Recovery Excavation and Archaeological Monitoring at the Tse-whit-zen Site*, vol. 1 (Gig Harbor, Wash.: Larson Anthropological Archaeological Services, 2006), 8.

4   Conquering the Last Frontier

1 *The Model Commonwealth* (Port Angeles, Washington), November 23, 1888, quoted in Paul J. Martin, *Port Angeles, Washington: A History*, vol. 1 (Port Angeles, Wash.: Pen Print, 1983), 44.

2 Martin, *Port Angeles, Washington*, 44.

3 Thomas Aldwell, *Conquering the Last Frontier*

(Seattle: Artcraft Engraving and Electrotype Company, 1950), 17–18.

5 Ibid., 19–20, 22–26.

6 Ibid., 68.

7 Ibid., 80.

8 Ibid., 111.

9 Washington State Archives, Surface Waters file, Elwha River folder, box 1010-38, accession number 1911-15.

10 Ibid.

11 Ibid.

12 Ibid.

13 Ibid.

5   The Big Mill

1 John McCallum and Lorraine Wilcox Ross, Port Angeles, USA (Seattle: Wood and Reber, 1961), 118.

2 Beatrice Charles and Adeline Smith, interview by the author, digital audiodisc, Port Angeles, Washington, March 2004.

3 Kaehler and Trudel, "Trading Posts to Timber Mills," in *Final Data Recovery Excavation and Archaeological Construction Monitoring at the Tse-whit-zen Site, Clallam County, Washington* vol. 1 (Gig Harbor, Wash.: Larson Anthropological Archaeological Services, June 2006), 21–22.

4 Ibid., 22.

5 H. H. Hill, "Built at a Cost of One and a Half Million Dollars, Is the Last Word in a Modern Methods of Handling the Manufacture of Lumber," *Tribune Times*, Prosperity Edition, "Greatest Lumber Mills in Pacific Northwest," May 15, 1914. Found in newspaper file in the artifacts storage facility of the Clallam County Historical Society, Port Angeles, Washington.

6 Patty May Hassel, "Sol Duc Hot Springs," in *Jimmy Come Lately: History of Clallam County*, ed. Jervis Russell (Port Angeles, Wash.: Clallam County

Historical Society, 1971), 415–19.

7   Aldwell, *Conquering the Last Frontier*, 142.

8   Ibid., 144–45.

9   Ibid., 145–46.

10 Barbara Lane, "Indian Use of Shellfish in Western Washington and the Indian Treaties of 1854–1855," May 10, 1984. Found at archives of the Lower Elwha Klallam Tribe, Port Angeles, Washington.

11 "Newsprint Mill Observes 20th Anniversary," *Crown-Z News*, November 5, 1940, Port Angeles, Washington. Found in Mills, Crown Zellerbach file, box 37, Clallam County Historical Society reference library.

12 McCallum and Wilcox Ross, *Port Angeles, USA*, 137.

13 Interview with Edward C. Sampson, June 1992. On file at Lower Elwha Klallam Archives, Port Angeles, Washington.

14 Beatrice Charles and Adeline Smith, interview by the author, tape recording, Port Angeles, Washington, March 2005.

15 *Port Angeles Evening News*, "Once-Thriving Lumber Mill Goes Up in Flames," January 22, 1940.

6   Collective Amnesia

1   Washington State Department of Transportation, dry dock facts circular. Found in permit file for Shoreline Substantial Development permit SMA 03-01, Department of Community Development, Port Angeles City Hall, Port Angeles, Washington.

2   Lynn L. Larson and Dennis Lewarch, *Archaeological Testing at the Daishowa America Port Angeles Mill Recycled Paper and Electrical Modernization Project Areas, Clallam County, Washington*, Larson Anthropological Archaeological Services, LAAS Technical Report No. 91-2, March 6, 1991, p. 18. Found at North Olympic public library, Port Angeles, Washington.

3   Ibid., 40.

7   This Ground Speaks

1   Elizabeth C. Reetz et al., "Field Techniques," in *Final Data Recovery Excavation and Archaeological Monitoring at the Tse-whit-zen Site*, ed. Lynn Larson, vol. 1, chap. 4, p. 7 (Gig Harbor, Wash.: Larson Anthropological Archaeological Services, July 17, 2006).

2   Ibid, 9–13.

8   Walking Together

1   Matthew E. Gill and Glenn Hartmann, *Burial Recovery at Tse-whit-zen* (Bainbridge Island, Wash.: Western Shore Heritage Services, 2006), p. 5.

9   Walking Away

1   Larson Anthropological Archaeological Services, *Data Recovery Excavation and Archaeological Monitoring at the Tse-whit-zen Site*, vol. 2 (Gig Harbor, Wash.: Larson Anthropological Archaeological Services, 2006), p. 111.

2   Gill and Hartmann, *Burial Recovery at Tse-whit-zen*, chap. 7, p. 2.

3   Ibid., chap. 7, p. 17.

4   Larson Anthropological Archaeological Services, *Data Recovery Excavation and Archaeological Monitoring at the Tse-whit-zen Site*, vol. 2, p. 48.

5   Ibid., 60.

6   Ibid., 53.

7   Ibid., 51.

8   Ibid., 59.

Notes on Sources

WORK ON THIS BOOK INCLUDED MANY HOURS OF INTERVIEWS DURING THE FALL
and winter of 2004 and over the course of 2005 and 2006. Some interviews were recorded
on digital audiodisc or audiotape, and some were documented by my own note taking,
as the situation demanded. All of the original discs and tapes are in my possession, at
my home, as are all of my notebooks and transcripts of the discs and tapes.

It took a little more than three years to do this book. Much of the work was done
for breaking news articles as well as a special series for the *Seattle Times*, published
in 2004, 2005, and 2006. Readers wanting to know more about the newspaper cover-
age should go to Seattletimes.com, where they will find the breaking news stories,
the series, and an online presentation, audio recordings, and a narrated slide show
about Tse-whit-zen in the special reports archives at http://seattletimes.nwsource.
com/news/local/klallam/.

This is a good place to make clear that I was hardly the first or only reporter to
cover this story. Brenda Hanrahan, a former reporter at the *Port Angeles Daily News*,
worked tirelessly to report story after story about every phase of the project. Anyone

curious to learn more about the project would do well to check out the Port Angeles paper. Back issues are archived on microfilm, available at any major library.

Those with an appetite for further exploration of historic photos of the region would also do well to visit the online trove at The Pacific Northwest Olympic Peninsula Community Museum, http://content.lib.washington.edu/cmpweb/index.html.

The interviews I did and books I used, cited here, only touch the surface of the impressions, experiences, thoughts, and feelings exchanged as I reported this book. Many interviews I did not note here were nonetheless important. There were many mornings, afternoons, and evenings spent with no notebook opened or recorder turned on that nonetheless shaped what appears in this book.

Many of the documents I relied on are restricted, and obtaining them requires special permission from the tribe. They are exempt from public disclosure. And much of what is documented in this book won't be found in any library or archive anyway: It's people's emotional journey, as offered in the moment, and oral history graciously passed on by tribal elders generous enough to share it.

I thought a lot about what I, as a nonexpert, had to offer in doing this book and why I wanted to do it. Ultimately, it was my belief in the value of this material. To me, these interviews are the heart of the book and its reason for being. I believed these voices needed a wider audience and a place of permanent, public record because the views they express set a marker for our development as a people and a region. They tell us who we are and who we are becoming.

A book like this never feels finished. Perhaps it will, however, provide resources and provocation for others to continue the exploration of what it means for people to walk together as this region finds its footing in a place we now all share.

For readers seeking to retrace the steps in my own exploration, here is an informal guide.

1   Buried Past Comes Alive

A few words about the bunker. The location is private and restricted. No one is allowed to visit this building without the permission of the Lower Elwha Klallam Tribe. I visited the bunker on several occasions and wound up spending most of an entire day and much of the night there in July 2005, going through box after box of the tribe's files on the dry dock project.

I kept a candle burning on a cafeteria lunch tray on the table as I worked, at the request of the tribe and out of respect for the ancestors. I also kept candles burning in the room where the burial boxes holding the ancestors' remains were stored, rising from time to time to make sure the candles had not gone out. I was alone for many hours in the building with my own thoughts and the presence of the ancestors in their burial boxes. I will never forget that honor or the trust bestowed by the tribe.

I lead the opening chapter with the feel and look of that room, that particular day. That description is built from notes I made as I walked around the bunker, touching nothing but observing it in detail, and from my thoughts about it over time.

My reflections on Port Angeles come from numerous trips there in the course of my reporting for the newspaper and my work on the book over three years. But the writing in this chapter stems especially from a visit I made there in March 2005. On that trip, I spent time on the Ediz Hook, at the gate to the site, and at a picnic bench by a gas station take-out counter, watching people come and go from a plywood plant.

Interviews by the author: Darrell Charles Jr., personal interview, Port Angeles, November 2004. Linda Wiechman, personal interview, Port Angeles, November 2004. Carmen Watson-Charles, telephone interview, November 2004. Derek Charles, personal interview, Lower Elwha Klallam Tribal Reservation (hereafter LEKT Reservation), March 2005; personal interview, LEKT Reservation, May 2006. Frances Charles, personal interview, Port Angeles, November 2004. Beatrice Charles, personal interview, LEKT Reservation, March 2005. Jerry Charles, personal interview, Port Angeles, November 2004.

2 Abundance

The description of the environment of the site and the Ediz Hook comes from a visit I made there in March 2005, when I recorded the sound of the tide at the beach and spent time reflecting on the site as I looked back at the land from the hook. I listened to that recording as I wrote the opening of this chapter.

I also relied on Robert Lundahl's documentary film *Unconquering the Last Frontier: The Historic Saga of the Damming and Undamming of Washington's Elwha River* (Evolution Films, 2000 and 2002).

Jim Allaway's report *Understanding the Elwha: A Strategy for Research and Education Programs on the Elwha River* (Bellingham: Western Washington University, Huxley College of the Environment, May 2004) was also a very helpful overview of the river and the dams' effect on the Elwha watershed.

I also relied on the final Environmental Impact Statement *Elwha River Ecosystem Restoration Implementation*, published in November 1996 by Olympic National Park, the National Park Service, and the U.S. Department of the Interior.

Other valuable information about the river from the tribe's perspective comes from the "Lower Elwha S'Klallam Tribe River Restoration Project" memo by the Lower Elwha Tribal Council and "A Recent History of the Elwha River." Both of these documents can be found at the Washington State Archives, in the Joe Mentor Donation, accession number 04-1-273, box 1, Lower Elwha Klallam Tribe file.

The story of the formation of the Ediz Hook and its use by Native people comes from Poster Three in a series of posters on the Tse-whit-zen site prepared by Larson Anthropological Archaeological Services for a presentation at the 58th annual Northwest Anthropological Conference, March 16–19, 2005. The authors of this poster are Sarah L. Sterling and Donald L. Tatum.

The linking of the salmon with the gift economy of the Coast Salish culture comes from biologist Jim Lichatowich's article "The Salmon's Gift," in *Peninsula Magazine*, Fall 1990.

The description of the work undertaken at the lab, analyzing the Tse-whit-zen site, comes from my observations at the lab during reporting trips in November 2004 and March 2005.

The discussion of use of native plants along the Elwha as well as of the creation site, the story of Thunderbird, and how the Elwha people got their name comes from an excellent slide-show presentation put together by Jamie Valadez and Carmen Charles-Watson of the Lower Elwha Klallam Tribe in June 2006.

Stories about the vision quests undertaken at the Elwha also come from this slide-show presentation.

The discussion of spirit helpers is from Erna Gunther, *Klallam Ethnography* (Seattle: University of Washington Press, 1927).

Interviews by the author: Dr. Michael Pavel, personal interview, Port Angeles, July 2005. Johnson Charles Jr., personal interview, LEKT Reservation, March 2006. Beatrice Charles and Adeline Smith, personal interview, LEKT Reservation, March 2006. Brian Winter, personal interview, Port Angeles and LEKT Reservation, March 2006.

3 Calamity

The Allen Library at the University of Washington Libraries' Special Collections is a trove for anyone curious to learn more about the exploration of the Northwest and its settlement by non-Indians. I relied on the Allen Library's resources for all of the following: The analysis of Quimper's notes as well as descriptions and explanation of the Coast Salish culture are from Wayne Suttles, "They Know No Superior Chief, The Strait of Juan de Fuca in the 1790s," pp. 251–64 in Jose Luis Peset Reig, *Culturas de la Costa Noroeste de America* (Madrid: Turner Libros, 1989).

The poignant quotes from the treaty council for the Treaty of Point No Point come from Charles M. Gates, "The Indian Treaty of Point No Point," *Pacific Northwest Quarterly* 46, no. 2 (April 1955): pp. 52–58.

For the discussion of smallpox, I relied on Robert Boyd, *The Coming of the Spirit of Pestilence* (Seattle: University of Washington Press, 1999). I also interviewed Boyd in March 2005 and again in October 2006 and benefited from his review of this chapter. All population estimates in this chapter are from Boyd.

"The Sun's Myth" is also from Boyd, *Pestilence*, pp. 58–59, and was collected by Franz Boas in 1891 as versified by Dell Hymes.

For the discussion of the treaties and removal of tribes from their homelands, I refer readers to a remarkably helpful booklet by Maria Pascualy and Cecelia Carpenter, *Remembering Medicine Creek* (Seattle: Fireweed Press, 2005). The booklet was prepared for the exhibit *Remembering Medicine Creek* at the Washington State History Museum in Tacoma in 1998. While there are many resources and histories on the treaties, treaty-making process, and history of this period, I know of few more locally relevant, readable, concise resources than this helpful booklet.

Also very useful, comprehensive, and readable is Joseph H. Stauss's *The Jamestown S'Klallam Story: Rebuilding a Northwest Coast Indian Tribe* (Blyn, Wash.: Jamestown S'Klallam, 2002).

For the account of the adaptation and survival of the Lower Elwha people after the cession of their lands, I relied on Barbara Lane's "Indian Homesteads in the Elwha Valley." This memorandum is found in the archives of the Lower Elwha Klallam Tribe and is archive ID number 358. I also relied on Lane's memorandum to the file of August 1, 1994, "Trust Indian Homesteads in the Elwha Valley and the Lower Elwha Reservation," on file with the Lower Elwha Klallam Tribe.

I also relied on the unpublished typescript by Jamie Valadez, "Elwha Klallam," an invaluable historical overview of the Klallam tribe circulated to tribal staff in January 2000.

Also important is Olympic Peninsula Inter-Tribal Culture Committee, *Native Peoples of the Olympic Peninsula: Who We Are*, edited by Jacilee Wray (Norman:

University of Oklahoma Press, 2002). This book is one of the few current histories of the tribes of the peninsula, written from a tribal perspective and with a chapter devoted to the Klallam people.

The account of Alexander Sampson comes from Harriet Fish's "Saga of a Sea Captain," in the *Port Angeles Daily News*, October 3, 1982. I also relied on his obituary, published January 29, 1893, in the *Port Angeles Beacon*.

Interviews by the author: Lynn Larson, personal interview, Gig Harbor, March 2005. David Rice, personal interview, Seattle, November 2004; telephone interview, November 2004; personal interview, Seattle, April 2005. Frances Charles, personal interview, LEKT Reservation, April 2005. Adeline Smith, personal interview, LEKT Reservation, March 2006. Beatrice Charles, personal interviews, LEKT Reservation, November 2004, December 2004, March 2005.

4 Conquering the Last Frontier

There is a wealth of information available for anyone who wants to learn about the damming of the Elwha River.

Among the best places to start is Thomas Aldwell's autobiography *Conquering the Last Frontier* (Seattle: Artcraft Engraving and Electrotype Company, 1950), from which I took all of the Aldwell quotations.

The account of the goals of the Puget Sound Cooperative Colony is from the Clallam County Historical Society's *A History of Clallam County* (Port Angeles, Wash.: Clallam County Historical Society, 2003).

The law prohibiting obstruction of fish-bearing streams is in *Laws of Washington 1889–1990*, p. 107, section 8.

Of all the files on the Elwha dams at the state archives—and there is enough to fill a pickup truck bed—the richest is the Surface Waters file in the Elwha River folder, box 1010-38, accession number 1911-5. It contains all the original correspondence between state fisheries officials and Aldwell sealing the fate of the Elwha and much more.

Bruce Brown's fine account of the deal made on the Elwha and its effect on hatchery policy is in his book *Mountain in the Clouds* (1982; Seattle: University of Washington Press, 1990), pp. 61–74.

A helpful tool at the Washington State Archives is Sharon Howe's "The Elwha River: An Annotated Bibliography of Selected Source Materials in the Washington

State Archives" (Olympia: Office of the Secretary of State, Division of Archives and Records Management, October 1994). This report includes an overview of the history of the river, a chronology, and a detailed bibliography.

More current materials, including primary sources documenting the science, politics, and debate about taking down the dams, are in the Joe Mentor Donation boxes. This astounding collection, acquired in 2006, includes what must be every report, press release, and flyer on the Elwha River circulated during the debate over taking down the dams. A good place to start is the Joe Mentor Donation, accession number 04-A-273, boxes 1 and 2.

Beatrice Charles's and Adeline Smith's comments about trying to rescue salmon smolts stranded in puddles and the tribe's connection to the river come from the transcript of an interview with Smith and Charles conducted by Aaron Scrol on June 9, 1997. The transcript is in the tribal archives, ID number 479. The quotations are on pp. 13 and 14.

Anyone seeking to learn more about salmon policy would do well to read Jim Lichatowich, *Salmon without Rivers* (Washington, D.C.: Island Press, 1999). This, to my mind, is one of the best books ever written on the notion that hatcheries and other technological fixes can be substituted for a living ecosystem. I would also recommend Joseph E. Taylor, *Making Salmon* (Seattle: University of Washington Press, 1999), and David Montgomery, *King of Fish: The Thousand-Year Run of Salmon* (Boulder, Colo.: Westview Press, 2003). Also invaluable on the Indian struggle for treaty fishing rights is Charles Wilkinson, *Messages from Frank's Landing* (Seattle: University of Washington Press, 2000).

Interviews by the author: Beatrice Charles and Adeline Smith, personal interview, LEKT Reservation, March 2005; personal interview, LEKT Reservation, March 2006.

5   The Big Mill

The account of Michael Earles's shakedown of the Clallam County commissioners for a free mill site and reduced taxes comes from G. M. Lauridsen and A.A. Smith, *The Story of Port Angeles and Clallam County, Washington* (Seattle: Lowman and Hanford, 1937).

The deed for the public tidelands sold for the mill is at the Clallam County Historical Society, in the Mills volume, folder A-Q.

The description of the Sol Duc hot springs resort and the fire that destroyed it comes from Jervis Russell's and the Clallam County Historical Society's *Jimmy Come Lately* (Port Angeles, Wash.: Clallam County Historical Society, 1971) pp. 408–19.

For the accounts of the importance of shellfish to the tribes, I relied on Barbara Lane's report, *Indian Use of Shellfish in Western Washington and the Indian Treaties of 1854–1855*, of May 10, 1984, on file at the Lower Elwha Klallam tribal archives.

I also used Karen James, *Klallam Use of Terrestrial and Aquatic Resources at Port Angeles Harbor and Ediz Hook*, a report prepared for the Lower Elwha Klallam Tribe, September 20, 2000, on file at the Lower Elwha Klallam tribal archives.

Another useful resource is Barbara Lane's *Identity, Treaty Status and Fisheries of the Lower Elwha Tribal Community*, prepared for the U.S. Department of the Interior and the Lower Elwha Tribal Community, July 25, 1975. This is Exhibit U.S. 91 in the Lower Elwha Klallam tribal archives.

The place-names in the Klallam language come from *The Papers of John Peabody Harrington 1907–1957*, Smithsonian Institution, in the microfilm collection at the Allen Library at the University of Washington, microfilm reel A 6952, vol. 1, reel 30, frames 154–57.

Beatrice Charles's recollections of her life growing up as a child at Pysht Village come from "A Day in the Life of Nine Year old Girl at Pysht in 1928," as told by Bea Charles, in a transcript provided to me by Jamie Valadez.

For the account of the destruction of the Klallam Village at Pysht, I relied on a transcript of an interview with Edward C. Sampson, June 1992, translated from Klallam by Beatrice Charles, Adeline Smith, and Timothy Montler and transcribed by Montler. It was published in the Lower Elwha Klallam tribal newsletter of September–October 1996. This transcript is on file at the Lower Elwha Klallam tribal center.

The account of the informality with which Indians secured their land—without taking title to it—and the destruction of Pysht also comes from an interview with Beatrice Charles and Adeline Smith, conducted at Smith's home by Aaron Scrol on June 9, 1997, Lower Elwha Klallam tribal archives ID number 479, pp. 1–7.

The burning of the settlement at Hollywood Beach is documented in Paul J. Martin's *Port Angeles Washington: A History, Vol. 1* (Port Angeles, Wash.: Pen Print, 1983).

Interviews by the author: Bea Charles and Adeline Smith, personal interview, LEKT

Reservation, March 2005; personal interview, LEKT Reservation, March 2006. Al Charles Sr., personal interview, LEKT Reservation, March 2005. Johnson Charles Jr., personal interview, LEKT Reservation, March 2006.

6   Collective Amnesia

The account of the difficulties encountered during the field survey of the site comes from notes taken during an interview of archaeologist Lara C. Rooke, on file at the Washington State Department of Archaeology and Historic Preservation, in Olympia, Washington, in the graving dock file.

The 1853 survey map is *False Dungeness Harbor, Washington*, U.S. Coastal Survey Map by the Hydrographic Party under the command of Lieutenant James Alden, U.S. N. Assist. It is on file in the maps storage room at the Allen Library, University of Washington Libraries, Special Collections.

The initial survey report of the site is by Jennifer Burns, Lara C. Rooke, and Glenn Hartmann, *Cultural Resources Survey for the Washington State Department of Transportation's Port Angeles Graving Dock Facility for the Hood Canal Bridge Retrofit and East Half Replacement, Clallam County, Washington*, December 10, 2002, revised on January 6, 2003. It is available through the Washington State Department of Transportation, technical report 0136, Agreement Y-7898, Task Assignment Document AX.

For a closely detailed account of the department's permitting and management of the dry dock project, I would also refer readers to Douglas B. MacDonald's *A Report to the Governor and Legislature of the State of Washington: The Hood Canal Bridge Rehabilitation Project and Graving Dock Program*, May 16, 2006. This exhaustive 224-page report includes a list of documents in appendix B that will be helpful to anyone who wishes to build an understanding of this project. Copies are available to borrow through the department's library at its headquarter offices in Olympia, Washington. Call 360-705-7750 to obtain a copy.

The letter from Frances Charles was written to Sue Roberds, assistant planner for the city of Port Angeles, on January 14, 2003. It is at the Port Angeles Department of Community Development, in the Shoreline Substantial Development file, SMA 03-01. The file is a good place to start looking for baseline documentation of the city's role in the project.

The staff report on the dry dock project by Port Angeles city planner Scott Johns is in the same file.

Interviews by the author: Port Angeles city councilman Larry Williams, telephone interview, November 2005; personal interview, Port Angeles, March 2005. Randy Hain, personal interview, Tumwater, July and August 2006. Glenn Hartmann, personal interview, Bainbridge Island, October 2006. Douglas MacDonald, telephone interview, December 2004; personal interview, Seattle, April 2005. Scott Johns, personal interview, Port Angeles, March 2006. Matt Bierne, personal interview, LEKT Reservation, March 2006. Frances Charles, personal interview, Port Angeles, March 2005. Beatrice Charles and Adeline Smith, personal interview, LEKT Reservation, March 2005. Dennis Sullivan, personal interview, Port Angeles, March 2005. Jamie Valadez, personal interview, LEKT Reservation, March 2005. Andrew May, personal interview, Port Angeles, March 2006.

7   This Ground Speaks

The report documenting an intact site is Dennis E. Lewarch's and Lynn L. Larson's *Distribution of Archaeological Deposits at 45CA523 Identified during Archaeological Site Assessment,* dated October 10, 2003. It is available through the Washington State Department of Transportation.

Interviews by the author: Dave Garlington, telephone interview, March 2005. LaTrisha Suggs, telephone interview, March 2005. Arlene Wheeler, telephone interview, July 2005. Glenn Hartmann, personal interview, Bainbridge Island, October 2006. Douglas MacDonald, personal interview, Olympia, August 2006; telephone interview, October 2006. Allyson Brooks, personal interview, Olympia, September 2006. Colleen Jollie, personal interview, Olympia, August 2006.

8   Walking Together

The archaeologist's weekly summary forms are on file with the Lower Elwha Klallam Tribe.

To gain a detailed sense of the back-and-forth that was required to reach the March agreements, I again refer readers to MacDonald's report, *The Hood Canal Bridge and Graving Dock Program,* of May 16, 2006. The report provides an exhaustive account of the negotiations, extensive quotations from press clippings that chronicled the talks, the full text of the department's side agreement with the tribe, and the memorandum of agreement with state and federal agencies.

Interviews by the author: Arlene Wheeler, personal interview, LEKT Reservation, March 2005. Douglas MacDonald, personal interview, Tumwater, September 15, 2006. Dennis Sullivan, personal interview, Port Angeles, March 2005. Verna Henderson, personal interview, LEKT Reservation, November 2005. Steve Reinmuth, personal interview, Olympia, August 2006. Randy Hain, personal interview, Tumwater, August 2006.

9   Walking Away

The quotes and account of the Centennial Accord meeting in December 2004 are from my attendance at the meeting.

Interviews by the author: Amy Carter, personal interview, Port Angeles, March 2005. Alysson Brooks, personal interview, Olympia, September 2006. Arlene Wheeler, telephone interview, April 2005. Mark Charles, telephone interview, April 2005; personal interview, LEKT Reservation, March 2006. Michael Q. Langland, telephone interview, April 2005. Carmen Watson-Charles, personal interview, Port Angeles, November 2005. Teresa Sanders, personal interview, LEKT Reservation, March 2005. Wendy Sampson, personal interview, LEKT Reservation, March 2005. Colleen Jollie, personal interview, Olympia, August 2006. Douglas MacDonald, personal interview, Seattle, November 2004; personal interview, Seattle, April 2005; personal interview, Olympia, August 2006. Frances Charles, personal interview, Port Angeles, November 2004. Beatrice Charles, personal interview, LEKT Reservation, November 2004. Mary Anne Thomas, personal interview, LEKT Reservation, November 2004. U.S. Senator Maria Cantwell, telephone interview, December 2004. Washington Governor Gary Locke, telephone interview, December 2004.

10   We Were Here—We Are Still Here

The quotes and observations of Douglas MacDonald come from attending a meeting at the union hall in Port Angeles in January 2005.

The city shoreline ordinance is from the Port Angeles Shorelines Master Plan, 1995, chapter 4, pp. 27–29.

Interviews by the author: Larry Williams, personal interview, Port Angeles, March 2005. Jim Buck, personal interview, Port Angeles, March 2006. John Brewer, telephone interview, July 2006. Andrew May, personal interview, Port Angeles, March

2006. Arlene Wheeler, personal interview, Port Angeles, August 14, 2006. Randy Hain, personal interview, Port Angeles, August 2006; personal interview, Tumwater, August 2006. Tim Thompson, telephone interview, September 2006. Leonard Forsman, telephone interview, April 2007.

Epilogue

Interviews by the author: Johnson Charles Jr., personal interview, LEKT Reservation, March 2006. Jamie Valadez, personal interview, Port Angeles, March 2006, Bea Charles, personal interview, LEKT Reservation, March 2005.

Glossary

The Klallam glossary was compiled from a superb Web site run by Timothy Montler, a linguist at the University of North Texas who has worked with the Lower Elwha Klallam tribe since 1990 to preserve its language. The site has a wealth of information about the tribe and its history, culture, and language and is a must for anyone interested in learning more about the Lower Elwha Klallam people. Visit http://www.ling.unt.edu/~montler/Klallam/.

To learn more about the tribe, visit its Web site, http://www.elwha.org/.

Index

Illustrations are indicated by boldface type.